1913

The Cradle of Modernism

Jean-Michel Rabaté

Blackwell
Publishing

BLACKWELL PUBLISHING
350 Main Street, Malden, MA 02148-5020, USA
9600 Garsington Road, Oxford OX4 2DQ, UK
550 Swanston Street, Carlton, Victoria 3053, Australia

The right of Jean-Michel Rabaté to be identified as the Author of this
Work has been asserted in accordance with the UK Copyright, Designs,
and Patents Act 1988.

First published 2007 by Blackwell Publishing Ltd

1   2007

Library of Congress Cataloging-in-Publication Data

Rabaté, Jean-Michel, 1949–
    1913 : the cradle of modernism / Jean-Michel Rabaté.
       p. cm.
    Includes bibliographical references and index.
    ISBN 978-1-4051-5117-7 (alk. paper)—ISBN 978-1-4051-6192-3 (pbk. : alk. paper)
    1. Literature, Modern—20th century—History and criticism.   2. Modernism
(Literature)   I. Title.   II. Title: Nineteen thirteen.

PN771.R33 2007
809'.041—dc22

                                                                  2006052663

A catalogue record for this title is available from the British Library.

Set in 10.5/13pt Dante   •
by Graphicraft Limited, Hong Kong
Printed and bound in Singapore
by Markono Print Media Pte Ltd

For further information on
Blackwell Publishing, visit our website:
www.blackwellpublishing.com

Contents

List of Illustrations

Acknowledgments

The author and publisher gratefully acknowledge the permission granted to reproduce the following copyright material in this book:

Illustrations

Figure 1: Armory Show poster, 1913, Hirshborn Museum and Sculpture Gallery, Smithsonian Institution, Washington DC.

Figure 3: Kazimir Malevich, *Elongation of the Suprematist Square*, 1913, pencil on paper, Kupferstichkabinett, Kunstmuseum Basel.

Figure 4: Italian policemen guarding the *Mona Lisa* painting in Florence, Roger Viollet / Getty images.

Figure 6: Marie Curie and Albert Einstein, 1913, Engadine, Switzerland. AIP Emilio Segre Archive.

Figure 8: Photograph for *The Star of Ethiopia*, W. E. B. du Bois Library, University of Massachussetts.

Quoted Texts

"Hic Jacet" by William Carlos Williams, New Directions Publishing (US rights), and Carcanet Press for UK and rest of world rights.

"In the Station of the Metro" by Ezra Pound, New Directions (US rights), Faber & Faber for UK and rest of world rights.

"Trumpets" translated by Robert Grenier, permission granted by Robert Grenier.

"Petersburg Stanzas" and "1913" by Osip Mandelstam, from Stone, translated by Robert Tracy, Princeton University Press.

"Pauis" translated by Darlene J. Sadlier, in *An Introduction to Fernando Pessoa: Modernism and the Paradoxes of Authorship*, University of Florida Press.

Every effort has been made to trace copyright holders and to obtain their permission for the use of copyright material. The publisher apologizes for any errors or omissions in the above list and would be grateful if notified of any corrections that should be incorporated in future reprints or editions of this book.

Finally, I should like to thank Eric Bulson, who kindly read a draft of this book and made countless useful suggestions.

Introduction

Modernism, Crisis, and Early Globalization

Could the year 1913 have brought us bad luck? If I have chosen to focus on one single year, 1913, to explore the emergence of modernism, it is not because this single moment looks, from a distance, like the last haven of peace before the universal conflagration of World War I, or seems to enact the absolute termination of what the French used to call *la belle époque* and the Americans *the gilded age*. On that view, 1913 would hold all the last snapshots of an old world contented with itself, basking in the enjoyment of hard-earned privilege and a successful industrial revolution. Rather than seeing this year as a last moment of innocence (which may be what had attracted me to it in the first place), I have come to the realization that it can be described more accurately as the inception of our modern period of globalization: 1913 marks the time when the impetus that delivered the first world war to enthusiastically cheering crowds was already perceptible, and when the same *élan* created so many masterpieces in the arts and literature; in that sense, we can agree that it has brought bad luck to the world, but that it has changed our perception of the new and the old for ever.

1912 + 1

In fact, the most sensitive of witnesses, the sharper-sighted artists and intellectuals, sensed this quite well in 1913. This is why, in a prescient book published in 1913, Morton Fullerton evoked the prophecy made to William I, Crown Prince of Prussia, by a an old lady from the village of Fiensberg: the woman asserted that the German empire would be destroyed in 1913.[1] The bad omen is also what led Leonardo Sciascia to devote a beautiful and sparse novel to this same year.[2] Sciascia's inspiration was triggered when he

1

found that he owned a copy of d'Annunzio's *Le Martyre de Saint Sébastien* which had been dedicated to a friend with a nice epigraph ("Every arrow is for salvation"), and was signed and dated: "Gabriele d'Annunzio. 7 juin 1912 + 1." More than superstition working for the author or for his intended reader, this reveals a wish to let 1912 linger on in 1913. Indeed, *Le Martyre de Saint Sébastien* had been quite visible in 1911, after it had been adapted by Claude Debussy for a ballet danced in Paris by Ida Rubinstein. Alas, the audience agreed that it was a glorious flop, the grandiose and wordy libretto unredeemed by the innovative impressionistic score. This was to be Debussy's first public failure; it announced mounting financial worries for the composer, whose first marriage was fast unraveling and who was already in failing health. By contrast with the care-free years of 1900–9, when cultural tourism reached a peak in Paris, a city that seemed to be intoxicated with its own festive spirit and endless revels as sung earlier by Offenbach in *La Vie parisienne* and *La Belle Hélène*, 1912 was marked by deepening shadows: warfare, rearmament, mobilization, and the Balkan wars were looming heavily on the central European front.

Music, painting, and literature can be taken as indicators of subtle changes in the zeitgeist, much as Modris Eksteins did in his excellent *Rites of Spring*.[3] For Eksteins, the 1913 premiere of Stravinsky's ballet *The Rite of Spring* unleashed a torrent of modernist primitivism in which one can understand that the Great War was inevitable. Stravinsky had intended to call his ballet "The Victim," and shocked people most by having the young maiden destined to be sacrificed agree to her own demise. Here, in a meditation on "primitive" rituals, we find the notion that creation and destruction have become inseparable, which was true not only of the artistic movement that aimed at a general revolution in the arts but also in everyday life. I will return to Stravinsky's famous ballet in the next chapter, and will limit myself here to an evocation of another revolutionary musician, who was to change music more durably than his Russian counterpart and one-time friend. When Arnold Schoenberg started experimenting with free atonality in the years 1908–11, he was impelled as much by an inner necessity as by his links with the German expressionists. The 1909 monodrama *Erwartung* is typical of a new atmosphere. The libretto had been written by Marie Pappenheim, a relative of the Bertha Pappenheim, who had been Freud's and Breuer's "Anna O." in the *Studies on Hysteria*. It is the monologue of a distraught woman who discovers at the end that she has murdered her lover out of jealousy. First, she does not recognize the woods and the corpse, and the music follows her hallucinations and anguished questioning in a series of fresh departures – each section last a few seconds and then stops on a climax;

there is no discernible thematic development; the rhythmic texture changes continually; the enormous speed corresponds to the impression that a whole life unfolds in a few seconds.[4]

What should interest us in this context is Schoenberg's superstitious character. He abhorred the number 13 and routinely skipped over measure 13 in his scores. He would often renumber page 13 as well. He even went to the extreme of deleting the extra "a" in Aaron's name from the title of his opera *Moses und Aron*, in order to have only twelve letters in it. There must be a link between this superstitious numerology and the decision made after the war to systematize atonality by creating the twelve-tone technique. His return to some sort of classicism in the twenties transformed anonymous and age-old superstition into a necessary composition rule, into laws of the new music. Indeed, born on the 13th of September, Schoenberg was afraid that he might die on a Friday 13th – as in fact he did, on Friday, July 13, 1951.[5] I will soon return, via Adorno, to the opposition between Schoenberg's "revolutionary" music and Stravinsky's neoclassicism after the war. Earlier, when they were still collaborating, Stravinsky was probably aware of Schoenberg's fear of the number 13. After all, he had gone to Berlin to attend the rehearsals and one performance of *Pierrot Lunaire* in December 1912, just at the moment when he was revising and completing the score for *Le Sacre du Printemps* (*The Rite of Spring*). In *Pierrot Lunaire*, the ultra-short section 12, entitled *Galgenlied* (Gallows Song), contains just 13 measures – it last approximately 15 seconds – while section 13 deals with Pierrot's "Beheading" by the moon's "naked scimitar."

In view of Schoenberg's later compositional legislation, the year on which this book focuses should not be seen in an exceptionalist light – true, 1913 was a fascinating and incredibly productive year; so are other important years that dot a half-century, at least, of international modernism. Modernism should be understood as a series of cultural and political punctuation points more than a sequence of red-letter days, but to grasp this one needs a synchronic or "simultaneist" (a term used by a number of artists then, as we will see) approach. Ideally this book should find its place in a series of "slices of century" that would follow the three phases of modernism upon which critics tend to agree: they divide half a century into "early modernism," ranging from 1900 to 1916, "high modernism," from 1917 to 1929, and "late modernism," from 1930 to 1945. By focusing on several more years, the main dates of a precise periodization would sketch as many titles of books waiting to be written: *1900, 1905, 1908, 1913, 1917, 1922, 1929, 1933, 1936, 1939, 1945, 1950*. Then, for whoever is in a hurry, the dodecaphonic series can be reduced further to a nucleus of four dates: 1905, 1913, 1922, and 1929. Apart

3

from a few exceptions (the year 1912 was productive too, especially in the German and Austrian context), these years would give due attention to the main masterpieces of early, high, and late modernism.

Now, I have just mentioned one year that has often been called the "annus mirabilis" of high modernism, and it is 1922: Michael North has treated it brilliantly in *Reading 1922: A Return to the Scene of the Modern*,[6] while Marc Manganaro has explored the simultaneous emergence of a term like "culture" to define the new spirit in 1922 in *Culture, 1922*.[7] On the other hand, none of the 12 years that I have mentioned coincides with the year chosen by Hans Ulrich Gumbrecht when he decided to exemplify a synchronic approach to literary history. His book, *In 1926: Living at the Edge of Time*,[8] chooses 1926 almost at random, for family reasons, it seems, in order to illustrate the principle that "the perspective of historical simultaneity does not depend on the choice of a one-year span."[9] Gumbrecht confesses that his method could as validly apply to the year 926! He excels at re-creating the lived feel of a period, called up by objects such as airplanes, automobiles, car assembly lines, gomina, and gramophones, its emblematic agents (engineers, hunger artists, Americans in Paris), its binary codes (action vs. impotence, authenticity vs. artificiality, center vs. periphery), and its conceptual frameworks (Heidegger looms large here). For 1913, it seems almost idle to reconstruct a hinge-year that has been so effectively monumentalized by writers as diverse as Proust, Musil, Wharton, Kafka, Rilke, Biely, Mandelstam, Apollinaire, Cendrars, or Gertrude Stein, whether they wrote at that time or reminisced about it a little later.

Mine is a different project, closer in sensibility to Marjorie Perloff's groundbreaking *Futurist Moment*.[10] There, Perloff focuses on the "language of rupture" typical of the pre-war avant-gardes, and moves rapidly between Paris, London, and Russia so as to sketch a "Futurist" sensibility. I have also been inspired by a few other books, beginning with the almost exhaustive collective undertaking edited by Liliane Brion-Guerry, whose three edited volumes devote more than two thousand pages to *The Year 1913*,[11] and followed by Frederic Morton's brilliant reconstruction of Vienna in *Thunder at Twilight: Vienna 1913/1914*.[12] To these I would add two older synthetic accounts, *1913: America between Two Worlds*,[13] by Alan Valentine, and *1913: An End and a Beginning*, by Virginia Cowles,[14] both of which are full of interesting details. The last three books move deftly between the anecdotal and the general so as to reconstruct the atmosphere of the period over one year, while Perloff ranges freely between 1910 and 1914 to highlight the creation of modernity. Brion-Guerry's unwieldy volumes analyze this year in order to treat in depth *all* the artistic manifestations observable at the time, but she explains that the choice of the date derived from its strategic position in a history of modernity.[15] Besides, even if some efforts are made in the direction of the United States and Russia, the volumes' bulk focuses on Europe. It is now time to question assumptions such as the one which opens a fine book documenting the "drift to world war" in the first decade of the twentieth century: "The world at the beginning of the twentieth century was a very different place from what it was to be two generations later. Primarily this was so because Europe was still the centre of the universe, both politically and economically, and Europe was still in the main the Europe of the *ancien régime*."[16] In order to avoid the trap of Europeanism, the best approach is to try and be as "comparative" as possible; this entails that one cannot provide an exhaustive account, and cover all countries at once. Hence, covering as much ground as possible while keeping a clear problematic in mind, I will take the category of "modernism" as my red thread.

By modernism, I do not mean simply an overarching label defining the "spirit" of an entire historical period, neither the listing of more radical ventures that were beginning to be known under the name of the "avant-garde." My leading question will be: how could one be "modern" in 1913, what were the conditions for the emergence of this modernity? What were the links between the modern and the awareness, then recent (at least since Goethe), that there was something like a world literature? Thus, I will not use "modernism" stylistically only. Describing "1913 modernism" on a world-wide scale renders it impossible to concentrate exclusively on the formal properties of the various achievements considered: the variations from medium to medium, from country to country, are such that no single standard of "advancement" could be defined. At the same time, the decision to stick to one year prevents one from adopting a teleological model in which one knows what the "progressive" factors would be, as opposed to their "regressive" counterparts. If innovation varied from genre to genre, from medium to medium, from country to country, there remained a common curve: each time, an old order was felt to be crumbling down, while new ethical and esthetic values were being promoted. It was often a confused aspiration for novelty that was expressed more than outright successful experiments (we will verify this when comparing William Carlos Williams' poems with Gertrude Stein's texts of the same period). Above all, the specific focus on this year, culture, and war will appear to posit an uneasy relationship, in a productive tension that can be ascribed to a new management of speed, communication, and technology.

Speed and War

Since the late 1970s, Paul Virilio has been pointing out the crucial role of speed in the intermeshed networks of war, technology, and communication.[17] He has coined the term "dromology" to define the accelerated speed of everything, especially in the domain of warfare, at the end of the nineteenth century. One might say that modern warfare begins when accurate and fast information can be transmitted. Thus, at the level of information theory, there was no great difference between the long-term uncertainty that surrounded the disappearance of King Sebastian of Portugal in the notorious battle of Kasar el Kebir in August 1578 and the delay concerning the outcome of the battle of Manila that opposed the American and Spanish fleets in May 1898. In 1578, the inexperienced king of Portugal had decided to support a Moroccan pretender; the "battle of the three kings" was a total defeat on the Portuguese side: both the army and the king were entirely obliterated. As nobody could believe that a king and an army could disappear without leaving a trace, the legend rose that Sebastian would come back, and messianic Sebastianism was still active in the nineteenth century, leaving an impact on a writer whom I will engage with later, Fernando Pessoa. Similarly, but on a smaller scale, the battle of Manila, during which the US fleet led by Admiral Dewey destroyed the fortresses defending the city as well as the whole Spanish fleet in the harbor, was one of the first undisputed victories of modern technology in maritime warfare (the Spanish were never able to hit anything, while the deadly accuracy of US guns was notable). Yet its outcome remained uncertain for a week: the Spanish side had sent premature cables reporting victory, after which Dewey had the undersea telegraph lines cut, which left the international press without news. For nine days, the wildest rumors circulated that a Spanish armada was going to attack New York, and this created panic in the US and elsewhere. In fact, the battle took place on May 1, 1898, and the full story of the American victory only reached European and American newspapers on May 10.

By contrast, it took very little time for the Western world to be apprised of the sinking of the *Titanic*, which hit an iceberg on the night of April 14/15, 1912. The *Titanic* was supposed to be the safest and fastest passenger steamer of the time, but was engaged, like all other luxury cruise ships, in an international race for speed records opposing especially Germany and England, which forced its captain to navigate recklessly in treacherous waters. The *Titanic*'s operator sent a wireless distress call at 12.15 a.m. on April 15 which was caught by ten ships navigating in the vicinity, but the *Carpathian*, the first ship to arrive, came two hours after the steamer had sunk with 1,522 passengers. A wireless station in Newfoundland picked up the message that the ship was sinking at 1.20 a.m., and the disaster made headlines world-wide by the early morning of the 15th. A few days later, the *New York Times* commented on the newly discovered power of electricity to link the whole world in an instant: "But for the almost magic use of the air the *Titanic* tragedy would have been shrouded in the secrecy that not so long ago was the power of the sea . . . Few New Yorkers realize that all through the roar of the big city there are constantly speeding messages between people sep-arated by vast distances, and that over housetops and even through the safe walls of buildings and in the very air one breathes are words written by electricity."[18] The increased speed in a decidedly world-wide circulation of information was used for political purposes during the two Balkan wars, whose cumulative effect was to bring about a general war in 1914. All the incidents were documented and often manipulated by public opinion. The Italo-Turkish or "Libyan" war, fought between the Ottoman empire and Italy from September 29, 1911 to October 18, 1912, had revealed Italy's new imperialist ambitions, and its systematic use of the press helped propel public opinion towards a nationalist and imperialist goal. This limited war awoke long pent-up nationalism in the Balkan states. Realizing how easily the Italians had defeated the Ottomans, the members of the Balkan League attacked the empire before the war with Italy was over. Moreover, the Italo-Turkish war was notable for its use of new technology in warfare. On October 23, 1911 an Italian pilot flew over Turkish lines to assess their positions, and on November 1 the first air-bomb was dropped from an airplane and landed on Turkish troops in Libya.[19] On 25 July 1913, during the second Balkan war, Romanian aviators took pictures of Sofia from their planes and dropped leaflets for the population. Sofia was thus the first European capital to come under the wings of enemy aircraft.[20]

If the claims of Italy over Libya dated back to the Congress of Berlin in 1878, the Italian press began a massive campaign arguing for an immediate invasion of Libya at the end of March 1911. Newspapers described the country as friendly to the Italians and pictured the coming war as a "military walk." War was declared on September 29, 1911; Tripoli was conquered in October. Early victories in Tobruk, Derna, and Homs were followed by difficulties in Benghazi. In November 1911 the battle of Tobruk almost annihilated the Italian expeditionary corps, and 100,000 new men had to be sent. The stalemate led to a war of position in which even the use of avi-ation was of little effect. On November 5, 1911 Italy declared its suzerainty over Libya and occupied the Dodecanese islands. In the summer of 1912,

Italian torpedo boats attacked the Turks in the Dardanelles. Bulgaria, Serbia, and Greece armed themselves against the Ottoman empire, and Montenegro declared war against the Turks. Italian diplomacy exploited the situation and obtained a favorable peace: a treaty was signed at Lausanne on October 18, 1912. The invasion of Libya had been costly for Italy but had demonstrated that lobbying powers working for an active political minority could change the politics of a country. The lesson was not lost on Mussolini or d'Annunzio after the Great War.

Another example of the increased role of the press and public opinion is the way in which Macedonian revolutionaries played with them so as to trigger the first Balkan war. The Internal Macedonian Revolutionary Organization, established in Salonica, had been trying to obtain autonomy for Macedonia from the Ottoman regime since the last years of the nineteenth century. In the first decade of the twentieth century, it launched uprisings and thus kidnapped Miss Stone, an American citizen, in order to create an international furor, a radical strategy which was successful in the end. Regular Turkish reprisals for guerrilla attacks in Macedonia galvanized the public. After a bomb exploded in a mosque on December 11, 1911, the Turks killed Macedonians at random, triggering a series of bombings, massacres, and tortures. The Organization had been instrumental in arousing public opinion and bringing pressure on the Bulgarian government so as to settle the Macedonian problem. Protest meetings were organized after each massacre. Finally, the Kotchana bombing in 1912, followed by other reprisals by the Turkish army, led Bulgaria to declare war against Turkey. This was the first Balkan war.

As at the end of the nineteenth century, the main European powers had regrouped themselves in two blocs, the triple Entente (Britain, France, and Russia) and the triple Alliance (Germany, Austro-Hungary, and Italy), they began to clash in many parts of the world, in Africa and the Balkans mostly. The first incident of the century took place in Morocco, a country coveted both by Germany and France. The 1904 "Entente" with Britain had granted France colonial "rights" over Morocco, but Kaiser Wilhelm II tried to prevent French expansion there. In March 1905, the Kaiser landed at Tangier, where he greeted the sultan of Morocco as an independent sovereign, promising German protection should France attempt to colonize his state. The following year, the conference of Algeciras was convened to clarify the status of Morocco. Germany was supported by Austria while France was supported by Britain, Russia, and the United States. France was given special privileges, and was allowed to control the Moroccan police, customs, and arms shipments. The diplomatic victory of the Entente over the Alliance left Germany dissatisfied: it felt "encircled" in Europe and hemmed in its colonial expansion in Africa.

The Balkans were the most troubled spot in Europe. Local nationalities were chafing against Turkish rule, even if, by the end of the nineteenth century, a few subject races had gained independence and formed nation-states as was the case for Greece, Serbia, Montenegro, Romania, and Bulgaria. These emerging nation-states wanted to expand by including fellow nationals still living in the Turkish empire or the Austro-Hungarian empire. The Balkan states were pulling at fragments of Turkey and the Austro-Hungarian empire in order to retrieve contested territories. Russia supported her Slav brothers in Serbia in their struggles against Turkey and Austria, while Austria tried to suppress all nationalist tendencies in the Balkans. The tense situation had been complicated by the 1908 revolution of the Young Turks that brought liberal reformers to power in the Ottoman empire. Under their pressure, the sultan had agreed to give a constitution. All of a sudden King Ferdinand of Bulgaria proclaimed himself king of Crete as well and decided to be united with Greece. Austria then annexed Bosnia and Herzegovina, which angered the Russians and the Serbians. Serbia, ready for war, asked for support from Russia. War was imminent until Russia backed down because England and France were unwilling to become involved, whereas Germany had promised her military support to Austria. Russia felt humiliated but immediately after the crisis intensified its armaments program. The annexation of Bosnia-Herzegovina had made Serbia the irreconcilable enemy of Austria. Serbian nationalists formed a secret society whose aim was to provoke revolts in Bosnia and ultimately war with Austria while Austria was looking for the first opportunity to crush Serbian nationalism.

In 1911, a second Moroccan crisis was triggered by the rivalry between France and Germany. The French had installed a pro-French sultan on the Moroccan throne. He was not popular and, in May 1911, French troops occupied Fez to suppress an uprising. The Germans responded by sending the gunboat *Panther* to Agadir, a port on the Atlantic coast. The British, fearing that this would turn Agadir into a German naval base on the route to the Cape, backed France. War seemed inevitable until, at the last moment, Germany gave in. France gained Morocco, leaving a small portion opposite Gibraltar to Spain. In exchange, Germany was given a strip of the French Congo. The Agadir crisis had showed how fragile the peace was in Europe, but unlike the earlier crisis of Fashoda which had pitted French against British imperialisms in Sudan at the close of the nineteenth century (1898) – then, if a war had erupted, France would have fought with Russia against Britain and Germany – the crises of the early twentieth century strengthened the recent Franco-British alliance. The Entente powers exchanged information about the conditions of their respective armies and navies. In 1912 Britain and France made a secret naval agreement: in the event of a war, the British fleet would guard the North Sea and the Channel, and the French fleet was to be deployed in the Mediterranean.

The Young Turk revolution had weakened the Turkish government, which was exploited by Italy when, as we have seen, Tripoli was attacked. The Balkan states, Serbia, Bulgaria, Greece, and Montenegro, had declared war on Turkey in October 1912. From October 1912 to May 1913, the Balkan League was victorious, allowing Turkey to keep only the area around Constantinople. Then the central powers intervened and imposed their settlement at the Treaty of London. It stipulated that a new state, Albania, should be created to prevent Serbia from getting a coastline on the Adriatic. To compensate for this, Serbia was given a large part of Macedonia. This settlement led to the second Balkan war in 1913. Bulgaria regarded Macedonia as her possession and her quarrels with Serbia over Macedonia escalated. Now an isolated Bulgaria was fighting against Serbia, Montenegro, Romania, Greece, and Turkey together. The war was quickly lost by Bulgaria, leaving Turkey and Romania to regain territories. But the second Balkan war led to the outbreak of World War I. Twice victorious, Serbia had swallowed a part of Macedonia and aimed at reuniting with its fellow nationals in a Slav state, including the 8 million Serbs and Croats who were subjects of Austria. This led to an inevitable collision as interrelated alliances tightened the conflict: the Kaiser assured Austria of his support, while the tsar, disappointed that Russia had not obtained Albania for Serbia, declared unconditional support for a greater Serbia. The assassination of the Archduke Franz Ferdinand and the Duchess Sophie by two Bosnian Serb students in Sarajevo on June 28, 1914 precipitated the final crisis.

The main cause of World War I was *Weltpolitik*, not only understood as the colonial policy of Kaiser Wilhelm II, who held that Germany had a right to become a global imperial power like France and Britain, but also as a global concept, a set of beliefs and tenets shared by all the European powers – and some American parties. In 1912 and 1913, the local wars in the Balkans had allowed Serbia to emerge as a powerful country. Austria could not tolerate this, and the third Balkan war started with the assassination of the Archduke Franz Ferdinand and his wife in Sarajevo, soon leading the central powers as well as France and Britain into war. Militarism, imperialism, and nationalism had each a role to play in the causes of the war, while the combination of these causes can be equated with the emergence of globalization – even if the term sounds like an anachronism.

Early Globalization

Was "globalization" really an anachronism in 1913? Recently, discussions have raged about the claims made forcibly by Michael Hardt and Antonio Negri that the main features of our late modernity are shaped by a globalized "empire" corresponding to North American world domination.[21] Critics such as Doug Henwood have expressed skepticism about the alleged novelty of the phenomenon, stressing that it had existed one century before under a similar British domination.[22] In fact, one might argue that the world was more unified under the British rule than it is now.[23] In order to bring fresh substance to the ongoing discussion, I will turn to the insights of a contemporary, a particularly astute observer of the pre-war situation in Europe and the rest of the world. This was Morton Fullerton, a Harvard-educated cosmopolitan intellectual, the one-time lover and then close friend of the American novelist Edith Wharton. In *Problems of Power* (*PP*), an inspired book published in 1913, Fullerton, who argues for peace, nevertheless begins ominously by quoting Bossuet: "When God wipes out, he is getting ready to write."[24] This conjures up the specter of a general war that will redraw all the lines on the map of Europe. He connects this quote with Bismarck's "clean slate" policy, and compares Napoleon and Bismarck, the two rulers who redefined Europe in the nineteenth century. Fullerton, a friend of Henry James and Oscar Wilde, had been the Paris correspondent of the London *Times* between 1893 and 1907, and he was one of the shrewdest and most knowledgeable observers of European affairs at the time. Perhaps only an American could understand so well the complex skein of passions, resentments, alliances, and aspirations that made central Europe a power keg. Early in his book, he quotes Count von Aehrenthal, the Austro-Hungarian Minister for Foreign Affairs, who in April 1912 described the political imbroglio of the new "world-situation" generated by the alliance between England, France, Italy, and Russia on the one hand, and Austria, Germany, and Japan on the other. For von Aehrenthal, such alliances testify to an increasingly interconnected world as they also look to Asia and Africa, which "brings into existence other points of contact and other zones of friction" (*PP*, 6). Fullerton discusses at some length the complex treaties that generated an international "dove-tailing" (*PP*, 62) of the world: "They bear witness, thus, to the most salient reality of modern civilization, namely the increasing predominance of economic laws, with the consequent interpenetration of peoples, a state of things that has multiplied zones of friction; the blind but ineluctable evolution towards a condition of "socialistic" reciprocity, coterminous with the circumference of the planet, and tending to annihilate national barriers" (PP, 6).

Why is Fullerton speaking of "socialistic" reciprocity? He was not a liberal, and, like Edith Wharton, supported Theodore Roosevelt, a president who was unabashedly imperialist and interventionist, whereas the recently elected Democrat President Wilson wanted to focus on interior political issues. However, Fullerton's philosophy of history often comes close to a Marxist view: he insists that economics is the determining factor in human societies; more precisely, he sees the end of the nineteenth century marked by a deepening clash between renewed nationalism, by nature particularistic, and the laws of the market, by nature universalistic. He gives the example of the Dardanelles straits, which were closed for a few months in 1912 by the Turks during the Balkan war: tons of Russian grain were left to rot in the Black Sea, while England, Romania, Bulgaria, and Greece lost some £20,000 a day. International traffic had to be diverted via the Suez Canal. Lord Lansdowne concluded that it was not tolerable to let a limited conflict strangle the trading interests of the whole world. The "trading community of the world" could not allow limited national wars to jeopardize their interests (PP, 7–8). Thus the state of the modern world described by Fullerton corresponds word for word with what Marx and Engels had seen in 1848.

In the *Communist Manifesto*, Marx and Engels had written those prophetic words:

> The need for a constantly expanding market for its products chases the bourgeoisie over the whole surface of the globe. It must nestle everywhere, settle everywhere, establish connections everywhere. The bourgeoisie has through its exploitation of the world-market given a cosmopolitan character to production and consumption in every country. . . . In place of the old local and national seclusion and self-sufficiency, we have intercourse in every direction, universal interdependence of nations. And as in material, so also in intellectual production. The intellectual creations of individual nations become common property. National one-sidedness and narrow-mindedness become more and more impossible, and from the numerous national and local literatures, there arises a world literature.[25]

This world literature emerged in full view of the public when for the first time the Nobel Prize in literature was given to a non-European, Rabindranath

Tagore, in 1913. At the same time, an American company like AT&T pledged a universal phone service expanded to all rural areas, the portable phonograph was manufactured, and sounds were recorded on cylinders, producing fairly accurate radio renderings of main political events. One can date from this year the moment when today's global world came of age, in the current intermeshing that we know between constant technological inventions, flows of international capital, and the reawakening of particularist claims, whether religious or national or both, that saw in war the only solution to their predicament.

Fullerton duly notes a recent upsurge of nationalisms almost everywhere: "The twentieth century tendency will almost uniformly be found to be towards a greater 'national' activity." (PP, 9), he writes, and contrasts this trend with the "passion for the planet" that was dominant in intellectual and political circles a quarter of a century earlier. As he insists, the national spirit manifests itself more strongly when it is threatened: he perceives clearly that the reawakening of nationalism is a reaction to the encroachment of the leveling tendencies of global capitalism. At least, he believes that the United States cannot be blind to the fact that it has become a world power (PP, 23) and thus will be unable to avoid being engulfed in a general conflagration. The geographical center of gravity has shifted from the Mediterranean world to the Caribbean world (PP, 310) and the United States cannot continue being naive about its responsibility toward the rest of the emerging nations. Fullerton sees the military and industrial rise of Japan, victorious over Russia in 1905, as a portent of new changes in the Asian world, while Russia seems closer to the old Europe than ever. Praise for a strong Republican president like Roosevelt is consistent with a rejection of socialism, and Fullerton, who quotes the text of the International and Karl Marx (PP, 196–7) and describes with some horror the mounting tide of social unrest, workers' strikes, and the myth of the "general strike," is no socialist fellow-traveler. Yet his vision of history, determined both by "money" (let us say economic power) and "public opinion" (let us say ideologies like nationalism) (PP, 195), defined as two "occult powers" behind governments, is not incompatible with the main lessons of Marx and Engels. Fullerton is not blind to the combination of those two forces as he sees them merging together in Germany: "Germany is a parvenu Power and full of Pangermans who want to 'make history,' and not merely to "make money" (PP, 210). He also observes that, in October 1912, the mills of Gary, Indiana, had to close because 2,750 workers of Slavic origin decided all at once to join the crusade of the Balkan states against the Turks (PP, 201 n. 1).

Unanimism and Global or Local Crises

It seems, in consequence of these new trends, that "unanimism" should stand out as the literary movement most attuned to this period. Jules Romains had launched *unanimisme* in 1905 with a number of critical articles, published *La Vie unanime* in 1908, and then added to this book so as to publish a new collection of poems in 1913, developing its Whitmanian and collectivistic mode, putting forward the life of "groups" in which individuals are molded, and defining as the new literary sites the streets, the theater, factories, dining halls, and the crowds in the metro.[26] Nevertheless, as we will see, "modernist" poets like Guillaume Apollinaire and his friends were to clash with Romains' generous but somewhat fuzzy poetics of the collective, and his appeal to common sense. What we tend to call "high modernism" today is mostly born out of a reaction – often critical, at times sympathetic – to three avant-gardist artistic trends that had come to the fore between 1906 and 1910, unanimism, cubism, and futurism. Their cumulative impact lasted longer, to be sure, and we find a confirmation of this in the fact that Ezra Pound adapted the French *unanimisme* when he launched a similarly French-sounding *imagisme* in London, mostly to avoid being confused with Italian futurism. In fact, the poetics of the "unanimist" group as well as the decision to situate modernity in an urban space goes back to Baudelaire and his symbolist admirers,[27] but the *unanimistes* wanted to break with the deliberately obscure and allusive style of the late symbolists. They wanted to write as simply as one speaks (a position shared initially by the London imagists) in order to address an audience as effectively as possible. They also derided pure experimentalism such as had been unleashed by Marinetti's inarticulate *parole in libertà*. But Anglo-American modernism initially refused the collectivist drift of the French unanimists in the name of "individualism." It is tempting to apply to the ideology of the arts the paradox outlined by Morton Fullerton: individualism flares up most when it is threatened, exactly as nationalism returns as the repressed – either of the old empires like the Austro-Hungarian double monarchy, or of a new economic uniformization of the world at the hands of international financiers.

In this framework, modernist globalization should not be seen as a recent factor associated with late capitalism as we tend to believe,[28] but as an older trend closely linked to the development of European and American imperialisms at the end of the nineteenth century, a development that reached a climax when the competitive logic of international capital and the explosion of newly unleashed nationalisms inevitably led to a world war. The world-wide web of the internet in which we think we see a pat allegory of today's globalized planet has its inception in an earlier historical process culminating in a world-wide war. In other words, we are not yet out of the modernist period, which is why it is so vital to understand its origins. My ambition will therefore be to provide an answer to simple questions. Was modernism already a visible and dominant trend in 1913? How international or cosmopolitan was modernism in 1913? Was it brought about by the same groundswell of nationalism that led to global war in the summer of 1914, or did the war kill its spirit of cosmopolitan generosity? If modernism was traversed from the start by a sense of crisis, was it unable to provide a solution because it needed the deployment of the crisis to thrive or because it could not avoid being a cultural symptom of a much larger cultural collapse?

Here, much more relevant than Romains' poetic *unanimisme*, would be W. E. B. Du Bois' famous journal *The Crisis*, which was launched in 1910. Du Bois had made himself noticeable as an agitator and a teacher, as the celebrated author of *The Souls of Black Folk* and *The Philadelphia Negro*. He embodied the radical vanguard of the black movement fighting for equal rights, which led to a clash with the politics of conciliation led by Booker T. Washington. The clash erupted when the National Association for the Advancement of Colored People (NAACP) chose him as its director of publicity and research. Du Bois left Atlanta where he had been teaching and moved to New York, where he founded *The Crisis: A Record of the Darker Races* in November 1910.[29] This very outspoken monthly was a tremendous success: the first issue of 1,000 sold out; the next month the run was 2,500, rising to 6,000 in March 1911. In April 1912 it had 22,500 subscribers, and was reaching 33,000 subscribers by 1914. The journal was devoted to the race problem, and its first issue dealt squarely with a vision that had horrified Du Bois: the unpunished lynchings of blacks in the South and even in Pennsylvania. He also documented the long-term history of Africa (I will return to this topic in chapter 5) and took sides with the suffragettes, asking his fellow militants to support the vote for women.

In a famous article of April 1913, "Hail Columbia!", he praises the 5,000 women who had braved the police horses and a rowdy crowd when marching in Washington, DC, stressing that they were showing the way to the black man in his quest for dignity and equality. He was as much of a feminist as he was a socialist, praising Eugene Debs, and hoping that the new President Wilson would take the black vote into some consideration (he was soon disillusioned). He had studied Kant and Hegel, but his rhetoric was closer to biblical verses and nineteenth-century poetry. The name of the journal came from an 1844 poem by James Russell Lowell which declaimed:

And the slave, where'er he cowers, feels the soul within him climb
To the awful verge of manhood, as the energy sublime
Of a century bursts full-blossomed on the thorny stem of Time.

Du Bois was skeptical of organized labor, knowing well that even the leftist "wobblies" of the IWW (Industrial Workers of the World) were reluctant to admit black workers, who were also steadily expelled from most organized labor unions. Du Bois was also a novelist of talent (I will return to his "economic" novel, *The Quest of the Silver Fleece*) and a tireless and convincing proselytizer. He had great hopes of the help that could be provided by international public opinion, especially in England and France, but his radicalism alienated some of his friends at the NAACP. I will return to the main tenets of his philosophy, limiting myself to noting that he saw very well in 1910–13 that the time was "a critical time in the history of the advancement of man." He also saw, with as much clarity as Fullerton, that the causes of the war were economic before being political – although he had not become a Marxist yet, as he was to do in the thirties. His later political radicalization led to his growing alienation from an American public consensus and his subsequent decision to spend the rest of his life in exile. He was aware that America was changing fast, and that the time was ripe for decisive political action. Fullerton had also insisted on this factor, stressing that if Londoners or Parisians went abroad for a while, they would go back to cities that were fundamentally identical, whereas a New Yorker would barely recognize his surroundings even after a short absence (*PP*, 13–14). Indeed, urban America changed more between 1890 and 1910 than in the whole preceding century, and this relentless transformation announced future metamorphoses in Europe.

We will see that this thesis is echoed and developed in Edith Wharton's *The Custom of the Country*. Let us simply recall that this time of change and crisis was also giving birth to the world as we know it now: an age when telephones, motor cars, electric light, central heating, X-rays, cinemas, radium, airplanes, or the wireless were known to most urban citizens of the first world. This is our present age of a globalized economy – when free trade transforms the whole globe, linking the farthest outposts in which cheap labor can be found with the hubs of international finance – with the difference that today these amenities are available to a larger segment of the population. We may as well notice with some nostalgia that a few perks known to well-off men and women of 1913 have disappeared. Thus the mail was delivered four times a day in Paris, and Proust could reach his correspondents in an hour thanks to the *pneumatique*. Proust also subscribed to the *théâtrophone*, a service that connected him by telephone with the opera and major theaters, allowing him to hear musical or theatrical performances at home in real time.

Meanwhile, Edith Wharton had taken the habit of rushing in and out of European countries and even Morocco in her famous "motor-flights" that terrorized Henry James. And Proust would lose his last true love, his one-time chauffeur Agostinelli, to the lure of faster airplanes: Agostinelli, who by that time called himself Marcel Swann, drowned in the Mediterranean in the spring of 1914 after crashing his training airplane into the sea. The roar of the engine barely allows us to overhear Richard Strauss and Hugo von Hofmannsthal as they discuss their joint opera, *Die Frau ohne Schatten*, during a rapid automobile tour of northern Italy in the spring of 1913. No doubt, the modern art form par excellence would be film: its reels of silently flickering frames would bring, along with a universal language of images accompanied by live music, the sense of a giddy acceleration of the whole world.

Chapter 1

The New in the Arts

In the chapters that follow, I will suggest a new way of reading modernism historically and internationally. It will engage with cultural history defined in a global context while providing precise readings of individual texts or artistic masterpieces. My aim will be to study the emergence of international modernism in literature and the arts by focusing on one single year that will function as a frame, a limit, and a global attractor of trends and currents. The constraint of limiting the investigation to one year recontextualizes dynamically the readings of canonical and non-canonical works alike. In a "slice" carved out from a productive historical period, cross-references multiply and interconnect. This approach will lead to an original assessment of the links between modernity, the avant-garde, and national or international artistic movements. Modernism will be inserted into the broader context of a newly "globalized" world literature, showing the "new" in literature and the arts, including film, the theater, music, and the visual arts as part and parcel of a resolutely transatlantic, comparatist, and multidisciplinary method. A new picture of cosmopolitan modernism will emerge from this pointillist mosaic.

The year 1913 was marked by two cultural shocks that made the modernity of modern art highly visible: the scandal caused by the premiere of *The Rite of Spring* in Paris and the uproar over the exhibition of modern paintings at the Armory Show in New York. Music and painting should have pride of place here, although cinema's emergence seems to be the proper emblem of the age. The medium itself was so recent that nobody was upset by its novelty – it was more a matter of adapting public taste to the new possibilities offered by technology.

Figure 1   Armory Show poster. 1913. Hirshborn Museum and Sculpture
Gallery, Smithsonian Institution, Washington, DC

Film

Late in September 1909 James Joyce gathered a group of businessmen known to have invested in the three cinema theaters of Trieste, and declared: "I know a city of 500,000 inhabitants where there is not a single cinema."[1] Immediately, they wanted to know where this investor's haven was to be found. The answer was Dublin, and Joyce was soon after sent with some capital to start cinemas in as many cities as possible in Ireland. The only cinema to open was the Volta in Dublin, a venture that did not meet with the expected financial success, although it did relatively well at first, partly because Joyce went back to Trieste less than three months after the opening, partly because Italian films like *Nero* or *Beatrice Cenci* appealed less to an Irish audience than to the Austro-Italian Triestine taste, but it reveals that by the end of the first decade of the twentieth century any major European city was supposed to have a cinema. For instance, Brussels had 115 cinemas and Paris some 200, while New York already had 986 cinemas in 1913. Indeed, the French and Italian film industries that had dominated the first decade were soon to be overtaken by the American and German centers of production in the twenties.

The main change that occurred in 1913 was the length of the films shown. Up to 1913 the standard length of a film remained one reel, which meant that the film lasted no more than 15 minutes. Film-makers believed that they were producing a popular art form for the masses, hence people whose attention-span was limited. The first feature-length film was *The Story of the Kelly Gang*, made in Australia. Directed by Charles Tait, it lasted 70 minutes, which was unprecedented when it was released in Australia in December 1906, and later in the United Kingdom in January 1908. Soon other multiple-reel films were released: *Queen Elizabeth* in France (1912) and, in Italy, *Quo Vadis?* (1913) and *Cabiria* (1914). *Quo Vadis?* adapted the best-selling novel by Henry Sienkiewicz about Nero's persecution of Christians in Rome and was directed by Enrico Guazzoni. It was made in 12 reels and lasted three hours, starring Christopher Young and Gustavo Serena. Guazzoni preferred staging huge dramatic tableaux, and had a colossal circus as a recurrent stage. There, one could admire many man-eating lions as well as racing chariots engaged in showy stunts, in a surprising anticipation of effects that we tend to associate with later Hollywood classics such as *Ben Hur*. *Quo Vadis?* was immediately a huge success in Italy, and it was soon imported to America, where it was reduced to eight reels. It was such a hit in New York (at the Astor theater people paid up to $1.50 to see it, much more than the usual ticket) that it demonstrated concretely the popular craving for full-length films. In

1913 Italy was the second largest importer of films, and it still set the standards of taste and technique. This was also the time of the first divas, such as Asta Nielsen, who starred in the erotic Danish film of Ole Olsen, *The Abyss* (1910), or Lyda Borelli and Francesca Bertini, the first Italian "stars" who performed to great applause in *Mark Anthony and Cleopatra* (1913). The Italian preference for "peplums" accounts for the wide appeal of *The Last Days of Pompeii*, a remake of an older version with more actors and more money directed by Mario Caserini in 1913. It was obviously the end of the first and heroic period of the cinema – the pioneer Georges Meliès realized his last film, *Le Voyage de la famille Berrichon*, in 1913, and was after that beset by financial and medical problems.

The evolution toward the multi-reel or "feature" film also marked the career of David Wark Griffith in America. In an advertisement published in the *New York Dramatic Mirror* on December 3, 1913, Griffith proclaimed himself the "producer of all the great Biograph successes, revolutionizing Motion Picture drama and founding the modern technique of the art." Born on January 22, 1875, in a Kentucky village, Griffith knew about bluster, self-inflation, and promotion. His role-model was a father who had been a farmer, a Confederate Civil War hero, an adventurer, and a Kentucky legislator. His mother, a devout evangelical Methodist, gave him a sense of stability and strict moral values. He began as an itinerant actor in 1895, acting in various locales for 12 years under pseudonyms. In 1907 he found work as an actor and scenarist for films in New York. He was soon hired by the Biograph Company's studio in New York, where he directed his first film in 1908. These were mostly one-reel nickelodeon comedies. Griffith also shot a number of historical films that were not very successful, and in 1912 shot *The Sunbeam*, a comedy that prefigures Chaplin's work. (Chaplin, who had been acting since 1912, shot his first films, such as *Kid Auto Races*, in 1914, and he achieved considerable popularity with *The Tramp* in 1915.) The 1912 *Female of the Species*, a Darwinian tale of survival and jealousy in the desert, was shot on location by Griffith with Claire MacDowell, Mary Pickford, and Dorothy Bernard. *An Unseen Enemy* (1912) features the film debuts of both Dorothy and Lillian Gish. He also indulged his taste for historical pageants, such as *Judith of Bethulia* (1913), with Blanche Sweet, Lionel Barrymore, and the Gish sisters – this was, after all, an age of pageants, as we will see with Du Bois' *Ethiopia*.

One of the most popular Biograph films, *The Musketeers of Pig Alley* (1912), announces the genre of gangster films by romanticizing gangster life. In this one, it was of course Lillian Gish who sparked off a gang war. *The House of Darkness* (1913), set in an insane asylum, is considered Griffith's darkest film. *Death's Marathon* (1913) is a short narrating the story of a man who embezzles funds to pay his gambling debts. A friend chases him as he toys with a pistol, talking meanwhile on the phone with his wife, played by Lillian Gish. Tod Browning starred in two 1913 short films, *Scenting a Terrible Crime* and *A Fallen Hero*. Other 1913 shorts include *The Battle of Elderbush Gulch*, *The Primitive Man*, and *The House of Darkness*, but Griffith was starting to move toward full-length feature films. A two-reel film from 1913, *The Mothering Heart*, is cloyingly sentimental, featuring Lillian Gish in her first major role (her husband betrays her with another woman while their baby becomes mortally ill). Her inspired acting transcended sentimentality, creating a deeply moving portrait of a woman and mother. In 1908 Griffith had "discovered" a pleasant, cheap suburb of Los Angeles, where he shot one film: *Hollywood*. Finally, at the end of 1913, Griffith parted with Biograph to go west, to work on feature films such as *Birth of a Nation* (1915) and *Intolerance* (1916). These two films would soon establish his reputation as a genius of the new medium. They would influence all other film-makers despite their deeply reactionary message. Even when Du Bois and his friends in the NAACP tried to have them banned, they had to acknowledge that they were beautifully made. The year 1913 had been a turning point for the American film industry. After 1913, Hollywood become America's indisputable movie production center, and it would soon dominate the whole world.

Like Griffith, Louis Feuillade had written and directed approximately 800 shorts, features, and serials in 18 years. He, too, was a pioneer of narrative, developing a filmic language adapted to the constraints of the moving image. Feuillade also filmed outside the studios, favoring open-air shooting, which replaced theatrical artifice and trick effects with an increased realism. In 1906 he became Gaumont's principal director. In addition to social dramas, chase films, comedies, and popular series, he invented the genre of the serial mystery film. He then decided to adapt *Fantômas*, the endless stream of best-selling crime stories that were penned jointly by Pierre Souvestre and Marcel Allain between 1911 and 1914.[2] In *Fantômas*, the eponymous hero is a daring criminal who accomplishes the most incredible thefts, crimes, and stunts and always escapes, most of the time by exchanging identities with his victims. One novelty in the serials *Fantômas* (1913), *Les Vampires* (1915), and *Judex* (1917) was that they were shot on location throughout France. These films captured the attention of a large audience, and after the war they thrilled the surrealists, who took them as emblems of a highly developed popular culture; they relished their disturbing reshuffling of identities, their reliance of plots on modernist pseudo-machineries, their creepy cynicism (the real hero is a hardened murderer), as well as their sudden epiphanies of pure urban poetry.

The new medium was ideally suited to adapt gothic horror stories. Poe's or Stevenson's tales were favorites. In Germany, *The Student of Prague* (1913), directed by Stellan Rye and Paul Wegener, depicted in two reels a poor student who had fallen for a beautiful countess and in consequence sold not just his soul but his own reflection to the Devil. The doppelgänger commits crimes of which the student is accused. The acting technique of Paul Wegener as the student was influenced by the Max Reinhardt company, developing expressionist techniques that made the drama still quite impressive. In the United States, the very prolific Irish-born director Herbert Brenon shot the first Universal Studios horror film with *Dr. Jekyll and Mr. Hyde* (1913). King Baggot, the main actor, conveyed very effectively Hyde's antisocial violence. This was not the first nor the last adaptation of Stevenson's classic, but it was one of Baggot's most haunting performances.

On the whole, people were rather optimistic about the consequences of a more and more widespread use of film. The French journalist René Doumic believed that film would bring about a more "democratic art" since it brought kings, emperors, and prime ministers closer to the people. Presidents like Poincaré and Wilson soon learned to use the technology to their advantage. For Doumic, the cinematograph was "a kind of popular annex to the Elysée Palace."[3] Even when Apollinaire claimed that the cinema was less international in 1917 than it had been before ("And notice that the cinema, which is the perfect cosmopolitan art, already shows ethnic differences immediately apparent to everyone, and film enthusiasts immediately distinguish between an American and an Italian film"[4]), he remarked that the new art was the current epoch's "popular art *par excellence*" and that it had reshaped the ways in which people perceived the world by forcing the general public to think in moving images.[5]

Music

I have already mentioned the Parisian scandal caused by the premiere of *The Rite of Spring* (*Le Sacre du printemps* – soon dubbed *Le Massacre du printemps* by Parisian wits[6]). It was the equivalent of the battle of Hernani in 1830, a fracas that consecrated the victory of the young Romantics over the classicists. As in Hugo's drama, the camps were drawn in advance at the premiere, and Stravinsky, Diaghilev, and the Ballets Russes figure as the heroes of the avant-garde. When they won, it looked as if music was the more advanced medium, at least because it clearly crossed national boundaries, with the dominant Russophilia in Paris, as well as historical and epochal limits: Debussy exclaimed, when he saw the score of Stravinsky's *Rite*, "This is negro music!" (*C'est une musique nègre*) – which may have been a qualified compliment. With different accents, all the major musical innovators in 1913 – Arnold Schoenberg in Vienna and Berlin, Ferruccio Busoni in Berlin, Claude Debussy and Erik Satie in France, Igor Stravinsky in St Petersburg and Paris, Charles Ives in America – expressed at the same time the urge to free themselves from the preordained rules of classical harmony, and to reject the cult of vertical and horizontal polyphonic integration that had obtained at least since Bach. To do so, they had either to look for earlier models, as Debussy did at one point, to opt for radical primitivism, as Stravinsky seemed to be doing, or to uproot systematically the whole musical language of tonality. No one had gone further in the latter endeavor than Schoenberg, who nevertheless was aware that this was less a revolution than an evolution that suddenly radicalized trends one could find in the later Beethoven, in Wagner's leitmotivistic chromatism, or in Brahms' orchestral polyphonies. Busoni, one of the first to endorse the experiments led by Schoenberg, Berg, and Webern, gave a theoretical framework to the movement when he published his *Sketches of a New Musical Esthetic* in 1907. This was followed by Schoenberg's publication of his massive volume *Harmonielehre* (*Treatise on Harmony*) in 1911, in order to prove to his detractors that he knew enough about harmony – before explaining that it was time to rethink it completely.

I have already mentioned *Pierrot Lunaire*, first performed in October 1912 in Berlin. There, Schoenberg experimented freely with contextual atonality, with *Sprechstimme*, a "speech-voice" or animated declamation in which the female singer speaks more than she sings – which seems to suggest that the voice leads the music. He also used *Klangfarbenmelodie* in the accompaniment of the voice by a small ensemble made up of a flute, a clarinet, a violin, a cello, and a piano. It has remained a classic of modern music, especially when it was revived by Pierre Boulez in the sixties to launch a second school of serial music. The work was a success in Berlin and Vienna, and so were the *Gurrelieder*, written between 1900 and 1901, and orchestrated in 1911. The premiere was given in March 1913 in Vienna, and led to the composer's first public triumph, with standing ovations that lasted 15 minutes. These "songs" compose a late Romantic oratorio whose lush polyphonic style calls up the later Mahler – they did not correspond to Schoenberg's more recent preoccupations. A few weeks later, it was the reverse: the Viennese audience erupted in general uproar and halted the performance of new music by Berg, Webern, and Schoenberg. This taught Schoenberg something about the limits of the public's acceptance when it came to atonality. He decided to return to Berlin, and in the autumn of 1913 completed *Die glückliche*

Hand, a precursor to his later opera *Moses und Aron*. This extremely condensed piece is a "male" companion to the earlier musical drama *Erwartung*. There, a generic man is seen struggling with workers in order to produce a gold ring for the ideal woman. The allegory is rather opaque, but the music is intense, sumptuous, elliptical, unexpected, and crepitating, and pushes Schoenberg's previous expressionistic forays toward a higher level of non-tonal contrapuntal organization. All commentators have stressed Schoenberg's decade-long silence after 1913 – no doubt the war had something to do with it – but also the need to formulate a new musical language.

Igor Stravinsky's progression was no less rapid. The young protégé of Rimsky-Korsakov found his way to European pre-eminence after he associated himself with Diaghilev, who since 1906 had been promoting the Ballets Russes in Paris. The triumphant success of ballets like *Firebird* in 1910 and *Petrushka* in 1911 led Stravinsky to a more ambitious project. Its gestation dates back to 1910 when, as he explains in his memoirs, he had a strange dream of a "pagan ritual" in which old men are sitting in a circle gazing at a beautiful young woman destined to be sacrificed to placate their gods. She is to dance herself to death, and to compose this new music Stravinsky worked with Nikolai Rerikh, a stage designer and painter who had done intensive research on early Russian themes, pagan sacrifices, and Slavic legends. Prehistoric folklore was a source of inspiration for many at the time, as is clear from the wide appeal of a novel like *The War of Fire*, published in 1911 by the brothers Rosny, who had made a specialty of primitivist romances set in prehistory with rough cave men discovering their humanity.

Thanks to Diaghilev and the exceptional qualities of his main dancer, Nijinsky, ballet – especially *ballet russe* – emerged as the main modernist genre after 1910: "Diaghilev had invented a new art form, the ballet as *Gesamtkunstwerk*: an entertainment, not more than an hour long, in which all the elements, the story (if any), music, décor, and choreography, were commissioned by himself to form a complete whole."[7] Whereas Wagner had wanted operas to become "total works of art" entailing long performances, entire cycles, and an almost religious fervor, the new Russian ballet was fast, stunning, elegant, and short. The decors and costumes by Bakst were as much admired as the grace of the ballerinas; and there was the incomparable Nijinsky. The triumph of *L'Après-midi d'un faune* in 1912, contrasted Debussy's subtle and fluid impressionistic score and the hieratic gestures of the nymphs and of the Faun, while Nijinsky ended with an accurately mimed orgasm to conclude with a "dying fall" – the Faun's erotic reverie had no doubt contributed to this new enthusiasm. Thus the year 1913 began well, but with unfortunate competition from Debussy's *Jeux*, opening on May 15, 1913, and

The Rite of Spring starting two weeks later. In *Jeux*, to Debussy's dismay, Nijinsky started experimenting with a new type of choreographic minimalism, and he barely danced, "letting the music pass." The theme was "modern" in that it used tennis-playing as a backdrop for elegant flirtation, which contrasted with the fierce wildness of *Rite of Spring*, simply choreographed by Nijinsky. Noticing that the Paris audience had not taken to *Jeux*, surprised by musical innovations that they could not follow, uncertain about the ironical stylization of the whole show, Diaghilev had carefully staged an "event" that was to look like a scandal. He had given free tickets to many young artists and sympathizers whose mission was to clap; he knew that Stravinsky's score was revolutionary and that Nijinsky's choreography, insisting on "prehistoric" body attitudes, with turned-in, bent knees and turned-in toes would set new standards, but he did not want to take chances.

One of the most condensed (if not totally reliable) descriptions of the scandal caused by *The Rite of Spring* even at the second performance can be found in Gertrude Stein's *Autobiography of Alice B. Toklas*:

> The performance began. No sooner had it commenced when the excitement began. The scene now so well known with its brilliantly coloured background now not all extraordinary, outraged the Paris audience. No sooner did the music begin and the dancing than they began to hiss. The defenders began to applaud. We could hear nothing, as a matter of fact I never did hear any of the music of the *Sacre du Printemps* because it was the only time I ever saw it and one literally could not, through the whole performance, hear the sound of music.[8]

Valentine Gross gives a similar account of the premiere:

> The theatre seemed to be shaken by an earthquake. It seemed to shudder. People shouted insults, howled and whistled, drowning the music. There was slapping and even punching. [. . .] I saw Maurice Delage beet-root red with indignation, little Maurice Ravel truculent as a fighting-cock, and Léon-Paul Fargue spitting out crushing remarks at the hissing boxes. [. . .] The ballet was astoundingly beautiful.[9]

The 34-minute work had scores of surprises for the audience: they could not recognize the bassoon that began with a weird solo, the rhythms were changing all the time, the choreography was arranged by Nijinsky, who shouted numbers – "17!", "18!" – to cue his dancers, and the idea of seeing a virgin sacrificed to a sun-god under the watchful gaze of the elders after a number of ritual dances was enough to stun a polite audience in 1913. But by the third performance the fracas had subsided, and the audience could enjoy the show with respectful attention. Almost everybody who was an artist, a poet, or a writer came to see it in those four performances of May and June 1913. The musicological analysis of the *Rite* has been done a number of times, but no one has been better able than André Boucourechliev to describe the interaction between dissonance and rhythm, showing how the dense polyrhythmic structure compensates for the lack of a definite tonality. As Stravinsky was to repeat later, unlike the Viennese composers, he had not followed any theory but his own ear.[10]

Jean Cocteau, who was a close friend and collaborator of Stravinsky at the time, saw in this ballet "the Georgics of a prehistoric age" echoing the violence of the Russian spring when the earth suddenly breaks free of its ice. We will return to Cocteau, who insisted on the aggressive theme of blood-rite barely sublimated as a "dance to death." The anthropological content seemed to justify or condone sheer primitivism overlaid with orgiastic overtones. Adorno writes that *The Rite of Spring* was to remain as Stravinsky's "most progressive composition" from the point of view of musical composition, while being the most "regressive" in the sense that it depicts human sacrifice as justified by the group in an "esthetic game with barbarism."[11] Like Debussy, Adorno tends to classify the *Rite* as *art nègre* with a Slavic slant, and in a section entitled *"Sacre* and African Sculpture" he compares astutely Stravinsky's ballet with a contemporary book by Freud, *Totem and Taboo*:

> In spite of the stylistic contrast between *Petrouchka*, the masterpiece of almost culinary design, and the tumultuous ballet, both have a common nucleus – sacrifice without tragedy, made not in the name of a renewed image of man, but only in the blind affirmation of a situation recognized by the victim. This insight can find expression either through self-mockery or through self-annihilation. Such a motif, which completely determines the manner of conduct of the music, steps forth from the frivolous mask of Petrouchka and appears in sanguinary gravity in *Sacre*. This belongs to the years when wild men came to be called primitives, to the sphere of Frazer and Lévy-Bruhl, and further of Freud's *Totem and Taboo*.[12]

A little later, Adorno compares the "deliriousness" of the ballet with the consequences of the Freudian prohibition of incest[13] – showing that the has grasped Freud's link between human sacrifices, early forms of religion, and the killing of the victim, who embodies the god in whom the murdered father of the horde has been transmuted. This explains why there is something regressive but also therapeutic in the ballet, whose formal paradox is that this ritual is accomplished "without tragedy" – unless we see in the tortured rhythmic form something comparable to the Greek tension between the world of gods and men, fate swaying over communal liberties.

Adorno's thesis is radical: only Schoenberg embodies real innovation; he accomplishes the synthesis of his major predecessors and pushes the evolution of music forward, toward self-conscious atonality. Stravinsky on the other hand, unable to found a new system, relies on nationalistic folklore and a Jungian concept of a collective unconscious (it was not an accident that the idea came to him in a dream). His modernism meets anarchism, but then peters out in archaism – infantilism is lurking behind the rebellion, for "the primitivism of yesterday is the naiveté of today."[14] Adorno realized after the publication of his first essay that he had over-systematized the opposition between the two composers: Schoenberg was not even flattered, but rather angry at the negative evaluation of his old friend Stravinsky; the latter remained Olympian and silent. Nevertheless, soon after the publication of Adorno's book he reverted to serialism.[15] Adorno is not so sure whether Stravinsky is to be called Freudian or Jungian, which, as will see, as early as 1913 was a real alternative. One can say that, on Adorno's view, Stravinsky repeats the evolution of Richard Strauss, who alternated between moments of sheer innovation – as with the ground-breaking *Salomé* (1906) followed by *Elektra* (1908), and by *Ariadne auf Naxos* (1912), the last two operas being too advanced for the public – and easier operas, such as the saccharine and easy *Rosenkavalier* (1910), which was extremely popular. I will return later to his collaboration with Hugo von Hofmannsthal on *Die Frau ohne Schatten*, begun in 1912/13 and completed in 1917, a project that eventually culminated in a neoclassicism similar to Stravinsky's work in the twenties.

Perhaps pushed forward by the rhythmic innovations introduced by Stravinsky's ballet, after the spring of 1913 the piano remained Debussy's privileged instrument of expression and exploration. Debussy's two books of *Preludes for Piano*, especially the second one, written between 1911 and April 1913, again play with ancient Greek modes as he had done earlier; they do not avoid dissonances and are generally considered to be his last masterpiece. The rivalry between Maurice Ravel, who had given a first public performance of Satie's second *Sarabande* at the Salle Gaveau to considerable public acclaim in 1911, and Debussy, who soon after also performed Satie's quirky pieces, had given an added twist to the old master's sudden fame. In 1913, very pleased to have been rediscovered for music composed in 1887 and 1888, Satie gave vent to his humoristic wit, producing piano works with untranslatable titles like *Embryons désséchés; I. D'Holothuries. II. D'Edriophtalma. III. De Podophtalma*, or *Croquis et agaceries d'un gros bonhomme en bois*. Moving from fin-de-siècle eccentricities to proto-Dadaism, he invented impossible instructions for his performers; a piece had the annotation "Like a nightingale with a toothache."[16] This irreverent spirit is a far cry from the "symphonic poems" that were also in vogue, with Scriabin's *Prometheus* in Moscow and Elgar's *Falstaff* in London. Scriabin and Elgar, closer in taste and style to Richard Strauss, had opted for a compromise between tradition and innovation – it was thus no surprise to see Sir Edward Elgar compose an official *Coronation March* for the British king in 1911.

These ceremonial pieces contrast with the new trend that was coming from across the Atlantic Ocean: jazz music. The first decade of the century was the time when a pioneer like Scott Joplin was desperately attempting to leave his mark in high culture by having his opera performed. Let us retrace his steps. Joplin had been made famous at the age of 31 by the "Maple Leaf Rag" (1899), a score that by 1909 had sold half a million of copies, and between 1900 and 1914 he authored more than 60 compositions, most of them "rags." He attempted to write a first opera in 1903, *A Guest of Honor*, to commemorate Booker T. Washington's famous dinner with President Roosevelt at the White House in 1901. In 1911 he moved to New York City and composed his magnum opus, an opera called *Treemonisha*. Based on the experiences of his second wife, who died at the age of 20, it told the tale of a young black woman from the South who tries to reject local superstitions and fights for self-improvement and education. In 1913 he was still trying to get *Treemonisha* produced, with no success, and while he composed *Kismet Rag* his health was failing – he died of syphilis in 1917, but had durably established ragtime as the new popular music. In 1913 imitators were legion: Charles "Lucky" Roberts, a Harlem pianist, had a first ragtime piece published as "Junk Man Rag," and everybody knew "hits" like "All Aboard for Dixie Land" or Jack Glogan's "The Airplane." Mark Sennet even directed a film called *That Ragtime Band* in 1913. But it was in 1912 that Gene Buck and Herman Ruby had composed the lyrics for a ragtime piece by David Stamper called "That Shakespearian Rag." Published in London in 1912, it quoted Shakespeare rather wittily if predictably (with "Friends, Romans, Countrymen . . ." and "My kingdom for a horse"). The chorus intoned: "That Shakespearian rag – Most intelligent, very elegant, That old classical rag has the proper stuff . . ." No doubt amused by these literary echoes, T. S. Eliot quoted it in the *Waste Land*, capturing in precisely onomatopoeic diction the new syncopation, a clear sing of modernist splicing of the of the old and the new: "O O O O that Shakespeherian Rag – / It's so elegant / So intelligent."[17]

Meanwhile a few composers were already attentive to those new rhythms – Stravinsky's frantic beats in *Rite of Spring* are unthinkable without the dual influence of Russian folklore music and early jazz. Debussy had written *Children's Corner* in 1906 (with the well-known "Golliwog's Cake-Walk"), and Satie had played with jazz rhythms in the first decade of the century. Charles Ives, too, was very attentive to the special cadences generated by small-town brass bands in Connecticut, always paying homage to his beloved father's career as the leader of the Danbury Brass Band, and mixing echoes of patriotic songs, the national anthem, Negro songs, blues, jazz, and ragtime to his more experimental chords "not tied to any key," as he said more than once. Like Schoenberg and Stravinsky, he always aimed at associating the vernacular and the cultivated, but he went further in just listening to the dancing but syncopated rhythms of early jazz music. Thus as early as 1902 he wrote "ragtime dances," an experiment in cubistic ragtime. A typical work of the early period is *New England Holydays*, composed between 1904 and 1913. Ives connects the four seasons with American official dates; winter is emblematized by George Washington's birthday, spring by Decoration Day (in which two bands play two different marches simultaneously), summer by the Fourth of July (for which we hear off-key and off-rhythm versions of *Yankee Doodle*, *Katy Darling*, the Battle Hymn of the Republic, gospel songs, and so on), and autumn is illustrated by Thanksgiving. Ives is thus both a radical experimenter like Busoni or Schoenberg's two main disciples, Berg and Webern, and an American Romantic, full of nostalgia for religious hymns, small-town marches, patriotic commemorations. His solutions are very close in spirit to those of the first Viennese school – the wish to let the inner life of chords control harmony and risk slipping out of it, by using chromatic, dissonant, or atonal chords that work their way to build a fully integrated musical structure. The irony is that most contemporaries, at least before the war, thought that Ives was simply untutored, a cranky amateur who did not know the rules of harmony and counterpoint, whereas he was desperately trying to bypass these. The result, so varied and pleasing to modern ears, gives us now the musical equivalent of American transcendentalism, the only truly American philosophy according to Stanley Cavell. It is thus no coincidence that Ives alluded so often to Emerson and Thoreau.

Painting

In 1913, more than ever before, the connections between painting, music, and literature were numerous and obvious. This led Jean Cocteau to describe *The Rite of Spring* as a pure "Fauvist" work: "When all is said and done, the *Sacre* is still a 'Fauvist' work, an organized 'Fauvist' work."[18] Fauvism was associated with Gauguin and Matisse, whose rebellion against the usual concepts of form and color had provoked an artistic revolution in 1903–5 – besides, a certain brand of primitivism was always associated with it. Adorno, who quotes Cocteau, systematizes the equivalences.[19] Debussy is the quintessential impressionist composer, while Stravinsky is either a "Fauve" or a "cubist." In the early Schoenberg, one witnesses the new expressivity of a subjectivity that at times withdraws into itself and at times attempts to encompass the whole universe; this would be enough to qualify Schoenberg as an expressionist, an affiliation that is immediately confirmed by a glance at his paintings. Schoenberg abandoned painting around 1913, to return to it much later – a sign that his thinking was evolving and that he was moving in the direction of pure abstraction. These descriptions are useful up to a point, as one can immediately see echoes between cubism and Stravinsky's simultaneous multidimensionality of rhythm, his *Rite* giving the rough equivalent of Picasso's faces caught through several perspectives at once. They beg the question of what cubism meant in 1913.

When discussing cubism, it is customary to distinguish between the first wave of so-called "analytical cubism" that started in 1907 with Picasso's *Les Demoiselles d'Avignon* and was systematized by Léger, Braque, and of course Picasso in 1909–10, from the second wave, "synthetic cubism," that began in 1912 and was practiced by Gleizes, Metzinger, Delaunay, Gris, and all the above-mentioned artists. This soon led to other types of experiments in 1912–13, as when Picasso and Braque started pasting bits of oilcloth, fragments of newspapers, or advertisements to the canvas, in the device known as collage.[20] In 1913 Apollinaire was asked by the German review of the expressionists, *Der Sturm*, to provide a survey of "Modern Painting" in that year. The article was published in February 1913,[21] just after a visit to Berlin by Apollinaire and Delaunay, and it maps usefully the various recent tendencies. Apollinaire knew well all the major painters in Paris, and was a close friend of Picasso, Matisse, and Delaunay. The two main schools that he sees as dominant in 1913 are cubism and orphism – the latter being Delaunay's own group. On Apollinaire's account, Picasso owed the discovery of cubism to Maurice de Vlaminck, who as early as 1902 collected African masks and imitated their stylized shapes, and André Derain, who followed suit. In 1905 Derain met Matisse; then one year later he became closer to Picasso. The fascination for Negro art gave young painters a new sense of colors and shapes. What Picasso, Braque, Metzinger, Gleizes, Léger, and Gris started painting in 1905–6 became more angular and rigid, and the new art was dubbed "cubist" by Matisse, a term that was soon after accepted by the painters themselves.

Out of this first cubism, which tended to analyze and decompose objects into their constituent planes, a new tendency emerged with Picabia and Duchamp, while Delaunay was inventing an art of pure color, playing with the prismatic derivations of light. Apollinaire makes the connection between orphism and the Blaue Reiter group that launched German expressionism, naming Kandinsky, Marc, Macke, and a few others: like Delaunay, they were interested in the spiritual properties of light and shapes. Picasso and Braque had started gluing to their canvases advertisements, letters, and other social signs because they wanted to call up the experience of the big city in which all the signs of publicity strike the eye. Finally, Apollinaire sees the Italian futurists as being generated by the crossing of cubism with Fauvism. All these schools share a common concern for the simultaneity of different levels of perception – and simultaneity was a key-word for Delaunay. Later that same year, Delaunay sent to the autumn salon organized by *Der Sturm* in Berlin a number of paintings whose titles are revealing: *Simultaneous Sun and Moon, Simultaneous Seine Tower Wheel Ball,* and *Simultaneous Representation: Paris New York Berlin Moscow the Tower.*[22] The esthetic effect of simultaneity corresponds to the possibility of blending not only the world's capitals but the arts. Apollinaire always insists that modern painters are following the same process as a poet when he is inspired: the wish to be a "realist," attentive to actual perceptions, does not prevent the painter from searching for "pure color."

Like Adorno and Apollinaire, Virginia Woolf's ground-breaking essay on the new period, written somewhat later, confirms the tendency to see a synesthetic cross-over from one medium to the other. Woolf says this in a piece in which she evokes the years from 1910 to 1914, and in which she shows how the direction went from the painterly to the literary. Her famous remark that the "new" spirit was born at the end of 1910 ("in or about December 1910 human character changed"[23]) is relevant for literary trends, as her aim is to divide her contemporaries into two camps, older writers, who are Edwardians, and younger writers, who are Georgians. Thus Wells, Bennett, and Galsworthy are "Edwardians" and belong to the first decade of the century, a decade identified with the reign of Edward VII, a moment still caught up in the ideals of the Victorian age. Forster, Lawrence, Strachey, Joyce, and Eliot are Georgians, as are all those whom we call "modernists." How could Woolf assert that the age changed drastically in December 1910? The date does not tie in with the death of King Edward (which occurred in May 1910) and the coronation of the new king. It high-lights the first of the two post-impressionist exhibitions of winter 1910/11 at the Grafton Galleries, which were organized by Roger Fry, a close friend of the Woolfs. Virginia visited the first exhibition, "Manet and the Post-Impressionists," in December 1910, and it had a deep impact on her – her remark means above all that *her* view of the world changed in December 1910, and primarily under the influence of modern painting.

"Post-impressionism" was a convenient term invented by Roger Fry in 1910 to lump together a number of important French painters, mostly from the end of the nineteenth century, who had not been exhibited in London. When in 1910 Fry exhibited Gauguin, Cézanne, Van Gogh, Seurat, Odilon Redon, and Toulouse-Lautrec, most French critics would have been hard put to find their common features or to put a name to them. True, in 1912 Fry came closer to the time's modernity by adding Matisse, Picasso, and Braque, but he still believed that there was a general movement of painters who were conscious of coming after impressionism and who would roughly encompass pointillism, Fauvism, symbolism, early cubism, and a French variety of expressionism. They were all French, and the distance afforded by the Channel allowed for such generalizations – soon questioned, as we will see, by artists who knew better, such as Wyndham Lewis.

Roger Fry is important perhaps most of all by virtue of his proximity to Virginia Woolf and to her sister Vanessa Bell. Woolf's moving testimony, simply called *Roger Fry: A Biography*,[24] surveys all the past period in what almost amounts to a posthumous autobiography. Woolf takes sides in the quarrel over the Omega Workshop, standing by her sister Vanessa, Roger Fry, and Duncan Grant, who had launched the collective venture: an artists' studio established along the lines of William Morris's Arts and Crafts movement, a generous project aiming at disseminating artworks and objects of everyday use conceived "in the new spirit." Their location in Fitzroy Square, in the middle of Bloomsbury, however, revealed that they were not that radical, and would spend as much time developing "post-impressionism" as creating new choreographies, dance costumes, theatrical sets, even collections of African folk art. At the time, a more serious group, led by Walter Sickert, was based in the working-class area of Camden Town – the Camden Town Group was started as the same time as the Omega Workshop, and was dominated by Sickert's magnetic presence, with members including gifted painters such as Spencer Gore and Harold Gilman. In 1913 they fused with the London group. Woolf, who rarely engaged with painting in writing, made an exception for Sickert.

Sickert would have been called a "post-impressionist" by Fry. In fact, he is harder to classify, yet is one of Britain's most important painters – a self-conscious modernist, and a difficult one at that. He gained autonomy early after rejecting his first master's teachings: he had started with Whistler, and soon outgrew the American exile's neo-symbolist pose to embrace a "French" position. He took as his model Degas, not Cézanne, Picasso, or Matisse, and appropriated Degas' distinctive esthetics of everyday life. He aimed at mixing the high and the low, the homely and the theatrical. Building on Degas' fascination for dancers, seamstresses, and street scenes, he took this to an extreme by insisting on a certain realism, at least in so far as painting was supposed to keep a concern for intelligibility by remaining a narrative art. Draftsmanship was crucial to judge a painter's training, and Sickert felt that Picasso, Matisse, and Lewis were cutting corners. Degas remained the model in all the aspects of the craft of painting. Sickert wrote in 1912: "It is just a quarter of a century ago since I ranged myself, to my own satisfaction, definitively against the Whistlerian anti-literary theory of drawing. All the greater draftsmen tell a story."[25] He never varied on this issue; for him painting was "a branch of literature."[26] But "literature" does not amount to high culture in this context, as he insists that "literature" can be found in daily newspapers, church sermons, musical-hall songs, or echoes of Shakespeare in ragtime lyrics bawled on a popular stage.

This idea convinced Virginia Woolf, who forgot what she had learnt from Manet, Cézanne, and the post-impressionists. In one of the rare essays that she devoted to a painter, Woolf, who knew Sickert and admired him, calls up a congenial spirit.[27] She praises the tangible materiality of Sickert's colors in his paintings devoted to Venice: "We long to lay hands on his clouds and his pinnacles; to feel his columns round and his pillars hard beneath our touch. One can almost hear his gold and red dripping with a little splash into the waters from the canal."[28] Such density of earthy colors and textures makes us perceive an intangible beauty latent in the simplest objects.[29] Even objects or buildings betray traces of humanity, a humanity that surges forth also in landscapes. This is because Sickert is fundamentally a "biographer" who steals visual snapshots of his characters, offering slices of lives that we are tempted to reconstruct since quite often his figures are seized "in a moment of crisis." Woolf applies the principle that "it is difficult to look at them and not invent a plot"[30] to one of Sickert's most celebrated paintings, the 1913 Ennui. It presents in stark contrast a middle-aged man, sitting and with a cigar and a half-empty glass in front of him, and a younger woman who looks at the wall behind him, her eyes half-closed, her body half-leaning on a chest of drawers. Both bodies are joined at the center in a single diagonal, gazing in diametrically opposite directions. This looks like an allegory of boredom, of the everyday hell of stuffy bourgeois interiors in which men and women have nothing left to say to one another. Woolf elaborates an entire scene with "the old publican, with his glass on the table before him and a cigar gone cold at his lips, looking out of his shrewd little pig's eyes at the intolerable wastes of desolation in front of him" and the fat woman who "lounges, her arm on a cheap yellow chest of drawers, behind him." She explains:

> The accumulated weariness of innumerable days has discharged its burden on them. They are buried under an avalanche of rubbish. In the street beneath, the trams are squeaking, children are shrieking. Even now someone is tapping his glass impatiently on the bar counter. She will have to bestir herself; to pull her heavy, indolent body together and go and serve him. The grimness of the situation lies in the fact that there is no crisis; dull minutes are mounting, old matches are accumulating and dirty glasses and dead cigars; still on they must go, up they must get.[31]

This reverie on the dreariness of life presupposes that the couple own a pub and have retired upstairs momentarily. The model for the older "publican" was Hubby, a reformed alcoholic; if the huge glass on the table was filled with water, one understands his *taedium vitae*. Hubby was a factotum who had been hired by the Sickerts, along with his wife Marie, in the hope of luring him away from pubs. They both figure in *Off to the Pub* (1912), in which one sees a man about to leave his house, his hand on the door-handle, while a woman is tensely glowering at him. Woolf may have heard something from Sickert himself. In *Ennui* one notices a stuffed bird in a glass case, which makes the situation even more stifling. There is also a painting on the wall, showing a beautiful woman whose shoulders are uncovered and who looks seductively straight at the spectator. This suggests the persistence, despite the prevalent tawdriness, of some order and beauty, and makes this painting qualify as a typically modernist work of art, even if its technique does not go beyond that of a Degas or a Rouault.

The important socialist magazine *The New Age*, to which I will return in the next chapter, asked Sickert to be a regular contributor, which he did in 1910 and 1913. He first appeared as one of the radical innovators in 1910, but in 1913 his views clashed with those of Ezra Pound and T. E. Hulme, who defended post-cubist artists such as Wyndham Lewis and Jacob Epstein. Orage, the general editor of *The New Age*, did not mind some controversy, and was genuinely open to divergent views. The younger "Vorticists" who took over at the end of 1913 were contemptuous of the mixture of expressionism and neo-realism that they perceived in Sickert's works. Besides, they felt that Sickert was too close to Fry, who was a personal friend, and that none of them could understand cubism. Still, in January 1914 one sees Sickert defending Fry's paintings against strictures by T. E. Hulme in the same *New Age*, distinguishing between Fry's qualities as an artist and his confusion as a critic – meanwhile making a few digs at Picasso and Matisse: "We must look at his [Fry's] canvasses unbiased by the recklessness of his career as an impresario and the obscurantism of his criticism. As a critic he would have us take seriously Monsieur Picasso's tedious invention of the puzzle-conundrum-without-an-answer and the empty silliness of Monsieur Matisse."[32]

This was something that Wyndham Lewis could not tolerate. After a stay in France (like Sickert, who had come back in 1905), Lewis had returned to London and devoted most of his energy to painting in the pre-war years. In 1911 he was among the members of the Camden Town Group. By 1913 the Camden Town Group had become the London Group. It held a group exhibition in Brighton, and Lewis wrote a foreword to the catalog. Roger Fry, after the two exhibitions at the Grafton Galleries, had invited Lewis and other members of the London Group to join his Omega Workshop. The association, begun in July 1913, was abruptly terminated in October: Lewis, Frederick Etchells, Cuthbert Hamilton, and Edward Wadsworth circulated a tract objecting to Fry's direction. They strongly dissociated themselves from Fry's "Post-what-not fashionableness." The war between Lewis and Fry, and by extension the whole Bloomsbury group, had just started.

On another front, Lewis clashed with Marinetti himself after Marinetti's very successful lecture at the Lyceum Club in the spring of 1910. In 1912 important paintings by the futurists were shown at the Futurist International Exhibition at the Sackville Galleries, and in 1913 Marinetti had lectured at T. E. Hulme's Poets' Club. Much as Lewis admired the plastic discoveries of artists like Severini and Balla, he regarded the futurist cult of the machine as misguided, as *passé* as the old world that they wanted to abolish, a belated adolescent Romanticism. One sentence suffices to dispel the hubristic illusion: "Man with an aeroplane is still merely a bad bird."[33]

This comes from the foreword written by Lewis for the exhibition of "English Post-Impressionists, Cubists and Others" which opened in Brighton in November 1913. In this short but very perceptive essay, Lewis distinguishes accurately between futurism, cubism and post-impressionism. First, he settles humorously his old account with Italian futurism:

Futurism, one of the alternative terms for modern painting, was patented in Milan. It means the Present, with the Past rigidly excluded . . . futurism will never mean anything else, in painting, than the art practiced by the five or six Italian painters grouped beneath Marinetti's influence. Gino Severini, the foremost of them, has for subject matter the night resorts of Paris. This, as subject matter, is obviously not of the future. For we all foresee, in a century or so, everybody being put to bed at 7 o'clock in the evening by a state nurse.[34]

The group with which he exhibited, his own group, consisted of Frederick Etchells, Cuthbert Hamilton, Edward Wadsworth, C. R. W. Nevinson, Jacob Epstein, and David Bromberg. They took cubism as their point of reference and avoided being labeled as "post-impressionists," a term that they found weak:

Cubism means, chiefly, the art, superbly severe and so far morose, of those who have taken the genius of Cézanne as a starting point . . . It is the reconstruction of a simpler earth, left as choked and muddy fragments by him. Cubism implies much more than this, but the cube is implicit in that master's painting.

To be done with terms and tags, Post-Impressionism is an insipid and pointless name invented by a journalist, which has been naturally ousted by the better term "Futurism" in public debate on modern art.[35]

What the group wants to do is both simpler and more radical:

All revolutionary painting today has in common the rigid reflections of steel and stone in the spirit of the artist, that desire for stability as though a machine were built to fly or kill with; an alienation from the traditional photographer's trade and realization of the value of colour and form as such, independently of what recognizable form it covers or encloses. People are invited, in short, to entirely change their idea of the painter's mission, and penetrate, deferentially, with him into a transposed universe, as abstract as, though different to, the musicians . . .[36]

For Lewis, even if they had hit on something, the activism of the futurists generated bad Italian melodrama, histrionic agitation for its own sake, a hysterical reawakening of late nineteenth-century concepts deriving from the industrial revolution – a novelty in Italy perhaps, but old hat in the United Kingdom. To believe that the solution lay in the estheticization of the machine was radically flawed thinking, even if it had generated interesting works of art here and there. The futurists insisted on a dynamic interplay of sliding planes and perspectives that called up the multiple exposures afforded by a camera, apparently harking back to the days of Marey and Muybridge. Vorticism was launched precisely at the moment when the London group wanted to go beyond the static image of "imagisme" without falling into the trap of the futurists. Ezra Pound's collaboration with the American photographer Alvin Langdon Coburn shows that the Vorticists saw new possibilities offered by photography. The active futurist Carlo Ludovico Bragaglia had just published a book on what he called *Fotodinamismo futurista* in July 1913. One would have to wait until 1916 to see Coburn experiment with a kaleidoscope and a camera in order to produce "vortographs," among which are the cubist photographic portraits of Ezra Pound.

This proves that Italian futurism was not dead in 1913. A rapid list of its activities that year is quite staggering. Severini painted *Plastic Rhythm*, and Boccioni produced one important painting, *Dynamism of a Cyclist*, and a bronze sculpture, *Development of a Bottle in Space*. Valentine de Saint-Point started her polemic against Marinetti's phallocratic conservatism in sexual matters; this began in January 1913 with her *Futurist Manifesto of Lust* in Paris, soon to be updated by Mina Loy's own manifestos (*Aphorisms on Futurism* and *Feminist Manifesto*) one year later. Like de Saint-Point, the futurist Italo Tavolato insisted on the value of sensuality, prostitution, and perversions like sado-masochism; he condensed this subversive ethos in *In Praise of Prostitution*, which led to his arrest for public indecency. When he was acquitted in Florence, the audience saluted the news with loud cries of "Viva il futurismo!"

In March 1913, a futurist evening took place at the Costanzi theater in Rome, with poetic readings by Buzzi, Palazzeschi, and Folgore, and speeches by Boccioni and Papini. In March, Russolo read *The Art of Noise*, mixing language and music. Marinetti published *Parole in libertà*, poems in the newly launched futurist magazine *Lacerba*; Severini's new manifesto was entitled *Plastic Analogies of Dynamism*, Carra's manifesto was called *Painting in Sounds, Noises and Smells*, and Marinetti's own manifesto campaigned for the *Destruction of Syntax: The Imagination without Constraints and Words in Freedom*. Pratella composed an opera, *L'Aviatore Dro*. But in 1913 both Marinetti and Papini were busy defining a futurist political program in a time of national elections. They insisted on nationalist irredentism in the Trieste and Fiume regions and on colonial expansion in Africa, and reiterated their elitist and anti-socialist stance. Thus, in spite of this frantic activity, and the broadening of the local basis from Milan to Florence and Rome, the appeal of futurism outside Italy seems to have faded in 1913, precisely because it was perceived as more and more local and jingoistic, if not yet entirely reactionary.[37] Yet the futurist cult of the machine had found an original technological application in Bragaglia's account of his photographic experiments with "photo-dynamics" in *Fotodinamismo futurista*, one of the most innovative futurist publications of the year.

Figure 2 Bragaglia, cover of *Fotodinamismo futurista*, 1913

In a similar manner, photography had played the role of a Trojan horse to bring the modern spirit to the dominant philistinism of New York, mostly thanks to the relentless efforts of Alfred Stieglitz. His domain was photography, and he was already a renowned photographer in both Germany and the US when he launched the influential magazine *Camera Work* in 1903, and two years later opened the little gallery of the Photo-Secession known as *291* for its location on Fifth Avenue. There, officiating as a self-appointed high priest of international modernism, he would showcase important photographers like Coburn (who had two solo exhibitions there in 1907 and 1908) or Steichen, but also present the work of European artists who had not been visible in the US, such as Matisse in 1908, 1910, and 1912, Toulouse-Lautrec in 1909, Cézanne and Picasso in 1911, and Picabia and then Brancusi in 1913.[38] The infectious Picabia was to establish an important link between the little world of the modernist esthetes gathering for regular discussions in the tiny rooms at *291* and the larger audience that was just being brought to contemporary art by the Armory Show – he had a solo exhibition just after the show closed, and remained very close to Stieglitz, paving the way for friends like Duchamp when they came to New York soon after.

By contrast, the Armory Show was a mammoth endeavor, and aimed from the start at being the biggest and most comprehensive exhibition of contemporary art ever – at least this was the substance of the opening speech by John Quinn, the fiery Irish lawyer who also became the patron of Pound and Joyce.[39] When it opened in New York on February 17, 1913, it was presenting 1,300 works of art to a bewildered American public, and the shock was such that American art was never the same again. Only one-third of the paintings, sculptures, drawings, and prints were from European artists, but these attracted more interest as they were usually more unconventional. Matisse's nudes were deemed to be scandalous, while Duchamp's 1912 *Nude Descending a Staircase* was thought to be pure provocation: to paint a nude was possible as long as he or she (one cannot tell the gender of the model, which attracted many salacious hypotheses) was immobile, but how could a nude be "descending a staircase"? Hundreds of cartoons joked about it, and it was even described as "an explosion in a shingle factory."[40] For many years after, Duchamp's reputation in the US was due to his being dubbed "the painter of the nude," a sulfurous reputation he managed to live up to during the festive years spent in New York during the war.

The Armory Show had been in the making since 1911, and the organizers had had the benefit of peeping at the second post-impressionist exhibition organized by Fry at the London Grafton Gallery in 1912. The only school not represented was the futurists, who only agreed to be exhibited as a group. And the German expressionists were under-represented, with just one abstract Kandinsky (titled *Improvisation*, it was bought by Stieglitz), one Kirchner, and three Lehmbrucks. Otherwise, the French schools were dominant: the Fauves with Derain, Dufy, Matisse (who had 13 paintings, one sculpture and several drawings), Marquet and Vlaminck; the cubists with Picasso, Braque, Léger, Gleizes, Picabia, Villon, Duchamp-Villon and

Duchamp. Older European artists included Van Gogh, Cézanne, Gauguin, Augustus John, and Odilon Redon. Sculpture was well represented with Brancusi, Maillol, and Rodin. The American groups that were most conspicuous included the "Ashcan school" with George Bellows, Jerome Myers, Glenn O'Colement, and American impressionists such as Childe Hassamm, Alden Weir, and Theodore Robinson. Whistler had four paintings, but O'Keefe, Dove, and Man Ray had not been included. The impact was tremendous on a whole generation of artists who could all at once catch up with the newest European schools. People realized that one could collect these recent painters – thus starting the craze for contemporary art that had made American museums and private collections such a repository of masterpieces.

The initially enthusiastic response of the cognoscenti gave way to a barrage of criticism in the press – what art critics could not accept was the non-representational character of cubism, the revolutionary use of color and the formal distortions of Matisse, the drift toward abstraction of Duchamp and Picabia. The press started a systematic denigration of the three older masters who seemed to be responsible for such a break with tradition: Van Gogh was insane – he had cut off his ear and had committed suicide; Cézanne was a misanthropic and reclusive self-taught banker dabbling in paint; Gauguin was a stockbroker who had deserted his family to enjoy the sensual pleasure of Tahiti's *vahines*. The general accusation of moral depravation and pathological insanity was a last-ditch battle of the conformists and reactionaries, along with the fear of having been duped by fakers and insincere *blagueurs* who abused the naive trust of the American public. It was thought that Matisse and Picasso were deliberately mystifying the viewer. Such inane vituperation subsided soon after; it soon dawned on everybody that modernism had won its battle in the New World.

The outcome of the Armory Show, which was much less of a triumph in Chicago and Boston, was that, by 1913, Duchamp and Picabia became more famous in New York than in Paris. Duchamp soon after moved to New York. In 1913 he was still working as an assistant librarian at the Bibliothèque Sainte Geneviève, where he would read the Greek skeptic Pyrrho and the left-Hegelian philosopher Max Stirner with passion, while discussing the "fourth dimension" with friends. After his stay in Munich in 1912, during which he had been exposed to Kandinsky's new abstract paintings and theories, he was busy constructing the "big glass" that eventually became *La Mariée mise à nu*. 1913 was also the year of the first "ready-made," with the bicycle-wheel on a stool. Duchamp declared that the object had a beautiful simplicity: it was pleasant to see, much more relaxing once it had been fixed on a stool. This ur-ready-made item (the word had not yet been coined) obtains its soothing effect less through esthetic contemplation than by enacting a conceptual paradox: a wheel has been "arrested" in its development, it turns without turning, speed becoming motionless by the wheel being up in the air and not moving on the ground. With a nod to Alfred Jarry, who idolized bicycles, the wheel functions here as a synecdoche, a part suggesting the principle of any locomotive machine. Its industrial status is a sign of the rapid disappearance of art as craft (looking at an airplane propeller in 1912, Duchamp had famously declared that no one could produce a better or more beautiful object). The wheel on a stool is a first "bachelor machine" (it is indeed "single"), and it is an industrial ready-made that freezes speed to suggest a double abolition in the vehicle that it both allegorizes and cancels.

The year 1913 saw Duchamp's turn from cubism (that of the famous Nude, which can be properly described as futuro-cubist) to a more radical conceptualism by which the artist rejects the purely "retinal" status of the work of art. The formalist American critic Clement Greenberg said in a later seminar that, prior to 1913, Duchamp was either a quasi-futurist or a pseudo-cubist, and not a very distinguished practitioner of either school. Duchamp relied too much on the illusion of depth given by perspective to grasp the inherent logic of cubism, which, according to Greenberg, was its tendency to pure flatness. His first neo-cubistic paintings suggest that Duchamp "had hardly grasped what real Cubism was about."[41] After which he followed Picasso's example and made a number of collage constructions with led to the first "found objects," like the Bicycle Wheel of 1913 and the Bottle Rack of 1914. This went in the direction of the object, which meant that Duchamp had not really understood what Picasso was aiming at in his collages, that is, a simple layering of flat surfaces. According to Greenberg's reconstruction, it would have been mostly out of frustration with his limitations in the medium of painting that Duchamp became so "revolutionary" in 1913.[42] Duchamp set out to attack formal and formalized art, although not always in a consistent manner. The point of subsequent work like the 1917 urinal was to "defy and deny any esthetic judgment; taste, the satisfactions of art as art."[43] Duchamp was at that time already erecting a whole anti-esthetic.

Tantalizing and provocative as these judgments are, a very different perspective on Duchamp's evolution can be gained if we move a little east and observe the complex development of the avant-garde groups active in Russia between 1904 and 1914. In that broader context, we observe that Greenberg's thesis is predicated on too restrictive a notion of modernism in painting, too squarely defined by flatness leading to bi-dimensional abstraction. A painter like Malevitch showed the same tendency to move toward a radical questioning of all values associated with traditional art like taste and esthetic judgment, while moving resolutely in the direction of an abstraction that is nevertheless contemporary with experiments in different techniques and mediums.

The Russian situation is enlightening because most innovative artists there understood that the key movements that they had either to imitate or overcome were cubism and futurism. This gave rise to a variety of cubo-futurist groups in Moscow, St Petersburg, and Kiev.[44] A major impetus had been provided by the failed revolution of 1905, during which Malevitch was on the barricades. In 1906, he considered himself an impressionist; in 1907 he was seduced for a while by Belgian symbolism. Then the Golden Fleece exhibition in Moscow, which showed paintings by Cézanne, Gauguin, Van Gogh, Degas, Matisse, Derain, Marquet, Van Dongen, Braque, Pissarro, Bonnard, Denis, and Vuillard, functioned as a wake-up call. Malevitch came closer to neo-primitivism under the influence of Cézanne's bathers, and was impressed by the energy of the emerging Blaue Reiter group in Munich spurred by Kandinsky. The neo-primitivist or nativist movement was represented in literature by Vassily Kamensky, whose novel *The Mud Hut* (1910) received a lot of attention (his well-publicized airplane crash in 1911 also acquired mythical status). With his friends Mikhail Larionov, Natalia Goncharova, and Vladimir Tatlin, Malevitch was looking for a way of combining rayonnism, cubo-futurism, and expressionism. The St Petersburg futurist poets Khlebnikov and Maiakovsky published a neo-futurist manifesto in 1912 ("A Slap in the Face of Public Taste"); meanwhile the Rayonnists insisted on the "Asiatic" or indigenous character of Russian culture – a theme that we will encounter again when dealing with the novelist Biely.

By 1912, Malevitch was negotiating between futurism and cubism. He wanted to translate *On Cubism* (1912) by Gleizes and Metzinger, while working like Duchamp on the paradoxes of the fourth dimension, under the influence of Piotr Ouspensky's *Novum Organum* (1911). He rallied the poets Khlebnikov and Kruchenykh, who had invented *zaum* (literally "transreason" or "beyond-sense"), a futurist literary practice similar to Marinetti's *parole in libertà*; it took language as a pure medium and worked by puns and distortions to make it both musical and subversive of "common sense." It was during a spring retreat in Finland, not far from St Petersburg, that Malevitch and Kruchenykh wrote a joint manifesto that was proudly if sarcastically entitled "First Pan-Russian Congress of the Bards of the Future." Dated April 15, 1913, it announced the need to "destroy" in succession the Russian language, old bourgeois commonsense, and anything that smacked

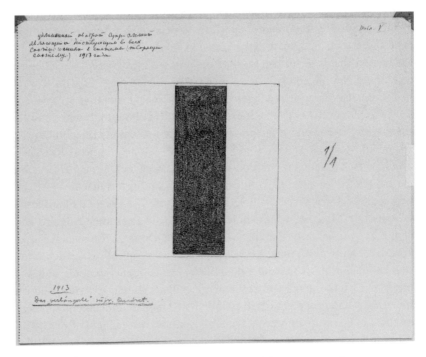

Figure 3 Kazimir Malevich, *Elongation of the Suprematist Square*,
Kunstmuseum, Basel

of beauty and complacency in the world of art. It is often taken as the first proto-Dadaist manifesto, and its aggressive tone is remarkable: "We have gathered here to arm the entire world against us. The time of the slap in the face has passed."[45] Rejecting a tamer verbal futurism defended by Khlebnikov and Maiakovsky in 1912, the new group is still futurist but with different slant – called "Avenirist," it aims not only at publishing different books by the same poets, but at radically transforming Russian theater, music, and language, as themselves part and parcel of the general overhaul. The Avenirist manifesto ends on a proclamation of war: "We need to sweep away the old mines and erect a skyscraper as stubbornly strong as a bullet."[46]

This is how, in the summer of 1913, the first collective production of the group, the neo-futurist opera *Victory over the Sun*, was conceived. The music was composed by Matiushin, the *zaum* libretto was by Kruchenykh, the sets, costumes, and choreography were made by Malevitch, while Khlebnikov wrote the preface. It was performed twice only, at the Luna Park theater in St Petersburg, on December 3 and 5, 1913. As the group had very limited funds, the musical production was quite poor, and there was only one old, out-of-tune piano to play on. Malevitch used to his advantage the fact that the theater had strong projectors: he devised startling white and black floors with geometrical patterns, while the costumes, quite varied but extremely stylized as cones and cylinders, would suddenly flare up in the strong head-lights and then fade in the dark. The opera took as its theme the struggle between the new creator, an aviator who tries to puncture the Sun, repres-enting old-world conservatism and the law of the father. Icarus-like, the hero finally crashes with his plane on the stage and steps out, unscathed, laughing: "Ha ha ha, I am alive. I am alive, only the wings are a little shabby and my shoe!"[47] The opera's general buoyancy was extraordinary, as it concluded on a note of defiance: "The world will die / But for us there is no end."

Despite the jeers and shouts which greeted the performances, the scandal was productive – at least Malevitch's career had found a sense of direction and autonomy, leading to the invention of suprematism. Its most famous emblem, the *Black Square on White Ground*, pushes painting toward total non-representation. Malevitch claimed that he had already invented the black square in 1913 – and indeed, in a cubist painting from 1913, *Cow and Violin*, one sees a white rectangle hidden beneath the violin, and some sketches for the opera show triangles within squares. A pencil drawing on paper from 1913 presents a first "Elongation of the Suprematist Square." Malevitch was already planning suprematism in 1913 (quite a number of the sketches for *Victory over the Sun* betray suprematist tendencies), while the first realizations of a totally non-figurative art came to the fore only in 1914–15. At least, we can consider *Victory over the Sun* as the perfect opposite of Stravinsky and Diaghilev's lush productions of ballets for the high society of international European capitals. It was the anti-*Rite of Spring*. Here, one had an intimation of a much later *arte povera*, of the wild explosion of Dadaism, and of the birth of a new concept that entailed the playful but determined negation of art by art. What defined this negation as more than passing nihilism was its radically collective production. Hence we will need to explore the collective agencies that brought modernism to that pass.

Chapter 2

Collective Agencies

On April 13, 1913, Jules Romains organized the kind of prank for which the Rue d'Ulm *normaliens* were known, one of their resounding *canulars*. The aged, self-taught, and semi-demented linguist Jean-Pierre Brisset had been suddenly pulled out of his obscure retreat in Angers to become the guest of honor at an award-giving ceremony to which writers, poets, and intellectuals had been invited. He had been elected "Prince of Thinkers" on January 6, 1913. This was a spoof on Paul Fort's election as the new "Prince of Poets" one year earlier. Aged only 40, Paul Fort officially replaced the unofficial former "Prince of Poets," Paul Verlaine. A huge banquet at La Closerie des Lilas had gathered the elite of French literati as Fort was well connected, friendly with Gide, Claudel, and Louys. The travesty that took Brisset as the butt of a students' prank started more modestly at the Gare Montparnasse, where Brisset was greeted with a welcome speech by Jules Romains. The group had a long lunch, punctuated by absurd perorations that generated the hilarity of all, except the dignified recipient. Then they all went to Place du Panthéon, gathering next to Rodin's *Thinker* statue, and Brisset gave a discourse of thanks. The old man, overjoyed at this long-delayed public recognition, accepted his "coronation" wholeheartedly, without guessing that it was a hoax. Louis Latzarus reported the event for the *Figaro* and described how, when Brisset exclaimed in the middle of the lunch that he was so happy that he was ready to die on the spot, a wave of embarrassment passed among the merry pranksters.[1]

In his speech, Brisset noted accurately that thinking demands less physical effort than Rodin implies with his muscular statue, and his talk was laced with idiosyncratic remarks like: "The military spirit and the religious spirit both come from the beasts who came before us and are our forefathers."[2] Later, a banquet was held at the Hôtel des Sociétés Savantes, with more tongue-in-cheek speeches. Without knowing it, Jules Romains and his "pals" (*copains*) had ushered in a new style of "banquet years," to quote Roger Shattuck's excellent book. Romains may have felt some remorse for a practical joke that was almost too successful since he later left money to organize an annual banquet in Brisset's name – Brisset died in 1919, and these banquets were held until 1939. By 1939, Brisset had been claimed as a precursor by the surrealists and not just a *fou littéraire*. He was one of the authors collected in André Breton's *Anthology of Black Humor* (1939). This double recognition establishes a link between a boisterous and humanistic *unanimisme* and one of the most enduring members of the avant-garde of the twentieth century.

The Linguistics of Delirium

Jules Romains had discovered Brisset's work by chance, but when he started reading books like *The Mystery of God* and *Human Origins* he found them so wildly entertaining that he could not resist showing them to his friends. Brisset had been an inventor, and patented a "flotation underpants-belt helping to swim" (an offshoot of his first book, *The Art of Swimming, Self-Taught in Less Than an Hour*, 1871) and a mysterious "calligraphic board." They did not meet with commercial success. Undeterred, he published, in 1878, *The Logical Grammar*, followed in 1900 by the *Science of God*. This was the beginning of his linguistic system, entirely based on the idea that human language comes from an archaic and onomatopoeic speech of pre-humanity which imitated the croaking of frogs, our ancestors. Only a Frenchman could arrive at this insight! By an entertaining series of puns, Brisset managed to make the whole French language derive from frog expressions, such as *koa koa* (which led to man's first interrogation: "Quoi? Quoi?") or *brekekekex* (the root of the fundamental issue, naming sex, since it generates: "Que sexe est?" also heard as "Qu'est-ce que c'est?"[3]). The relentlessness of his word concatenations is hilarious and untranslatable, and begins a long French tradition of conceptual punning that culminated with Jacques Lacan. Brisset's ambition was to reach back to a prelapsarian paradise, in an Adamic reverie aimed at returning to an idyllic time when men and animals would converse together peacefully. Brisset's involuntary ur-Dadaism is not fortuitous, for indeed his works may have been the origin of the name Dada – still a debated issue – as Brisset included it in the "language of the gods." This is based on the dominant fantasy, expressed in a painting by Douanier Rousseau, where the gods frolic in a primeval forest with wild beasts whom they cuddle and call their *dadas*. Noting that the usage of *dadas* to refer to animals was current in French and German, Brisset assumes that *dada* embodies the concept of a terrestrial paradise enabling a supreme state of linguistic and existential innocence. When linguistic bliss reigned, death did not exist – until, one day, the *dadas* started being killed . . .[4]

Jules Romains had taken the idea of ludicrous but entertaining banquets from Douanier Rousseau's unique dinner parties, at which he was an occasional guest. An incorrigible *naïf* in life as well as in art, Rousseau's ingenuous personality had been severely tested by all his acquaintances, as he found himself awarded pseudo-prizes of a ludicrous nature or invited to official luncheons, one with the President of the Republic, only to be turned away. Yet he persisted in organizing huge dinner parties in his studio, and held his *soirées familiales et artistiques* every Saturday. There, amid the wholehearted drinking and fun, the tables could be turned on the guests, since what mattered for the genial Rousseau was simple fun, especially late at night when the parties turned to bacchantic revelry.[5] Moreover there are endless stories of hoaxes greeting the discovery of Rousseau's naive paintings, whether they stemmed from Apollinaire, who claimed that Rousseau had fought in Mexico, or from Jarry, who asserted that it was he who had advised Rousseau to start painting. Jules Romains had learned from Rousseau's mixture of naivety and self-promotion, and no doubt made the connection between Rousseau and Brisset. At least, this was Marcel Duchamp's assessment: he considered Brisset the "Douanier Rousseau of philology,"[6] and it is no accident that Brisset reached the radar of the young avant-garde just at the time when Raymond Roussel started attracting their attention.

The second series of the theatrical performances of Roussel's *Impressions d'Afrique* had taken place in May 1912 at the Théâtre Antoine, after two or three failed performances at the Théâtre Fémina in September 1911. The play adapts rather literally a bizarre novel, and presents a series of scenes that stage the most curious machines: a statue of whalebone advances on rails made of veal lights (*mou de veau*), an automatic orchestra converts flows of electricity into temperature, a worm releases mercury-like drops on a zither to play popular melodies, a one-legged Breton plays the flute on his own tibia, Dizmé, a black woman, gets voluntarily electrocuted by lighting, a whole wall is erected with stacks of dominos to look like priests . . . In the novel, such proto-surrealist contraptions were generated by invisible puns loosely linking two similar-sounding sentences, as Roussel later explained in *How I Wrote Some of my Books*. Similar to the rebus-logic of dreams discovered by Freud in the *Interpretation of Dreams*, the staging of such linguistic hybrids gave birth to chimeras, monsters of the technological imagination. Duchamp attended one of the performances and kept the memory alive for ever: "It was wonderful . . . it was pure bizarre madness."[7] He later confessed that this play's deadpan delirium had acted like a trigger, inspiring him to begin work on *La Mariée mise à nu par ses célibataires même*. Meanwhile the audience, not understanding a thing, would hiss and heckle the actors. Roussel then decided to perform with his actors (being prodigiously rich, he could afford to waste fortunes to promote the idea that he was a very popular playwright). At the same time, Roussel was writing an even more surprising novel, *Locus Solus*, which he completed in 1913, and had serialized in *Le Gaulois du dimanche* in December of that year, where it went totally unnoticed.

Two other *normaliens* interested in the production of mad language, Michel Foucault, who rediscovered Brisset in the sixties and made the crucial connection with Raymond Roussel, and Jean-Jacques Lecercle,[8] have pointed out the modernity of this discourse, even though it is clearly a psychotic discourse in both cases. This foregrounding of the creative power of language even via absurd demonstrations illustrates modernity's specific "linguistic turn," just at the time of Ferdinand de Saussure's untimely disappearance. Saussure, who died in 1913, his famous *Course in General Linguistics* still unpublished, is widely credited with having invented modern linguistics and having spawned structuralism. He also left other notebooks that dealt with "anagrams" of proper names that he thought were hidden in famous Latin poems.[9] His associative logic seems at times as specious as Brisset's wild etymologies. At least on this point Brisset was more radical: according to him, Latin did not exist. It was an artificial language similar to children's games that invert letters in words and words in sentences; or, at best, it was a grammarian's invention – he even demonstrates that nobody in his senses would ever have used words in such a random order![10]

Unanimism and Collective Action

Jules Romains had all the right intuitions, but often ruined them by the excess of his irrepressible verve. He first wanted to be a poet, as we have seen, but realized that he was a better novelist and playwright. The novel that he published in 1913, *Les Copains*, is still readable today, and even highly entertaining. The plot is simple: seven male "pals" or drinking "buddies" who regularly carouse all night decide at the end of a drunken party to choose two cities at random, and then wreak havoc. Their goal is to create excitement, to make something happen in the midst of French provincial blinkered drowsiness. They select two small cities in the Massif Central,

Issoire and Ambert. The three natural leaders of the group have each devised an action. In Ambert, Broudier disguises himself as an unspecified Minister accompanied by a Secretary and a Director, and they startle the officers of the local garrison when they announce first that they have come for improvised night exercises, then that they have a theme: quelling a rebellion, assuming that armed conspirators have seized the city hall and are holding the mayor hostage. They are so convincing that the whole regiment is woken up and performs night exercises with blanks – and they end up creating so much of an uproar and confusion that the whole town wakes up in fear. The four other "pals" observe the inhabitants' panic and witness how Ambert can shed its provincial timidity to produce a new "mass" of people. What they have done is not only *épater les bourgeois* but force them to exist as a group and take possession of their city at last.[11]

It is now Bénin's turn with Ambert. The following Sunday, he passes himself off as Father Lathuile, a famous Catholic theologian just arrived from Rome where he has been the Pope's confidant. He ascends the pulpit and delivers such a persuasively liberal homely on sexuality and the need for Catholic families to grow and multiply that the whole audience gets increasingly sexual, more and more aroused, until at the end the young and the old clasp and kiss each other while the "pals" sitting among the pews fondle nice-looking women whom they have chosen as "neighbors." That same day, they move to Issoire, where the group has arranged the unveiling of an equestrian statue of Vercingetorix. The local deputy gives a speech while the statue is revealed. It is a hyper-realist Vercingetorix, painted in bronze but nude, with just a shield at the back and a bag. When the deputy apostrophizes Vercingetorix directly and takes him as a founder of the French nation, unleashing a string of clichés typical of the Third Republic, the statue comes alive, insults him in the most obscene manner, and then pelts the fleeing audience with boiled apples.

The "pals" are seen celebrating their "victory" in a last scene in which they go to a mountain refuge where they cook a sumptuous meal and drink vast quantities of good wine. In conclusion, Bénin delivers a long and drunken harangue in which one recognizes the main tenets of Romains' unanimist philosophy: the young men are stronger and more alive when acting together, since at those moments they feel uniquely relevant to the order of things, and act toward progress. Romains' central philosophical tenet was that the group condenses life, and that such collective life, if perceived in all its intensity, will make one approximate divine intelligence. The individual needs to find the source of strength and become one with it by reaching back to a godlike unanimism. A preliminary for this undertaking is the destruction of bourgeois complacency and the ending of limited individualism. By their pranks, the *copains* have "created Ambert" and "destroyed Issoire," thus balancing creation and destruction. They have followed the principle of a "pure act" which is tantamount to "pure arbitrariness"; nevertheless such arbitrariness had a purpose (p. 152). By organizing an united action, they have come closer to God; thus, the pals are told: "Tonight you are a unique god in seven persons" (p. 153). They embody a collective present, and while they are in that state the world belongs to them. Since eternity does not exist, not even for this sevenfold "god," the best that they can do is toast this wisdom while laughing and drinking as much as they can.

Romains' *A Manual of Deification* provides a blueprint for this short and engaging novel: one should look for the unconscious forms of unanimist life in streets, squares, and monuments, move on to the conscious forms of the same life in cafés, restaurants, libraries, theaters, churches, and so on before passing to the superior stage, the "divine surprise" provided when a group becomes conscious of its own collective life and brings other people to share this consciousness. By staging a subversion of everyday life that could announce the practices of the situationists in the late fifties and the sixties, Romains develops a program of urban revitalization using shock tactics, in consequence of which a dormant community will be shaken to its deepest roots by the concerted action masterminded by a few committed esthetes. The result is of course laughter, and a corrective laughter. Was this a spoof on the avant-garde? No, Jules Romains was quite serious, and sounds all too serious each time his inflated lyricism is given free rein, as when the "pals" ride on bicycles through beautiful landscapes and gushingly express their sense of being at one with the world. They will create the god-in-the-world by destroying some of it, which is why their collective dynamism always contains traces of dynamite. The pantheistic religiosity of these moments is founded on a concept of male comradeship that is definitively Whitmanian. It entails a need for the rethinking of a "politics of friendship," since collective action is indispensable for friendship to keep its direction and relevance.[12]

In the French context, such a political program was not hard to pigeonhole since it was in line with the main tenets of the socialists or the anarchists, which is confirmed by the spoofs of the Catholic Church and the army. Indeed, in their very physical description, Broudier, Bénin, and Lesueur, the leaders of the seven *copains*, call up Croquignol, Filochard, and Ribouldingue, the three anarchist tricksters invented by Louis Forton in 1908, whose rambunctious adventures in cartoons delighted the readers of *L'Epatant* – and they were not all children! In 1913, the Pieds Nickelés had once more

escaped from jail, fleeing to Serbia and Bulgaria, disguised as the most
varied nationals of the then ongoing Balkan war. Unlike Forton's, Romains'
version offered a highly literary variety of anarchism: what stands out in
the novel are the lyrical moments interspersing the action, when by smaller
groups or all together the seven men exult in their comradeship. They are
used to harangue in fake Latin, to compete by exchanging rhymed poems,
their glee triggered by heady amusements, such as producing in a few minutes
a pastiche of Mallarmé on the subject of camembert. Their main weapons
are elaborate disguises and eloquence, allied with a sense of purpose.

Surprisingly, there was one person who resented this attitude: Guillaume
Apollinaire. This was all the more surprising because he and Romains had
been friends for some time, had similar literary ambitions, and had noted
the coincidence that they had been born on the same day, five years apart,
Apollinaire in Rome, which made him a "Romain." Besides, Apollinaire almost
never wrote negative reviews. He opened fire in April 1911 after having
seen Romains' play *The Army in the City*, in which a local revolt in a city is
quelled by an occupying militia. In a particularly harsh review published
in *La Nouvelle Revue française*, Apollinaire attacked the very terms used by
Romains in his preface; Romains looked for an art that would be both
"classical and national," that was keeping in touch with French tradition.
Against these claims, Apollinaire objected that the play had "no truth," that
it was "botched" and devoid of style, with bad dialogue and stilted purple
patches, the whole sinking to the level of poor historical melodrama. He
viciously quoted Romains' *Manual of Deification*, a concise guide to unanimism, in which Romains gave the rationale for *Les Copains*, explaining that
he loved "waking up groups from their somnolence" by "doing violence"
to them,[13] for instance by speaking loudly in the street or opening an
umbrella when the sun is shining. This violent rejection terminated
Apollinaire's contract with the review – he was never to publish in the
Nouvelle Revue française again.

In another critical review of the same month, Apollinaire quotes the same
passage as a "confession" in which Romains admitted that he was fascinated
by organized violence – this was no excuse for writing that was mechanical,
predictable, accomplished like a chore. The condemnation was political
and harsh: Romains had the "tone of a trade-union leader proclaiming class-
war,"[14] and he churned out dull plays and trite poems just as he would
organize pranks – in a military manner. The clash between two forms of
early French modernism, both of them aiming at syncretic gatherings, could
not have been more obvious: on the one hand, Romains' modernism was
geared toward a common humanity, men of the crowd who have to be

educated by the avant-garde, even if it means using violence on them; on the other hand, Apollinaire's modernism followed in the steps of symbolism, and took the medium of art, whether linguistic, musical, or visual, as the only valid site of the effort; this would entail experimentation, which might risk losing the link with the audience, but one could assume that the public would want to educate itself if it wanted to follow, and would do this all the more willingly when it understood the beauty and the necessity of the experiment.

Romains' programmatic or pedagogical pranks call up a slightly earlier practical joke that involved Virginia Woolf. In February 1910 Virginia, her brother Adrian, a friend named Horace Cole, and a few others disguised themselves as Abyssinian diplomats and Foreign Office dignitaries in order to gain access to the *Dreadnought*. They were not discovered – their exotic garb and painted faces as well as their mock Abyssinian impressed the warship's officers. Did that entail a message of solidarity for the beleaguered Abyssinians at a time of tension with Italy? Not really. Empty as it may have been, the prank left above all the sense of having accomplished something subversive, even if, in retrospect, the result might be derided. This is also the sudden impulse that seizes Lafcadio when, in a famous scene of André Gide's *Vatican's Cellar* (a novel completed in June 1913 and published in 1914), the young man pushes the ludicrous character Amédée out of a speeding train. Amédée dies, and no one traces the murder to Lafcadio, who enjoys the intellectual benefits of a "gratuitous act." All this in the context of a bizarre hoax, a swindle rather, in which Protos, Lafacadio's boss, manages to extort money from a gullible countess when he has her believe that the Pope has been abducted and is a prisoner in his own cellars. As Gide said, this was to be a "demoralizing book," an undoing of any bourgeois morality testifying to a deep sense of crisis, more than just a literary parody of the picaresque novel.

By contrast, the unanimist utopia of *Les Copains* attempts a different type of action – it is the work of a small and determined group capable of achieving complex commando operations in a given locality. Romains, and his friends from *L'Abbaye* like Duhamel and Vildrac, believed that they were the guardians of a French Cartesian tradition that emphasized clear logic and appealed to humanity's "common sense." Working from this commonality, a small group united by a joint fervor wakes up an inert social mass by using violence if necessary. The mass lacks passion, and any passion is preferable to indifference. This may have been a dangerous position in times of nationalistic furor. Against this activism, Gide's grating novel focuses on an isolated individual so as to question collective myths and values. Like Proust attacking

Romain Rolland for his emphasis on social realism and the representation of simple "life," which requires works written without style,[15] Apollinaire did not believe that one could do something positive for the masses by exhorting them directly – that is, in a language that would be immediately comprehensible to all – to an awakening.

Romains' *unanimiste* program was encountering delicate problems similar to those that agitated Lenin in 1913. At that time, he debated hotly with other socialist revolutionaries about the role of the party and the limits of internationalism: "You speak of a socialist party educating the proletariat. In the present struggle, *the very* question at issue is that of defending the *basic* principles of party-life."[16] Another related issue was whether the Communist Party should be an "open party" as the Liberals wanted or an "underground party" ready to use political action to radicalize the crowds, as when St. Petersburg's 62,000 workers went on strike in the summer of 1913. By a striking coincidence, well exploited by Frederic Morton,[17] in January 1913 Lenin, Trotsky, and Stalin were all three in Austria; while Trotsky was enjoying the cultural life of the vibrant cafés of the capital, Lenin was plotting and writing in Cracow; a young man named Joseph Dzhugashvili, a former theologian, expelled from the Tbilisi seminary in 1898 for his communist leanings, subsequently deported five times but always escaping, had joined the Bolshevik central committee late in 1912. He spent barely five weeks in Vienna, and remained impervious to the night life and the cafés, concentrating on his mission: he had been sent to compare the way the double monarchy dealt with nationalist agitation with the Russian policy. He wrote, in one month, the canonical essay on "Marxism and the National Question,"[18] dated Vienna, January 1913. There, Stalin, who began like Ernest Renan by asking "What is a nation?", contrasted regressive "bourgeois nationalism" with a more open communist program. If socialism was by nature international, it would not be opposed to "regional autonomy" and would promote local "self-determination," a plan that relocated the Austrian solution (as we have seen, it was temporary and its tensions triggered the war) to the nationalities issue in a Russian context. The main conclusion was that nationalities would be relatively independent under socialism. Such a deft compromise elicited Lenin's admiration, and for a long time Stalin was to be the party's expert on national questions. Lenin preferred this sturdy realism to Trotsky's pure but quixotic idea of the international contagion of a world revolution. Soon after his return to Russia, Stalin was arrested, being poorly disguised as a peasant woman. He began his sixth and longest deportation. It was also in 1913 that he had chosen the evocative party name of "Stalin," the "man of steel."

The "New Spirit," or Early Modernism in Paris

The spirit of jokes or *esprit fumiste* that had marked the humor of the Mont-martre cabarets so famous in the last decades of the nineteenth century, and that so much defined Erik Satie's brand of wit, was not unknown to Apollinaire, who displays it in his narration of Walt Whitman's burial on the revealing date of April 1, 1913. The "Anecdote" of "Walt Whitman's Burial as Narrated by a Witness" deploys a grotesque and Rabelaisian scene that took place in 1892 at the Camden graveyard, where more than three thousand people had congregated, with enormous vats full of beer and whiskey, forming a long procession led by ragtime players, until the coffin, too large to pass through the door of the mausoleum, had to be hoisted up by totally drunk bearers. Apollinaire makes fun of the *comerados* who had gathered there, as Whitman had not "hidden his taste for pedophilia" and the "pederasts had come in huge numbers,"[19] led by Peter Connelly, a handsome Philadelphian tramway driver who had been the old bard's lover. Yet, this mock-epic scene was not a total invention, in spite of the date: the "witness" was none other than Blaise Cendrars, or Frédéric Sauser, who had been told that story, he claimed, by an old carpenter in New York, while he was frequenting the Ferrer School in which his girlfriend, Fela, was working in the winter of 1911/12.[20] Apollin-aire, as he often did, had only to expand the short vignette and give his fancy free rein. He later had to defend himself when supporters of Whitman com-plained, and swore that Cendrars was the originator of the "tall tale."

There was a time when the pleasure taken in elaborate farces turned dangerous; this happened in the summer of 1911, when Apollinaire was given a few Phoenician statues stolen from the Louvre by an acquaintance of his, Géry Pieret. Pieret had stolen twice from the museum, and sold at least one statue to Picasso, then a close friend of Apollinaire. On August 29, Pieret tried to sell more to the *Paris-Journal*, leaving them in Apollinaire's apartment before disappearing. He argued that he meant to alert public opinion to the fact that security was faulty in French museums. Such an alert had taken place on August 21, when the theft of the *Mona Lisa* was noticed. This made headlines all over the world. Terrified that they could appear responsible, afraid that they would be deported as foreigners, Picasso and Apollinaire got rid of the compromising objects, but clumsily, by depos-iting them on the *Paris-Journal* doorstep. The police soon traced the objects back to Apollinaire, who was arrested on September 7. He spent a week in jail, writing poems worthy of Villon and Verlaine. Meanwhile the press denounced him as "the chief of an international gang that has come to

France to rifle our museums." When Picasso was confronted with him, he denied even knowing the poet! Meanwhile, his enemies were dredging up old sins and offenses, the cabal ultimately leading to a painful break-up with his current lover, the young painter Marie Laurencin, whose mother forbade her to associate herself with such a disreputable con-man who was not even French. Apollinaire managed to prove his innocence and clear his name, yet the blow had been hard, and changed him deeply. The final break with Marie Laurencin occurred in 1913. A number of critics have surmised that his subsequent turn to experimental poetry with *Zone* and after had been due to the upheaval created by the incarceration – at least many poems of the times dramatize his plight as a rejected misfit, always unhappy in love, the *mal aimé* in perpetual exile, ready to try out new sources of stimulation.

The spirit of derision always accompanies the most solemn moments defining historical trends, and once in a while, hits a nerve in the zeitgeist's loose articulations. Vincenzo Perudia, who had stolen the famous painting, claimed that he had acted out of patriotism, in order to give back the masterpiece to its native country. In 1913 a Florentine art-dealer had offered money for rare pieces, and heard from Perugia who was still in Paris; the latter came to Florence with *Mona Lisa* hidden in a false bottom of his trunk. Perugia was immediately arrested, after which *Mona Lisa* was displayed in the Uffizi and then toured around Italy, to be finally given back to France: it reached Paris on December 31, 1913, and was hung in a new room of the Louvre five days later. Six months later, the trial of Perugia in Italy ended with a lenient sentence; he was almost immediately released, hailed by the crowds as a nationalist hero. In France, the alarm caused by the temporary loss of a national treasure triggered a da Vinci craze. This was partly halted by the war, only to resume in 1919, which happened to be the 400th anniversary of Leonardo's death.

This context is important and helps us understand why Marcel Duchamp made fun of the icon in the fall of 1919, when he bought a cheap reproduction of the painting, gave the lady a pair of moustaches and a goatee, and titled this *L.H.O.O.Q.* (an obscene pun on "she's hot in the ass."[21] By then, the spirit of Dada had come and was there to stay for a while, and Mona's real gender was a moot point. As to Apollinaire, the panic at being arrested and the fear of being deported were determining factors in the feature that struck his friends during and after the war, the strong upsurge of French nationalism and even bellicism that seized him. While Marie Laurencin had defiantly married a German artist and fled to Spain at the outbreak of the war, Apollinaire, who could have avoided being drafted, insisted on being a soldier in the French army. The first "surrealist" drama ever, *Les Mammelles*

Figure 4   Italian policemen guarding the *Mona Lisa* in Florence. Photograph
Roger Viollet / Getty images

de Tiresias, was conceived as a delirious futurist show that nevertheless aimed
at conveying a nationalist message.

This is why it is important to assess Apollinaire's drift to futurism in 1913,
and his specific neo-cubism. In 1913, Apollinaire published two books that
testify to an intensification of his already frantic activity and put him on
the map as France's most important poet, the poetic collection *Alcools* and
the collection of essays *Esthetic Meditations, Cubist Painters*, which included
reproductions of 40 cubist paintings. Then, in June 1913, he wrote and dated
the manifesto entitled "The Futurist Anti-Tradition,"[22] to be published in
the Italian magazine *Lacerba* in September 1913. It is a disconcerting piece,
in which he lists names and concepts that should be destroyed and those
that should be saved: from the bipartition in "Destruction" and "Creation,"
followed by a rigorous dichotomy in *Mer . . . De* (Shit . . . To), to a list of
names such as Dante, Shakespeare, Tolstoy, and Goethe (he deleted Racine
at the last minute), followed by a "ROSE" to be offered to an even longer
list of artists and poets, which includes Marinetti, Picasso, and all the main
futurists; it goes back to most of the futurist manifestos since 1909 and
prefigures *Blast*, with its opposition between "Blast" and "Bless." Ironically,

in the manifesto he wants to destroy the "artistic sublime," while the *Esthetic Meditations* state on the second page that a flame "has the sublime truth of its light that no one can deny."[23] In spite of this discrepancy in the vocabulary, both texts assert the same thesis – in the more conventional language of *Esthetic Meditations*: "One cannot carry everywhere with oneself the corpse of one's father." He adds: "But it would be in vain that our feet detach themselves from the soil that holds the dead."[24]

This underlines the fact that even if Apollinaire's manifesto mimics very literally all the avant-gardist gimmicks of the futurists (with its bold capitals, experiments with typography, juxtaposition of several levels on one page, elliptic syntax), he is still talking of a "tradition," even if it is an anti-tradition. This fits in very well with a little magazine like *Lacerba*, whose title was not simply a condensed wording of *L'Acerba* (The Acerbic One) but also a literary allusion to Cecco d'Ascoli, a poet who was burned at the stake by the Inquisition as a heretic in 1327, and whose didactic poem *L'Acerbo* was published posthumously in 1476. Each issue in 1913 had the same epigraph from Cecco d'Ascoli, "Qui non si canta al modo delle rane" (Here, one does not sing in the manner of frogs), which would have delighted Jean-Pierre Brisset. When baffled readers were bold enough to ask the reason of the strange spelling of the title which omitted an apostrophe, the editors attacked the "amazing literary ignorance of the Italians."[25] *Lacerba*, although considered as a purely futurist review, was not a party organ and published texts that at times were at variance with each other, sometimes even violently so, as was the case of Papini's "Against Futurism" in March 1913. This is why it is not astonishing to see Paul Fort, the "Prince of Poets," Roger Fry, Max Jacob, Kandinsky, and Stravinsky offered a rose along with the main futurists.

Among those who pushed Apollinaire toward the "modern spirit," none had a more direct impact than Blaise Cendrars. Cendrars was back from his travels to Russia and the United States, and the poem that he had written in New York (*Easter*) had been printed in Paris in November 1912, later retitled *Easter in New-York*. Cendrars read *Easter* to the Delaunays in their studio while Apollinaire was present, and Apollinaire was immediately struck by the novelty of the loosely imagistic autobiographical thread, the mythical and religious comparisons always offset by irony, the steady pulse of a metropolis providing an offbeat rhythm, and the gradual transformation of the speaker into a sort of anarchist Christ who greets prostitutes, destitute Jews, and all sorts of misfits.

According to witnesses, Apollinaire turned white after the reading and declared that his own poetic sequence sounded very tame by comparison. Then he dashed off "Zone" in one night, a partly derivative autobiographical poem, which he recited to Duchamp, Picabia, and other friends in October 1913. In fact, *Pâques à New York*, written at full speed by a lonely and sick young man in a New York room on Easter Sunday 1912, is still a conventional poem divided into strophes, written for the most part in rhymed alexandrines with very regular and predictable rhythms. Apollinaire managed to condense the gist of Cendrars' poem and made "Zone" much more daring. And finally, in November, he decided at the last minute to take out all the punctuation signs from the second proofs of the poem (he had also published "Vendémiaire" as an unpunctuated poem that same month, and the poem closed the collection as a companion to "Zone"). He also added to the proofs the shortest poem ever to the collection, the brilliantly resounding but mysterious one-liner "Chantre" – "Et l'unique cordeau des trompettes marines" (And the single string of the seatrumpets). "Zone" magnificently opens *Alcools*, finally published in April 1913:

> In the end you are weary of this ancient world
>
> This morning the bridges are bleating Eiffel Tower oh herd
>
> Weary of living in Roman antiquity and Greek
>
> Even the motor-cars look antique
> Religion alone has stayed young religion
> Has stayed simple like the hangars of Port Aviation[26]

The instability of the personal pronouns – the speaker is addressed alternatively as "You" and "I," both pronouns engaging in a schizophrenic dialogue – as well as the dominantly urban setting (the scene takes place in Paris with snapshots of Nice, Marseilles, Koblenz, Rome, and other cities) make it a prototype of the imagist poem. The Eiffel Tower turns into a shepherd watching the flock of bleating bridges over the Seine ("Bergère ô tour Eiffel le troupeau des ponts bêle ce matin"[27]). The lyricism of place-names ("I love the grace of this industrial street / In Paris between the Avenue des Ternes and the Rue Amont-Thieville") had never been rendered so effectively. The novelty lies less the lack of punctuation (after all, Mallarmé's *Un Coup de Dés* was not punctuated) than in the mixture between a lyrical voice always close to Romantic *Lieder* avoiding the rhetoric of poetic diction and a series of imagistic juxtapositions. By playing on all the registers of French literature, from the very colloquial to the highly literary, Apollinaire takes full stock of a modern world-view, in which literature can be found everywhere, but not primarily in books:

You read the handbills the catalogues the singing posters
So much for poetry this morning and the prose is in the papers
Special editions full of crimes
Celebrities and other attractions for 25 centimes[28]

Alcools has remained a popular collection that contains in germ the lyrical poetry of a century, paving the way to poets who remained close to a broad audience like Eluard and Aragon, or even Prevert and Brassens. It is no wonder that these poems were so often set to music.

Two months after the publication, Georges Duhamel who had not forgiven the insulting review of his friend Romains' play in 1911, wrote a scathing review. Fundamentally, Duhamel accused Apollinaire of a lack of originality, of recycling old clichés – and, more pointedly, of betraying a "Jewish" preoccupation with cheap exoticism:

> I call it an old junk shop because a mass of heterogeneous objects has found a place there and, though some of them are of value, none of them has been made by the dealer himself. That is just the characteristic of this sort of industry: it resells, but it does not produce. [. . .] The rest is a collection of faked paintings, patched exotic garments, bicycle accessories and articles of intimate hygiene. A truculent and bewildering variety takes the place of art in this assemblage. One barely catches a glimpse, through the holes of some moth-eaten chasuble, of the innocent and ironic eye of the dealer, who is part Levantine Jew, part South American, part Polish gentleman and part *faccino*.[29]

Thus the *unanimistes* were finally exposing their ugly side – a mixture of nationalism, anti-semitism, and smug traditionalism. The personal affront was too much for Apollinaire, who dispatched his close friend Max Jacob to challenge Duhamel to a duel. The affair was settled peacefully in the end, but it marks a clear division in the Parisian "new spirit." What is comical in hindsight is that the terms used by Duhamel for his rejection of *Alcools* would apply entirely to a rag-bag novel full of heterogeneous objects like Joyce's *Ulysses*. In 1922, even with the silly racial slur, the same account would ring positive.

The other poetic experiment of the year was the production of Blaise Cendrars' *Prose du Transsibérien et de la petite Jehanne de France* as a unique book-object with its pages illustrated by Sonia Delaunay. As we saw in the first chapter, the Delaunays had been experimenting with "simultaneism" since 1912, and this beautiful art book was to be the "first simultaneous book." It consists of a single sheet of paper folded up like an accordion in 22 panels that, when laid flat, total a length of 2 meters. Hence the entire run of

150 issues would reach the height of the Eiffel Tower, if one were to paste them together. The right-hand side of the pages contain the text of free verse poem whose divisions are marked by colored half-pages; virtually all the empty spaces are taken up by similar pochoir pastels that look like watercolors. The left-hand side is painted, and looks like semi-abstract forms in bright primary colors that slowly let precise shapes materialize at the bottom, where one sees the Eiffel Tower penetrating a great wheel painted in orange and green. What is essentially a travel poem finds its resolution when the narrator comes home to Paris, called the "city of the Tower . . . and the Great Wheel."[30] In her close reading of the book, Marjorie Perloff argues convincingly that the book is the best emblem of the futurist spirit, even though both Cendrars and Sonia Delaunay refused the epithet. They wanted the book to illustrate the spirit of *simultanéisme*, a notion that Robert Delaunay had found in a scientific treatise written by Michel Eugène Chevreul on *The Law of the Simultaneous Contrast of Colors*, published in 1839, the very year when the invention of photography was made available to all by the French government. Chevreul, a chemist, had discovered that adjacent colors tend to appear as dissimilar as possible, and he systematized in a number of tables, circles, and spheres the "laws of the harmony of contrasts" and the "laws of the harmony of analogy." One idea that the Delaunays derived from his theories was that opposing complementary colors brighten, which accounts for the way Robert and Sonia would use primary colors in a prismatic manner in their cubistic paintings. Thus *Prose* is a book before being either a poem or a painting, one that is it is to be both read *and* viewed as a picture. While the text, with its strong lyrical impetus, goes down the page, one has to see it laterally and then as a whole. Marjorie Perloff is right to assert that the spirit of the joint creation is futurist, although it is a softer and later futurism, imbued with a delicate grace and a rare balance between words, colors, and shapes thanks to Sonia Delaunay's creative adaptation of the work.

This French futurism would thus be more mature, it stops shocking people for the sake of it and even leads to something like a feminist futurism, even though the poem's meaning is underpinned by the male speaker, who stands out as the seeker and heroic wanderer. The refrain is Jehane's naive question: "Tell me, Blaise, are we very far from Montmartre?". The double title gives a crucial function of counterpoint to the feminine voice, and the medieval spelling keeps a trace of the mythical "Jehane" or Joan of Arc. The conceit is of course to turn the Virgin Joan of Arc (*la pucelle*) into a modern underage Montmartre prostitute. The poetic "prose" is well suited to a lyrical journal retracing the train travels Freddy Sauser took as an adolescent to the heart of Russia; this was in the spring of 1905, just after the disastrous war with Japan and the fall of Port Arthur; Cendrars also evokes the revolutionary days of 1905 in St. Petersburg.[31] All these exotic images contribute to a dialogue in the present with a feminine France, part prostitute, part idealized nation, a dialogue carried only half-way, leaving an image that glows in the dark like a precious icon. "The little Jehane de France" of whom the poet keeps thinking "in spite of himself" at the end testifies to the obdurate dialogism of the poem.

The New Spirit in London: Imagism and the *New Freewoman*

In parallel, another dialogue between the male poet as heroic exile and the feminine will occupy me in the last section of this chapter. It is the unlikely dialogue between Ezra Pound, an arch male modernist poet, with feminist writers and thinkers such as Dora Marsden, Harriet Shaw Weaver, Harriet Monroe, and Rebecca West. I will focus on Ezra Pound because, like Apollinaire and like Diaghilev, he can stand out as one of the few "impresarios" of modernism, those who not only felt the changes that were to bring about the new, but who also knew how to work with many other artists and learn from them. Apollinaire was called the "impresario of the avant-garde" by Roger Shattuck,[32] and the term has been used by all the biographers of Pound. Pound and Apollinaire shared similar characteristics: a certain evasiveness in their theoretical pronouncements, contrasted with the assured tone in which they were couched; both would flaunt their erudition while barely concealing huge patches of ignorance; and both were gifted with an abundance of wit and personal warmth, while once in a while being tempted by moments of harsh rejection and ideological polemics. Thus, as we saw, Apollinaire lashed out suddenly at Romains, and Pound would rail against so many people that it would be hard to list them, but one might think of his fight against Amy Lowell, who had tried to appropriate imagism. Meanwhile, both had a strong sense of fidelity with old friends.

Symptomatically, Pound started his poetic career – that is, after he had left the United States in the spring of 1908 – by working as a self-appointed impresario for Katherine Heyman, a pianist then playing in Venice. It was in Venice that he published his first collection of poems, *A Lume Spento*, before moving to London. In 1909, Pound divided his time and allegiances between Yeats' salon, in which one discussed myth, theosophy, and the perfect lyric, and Ford Hueffer's evenings, in which the issue was to create a new and exact prose, following Flaubert's example. He published more essays and

by an excessive, if diverting, admixture of meridional eloquence."
(This places the poets of commerce in their heaven and all's
right with the world once more.)

· · · · · · · ·

To compare these " empyreal spirits " with Whitman is, of course, absurd on the part of " Poetry
and Drama." Whitman may have found inspiration
in queer places just as Paolo Buzzi in his " Song of
the Imprisoned " (included in the present volume)
finds it in brothels, hospitals, prisons, asylums and
graveyards. But he did not help himself liberally to
city furnishings, " telegraphs, telephones, gramophones, cycles, motor-cycles, motor-cars, kinemato-
graphs," and the mechanical appliances heavily cata-
logued in " The New Futurist Manifesto." Such
things it seems are necessary to awaken the
" Futurist Consciousness " by acting upon a
feverishly nervous organisation. Whitman was an
individualist conscious of the infinite, and his sensations were stimulated by the Spirit of Life with
which he drenched his subjects. The Italian Futurists
are poets and painters of paroxysm and hallucination
who are frequently found " invoking all the furies
of madmen." They never go beyond the finite, and
their sensations are stimulated by the Spirit of Wireless Telegraphy, and their works are inspired by
" man multiplied by the machine." If we recollect
that it was Watts' condenser which saddled man
with a machine, we see how far the Futurists are
justified in ranking as such. What they are really
doing is handing legacies from the dead to the dead.

· · · · · · · ·

The Marinetti Futurists then, are pre-occupied
with corruption not with creation. It has been said
that the Futurist painters have inaugurated a new
period of caricature, and their quaint sympathy with
the phenomena of electric civilisation has doubtless
opened the door on some varieties of absurd and
macabre invention. Of course, it is not unjust to
caricature to assert that Futurism has been largely
responsible for bringing about its renaissance.
Caricature cannot go beyond the re-externalisation
of externals; like Futurism it remembers always the
earth. We have only to turn to the " New Age "
for proof of this. As all the world knows, the " New
Age " is a journal which, like " Punch," is welcomed
because of its middle-class nursery pictures. The
" New Age " pictures have the additional merit of
being produced by a person standing with his feet
deep in the clay. In this unromantic position in
he may be seen seeking to sum up the political situation in
well-known personages who, for the purpose, he
provides with samples of comic hair, comic noses,
comic chins, faces of pigs, bellies of the beer-barrel
order, ratty legs and assertive feet,—the stock-in-
trade in fact of a whiskey-drinking circus clown.

HUNTLY CARTER.

EDITORIAL.
Letters, &c., intended for the Editor should be
personally addressed : Ainsdale, England.

PUBLICATION.
All business communications relative to the
publication of THE NEW FREEWOMAN should be
addressed, and all cheques, postal and money
orders, &c., made payable to THE NEW FREE-
WOMAN LTD., Oakley House, Bloomsbury Street,
London, W.C., and should be crossed " Parr's
Bank, Bloomsbury Branch."
Terms of Subscription.—Yearly, 14/- (U.S.A.
3 dollars 50 cents); Six Months, 7/- (U.S.A.,
1 dollar 75 cents); Three Months, 3/6 (U.S.A.,
90 cents). Single Copies 7d., post free to any
address in the Postal Union.

ADVERTISEMENTS.
All orders, letters, &c., concerning advertise-
ments should be addressed to the Advertisement
Manager, THE NEW FREEWOMAN, Oakley
House, Bloomsbury Street, London, W.C.

Figure 5   *The New Freewoman*, December 1, 1913, p. 239

translations than his own poetry in those last Edwardian years, and many of the poets Pound started being associated with are considered as "Edwardian" today (Laurence Binyon, Victor Plarr, Ernest Rhys, Selwyn Image, F. S. Flint). The new friendship with Wyndham Lewis and T. E. Hulme pushed him forward, and in 1912, he contacted Harriet Monroe, who was launching *Poetry* magazine in Chicago, with the hope of promoting his newly launched school of *imagisme*. He became the foreign correspondent of *Poetry*, in which he included poems by Yeats, Tagore, Aldington, and Hilda Doolittle published, along with his own "Contemporania." It was also in *Poetry* that he defined his esthetic early in 1913: it was to be a compromise between Yeats' post-symbolic esthetic and Hueffer's cult of the *mot juste*. The March issue of *Poetry* published his famous manifesto of *imagisme*, which is based on a "Few Don'ts" (not to use superfluous words, how to avoid abstractions, ornaments, or poetic diction) and a new definition of the image as "that which presents an intellectual and emotional complex in an instant of time."[33] And the main authorities invoked by Pound, besides W. B. Yeats and Ford Hueffer (whose opinions systematically diverged, for example Yeats was promoting Tagore whereas Hueffer was promoting D. H. Lawrence) were the French *unanimistes* Charles Vildrac and Georges Duhamel, whose *Notes on Poetical Technique* is often quoted.

In April 1913, *Poetry* printed Pound's famous haiku, "In a Station of the Metro," and it appeared in the *New Freewoman* in August that same year. Both journals paid attention to the special typographical arrangement:

IN A STATION OF THE METRO

The apparition   of these faces   in the crowd   :
Petals   on a wet, black   bough   .   [34]

The spacing after the colon and the period is essential to the sense of an organ music's pause or rest; here, the expansion of the line as a spatial unity is identical with the aural suggestion produced by a musical score. I will return to Pound's fascination for Japanese and Chinese models in chapter 5, and the history of imagism has been often recounted. All through the end of the year, Pound was composing an anthology entitled *Des Imagistes*, which was published in March 1914, with poets like Aldington, Flint, H. D., Hueffer, Joyce, Lowell, and Williams. However, the worm was already in the apple since Amy Lowell was trying to control the group and get rid of Pound. By then, Pound had moved further and launched Vorticism with Lewis and Gaudier-Brzeska, whom he met in 1913.

In all the poems published in 1913, Pound turns away from the rather archaic persona of the troubadour that he had adopted and takes the role of a cultural critic, who lambasts the smug provincialism and inherited timidity of middle-class England and America. In March, Harriet Monroe objected to the lines "Speak well of amateur harlots / Speak well of disguised pro-curers," and found risqué lines like "Go! and make cat calls! / Dance and make people blush, / Dance the dance of the phallus," but accepted them after Pound had complained that one should not "emasculate literature utterly."[35] These poems were collected in *Lustra* three years later. Pound always insisted on blending the national, that is by helping promising young writers with the hope of unleashing an "American Risorgimento" soon to come, and the international, by insisting on "a universal standard which pays no attention to time and country – a Weltliteratur standard."[36] In 1913, Pound's strategy seemed to pay off at last – he had gathered the best writers in English on both sides of the Atlantic and was able to promote their work and his in two avant-garde magazines. In August 1913, Pound presented *The New Freewoman* to Monroe as "our left wing," and explained that he had taken charge of the literature department.[37] Left-wing it was, with a specific emphasis on anarchism and feminism – and yet, the esthetic program of Pound and that of the editor, Dora Marsden, were almost identical.

There could not have been two more dissimilar characters than Pound and Marsden. She has been described vividly and sympathetically by Rebecca West: "She had, to begin with, the most exquisite beauty of person. She was hardly taller than a child, but she was not just a small woman, she was a perfectly proportioned fairy. She was the only person I have ever met who could so accurately have been described as flower-like . . ."[38] Marsden, who had been head of a teachers' training college in Manchester, was also a militant feminist. Yet, today, she is more known for her contribution to high modernism than to feminism, and without her publishing of Pound, H. D., Aldington, Joyce, and Wyndham Lewis in the columns of her magazines, she might well be forgotten. Bruce Clarke's *Dora Marsden and Early Modernism*[39] has shed a better light on the rationale of the transformation of a small feminist magazine into one of the most active organs of high modernism, especially when the magazine was rebaptized *The Egoist* in January 1914. The metamorphosis can be explained by Marsden's personal evolution. She had been a classmate of Christabel Pankhurst in 1900 at the Manchester Victoria University, after which she remained associated with suffragism. A militant in the Women's Social and Political Union (WSPU), she was one of the keynote speakers at the huge rally that took place in June 1908 in Manchester, a meeting that drew 150,000 people. By 1908 she was a salaried organizer of the movement. She drew public attention by her spectacular harassment of Winston Churchill at the Southport Empire Theater in December 1909: she shouted insults and propaganda from a skylight in the dome and would have fallen to her death if the police hadn't caught her. She was repeatedly jailed, and force-fed through the nose like many other militant suffragettes. After "Black Friday" in November 1910, when two women died as a result of police brutality, Dora Marsden was thought to be too radical, and was denounced and condemned by the Pankhursts.

This led her to take a less militant attitude in 1911, and she decided to devote her time to the study of philosophy. She resigned from the WSPU, moved to London with her friend Grace Jardine, and enlisted Harriet Weaver, a liberal Quaker who had some money of her own, to found *The Freewoman: A Weekly Feminist Review*, that lasted from November 1911 to October 1912. *The Freewoman* was a unique forum for suffragists, feminists, anarchists, socialists, and Uranians (the gay liberation movement of the period). It also included spiritualists, money-reformers, poets, and esthetes. It went bankrupt in 1912, to be resuscitated under the name of *The New Freewoman: An Individualist Review* in June 1913. Then Dora Marsden and Harriet Weaver (who was still financing the journal) opened its columns to new writers such as Rebecca West, Ezra Pound, and Richard Aldington. Rebecca West deserves a special mention since she was at first the one who allowed Pound and his friends to get a footing in the magazine. She too had been a staunch suffragette, and in 1911 joined the staff of the *Freewoman*, agreeing with Marsden that the original movement led by the Pankhurst sisters was losing credibility and needed a broader scope. There had been an increased tendency to avoid sexuality, and it was reinforced when Christabel Pankhurst published her famous book on venereal disease, *The Great Scourge and How To End It*, in 1913. Unlike the Pankhursts, Marsden and West were very explicit about sexuality, and published some of the frankest discussions of prostitution, frigidity, and unfaithful spouses one could find in an English periodical at the time. In the second issue of the *New Freewoman*, West published a short story entitled "Nana," in which she narrates her visit to a sordid striptease club in Seville. When the woman whom she calls "Nana" (by reference to Zola) finally strips naked and sings, West grows rhapsodic:

> This was inspired nakedness. As the gaslight glowed off her body, whose wholesomeness immediately frustrated her attempts at indecency, and the lines of her trembled because she continued to sing deeply from the chest, I remembered how I once saw the sun beating on the great marbled loins and furrowed back of a grey Clydesdale and watched the backward thrust of its thigh twitch with power.[40]

The message of this offered flesh – here compared with a typical Scottish horse – is that the woman is for a while nothing but flesh and blood, a "refreshing" gift allowing one to leave behind all intellect. West craves to touch her and applauds frantically, but is then forced to leave because of the lewd looks thrown at her by the men in the bar.

West was not only a brilliant stylist and an untiring feminist propagandist, she had also chosen the camp of modernism and did all she could to promote Pound and his friends. Thus in August 1913 she introduced *imagisme* by referring to Pound's *Poetry* manifesto, which she quoted. In one sentence, she deftly opposes *imagisme* to post-impressionism and futurism, as being "not revolutionary" since they are really in love with the past. Yet this apparent passé-ism is also prospective and looks to the future: "Just as Taylor and Gillbreth want to introduce scientific management into industry so the *imagists* want to discover the most puissant way of whirling the scattered star dust of words into a new star of passion."[41] One detects a vague reluctance to let Pound have his way and make the business of poetry too professional, a technique to learn and apply. In September, H. D., Aldington, William Carlos Williams, Flint, and Amy Lowell are gathered under the heading of "The Newer School." And as if to confirm what West had to say about the "taylorization" of poetry, on October 15, 1913, Pound published the first installment of "The Serious Artist" as the lead article, followed by his "credo" on religious issues, "Religio"; the issue also features Aldington, Byington, Upward, and Rémy de Gourmont. There, Pound yokes violently esthetics and ethics when he states that "Bad art is inaccurate art."[42] For Pound, the cult of beauty has a hygienic function, it allows us to live better; conversely, a bad artist who does not pay attention to his skill is like a bad doctor who kills his patients. By that time, West had already left the magazine, displeased with its mixture of philosophy (Bergson and Upward are included in later issues) and experimental texts by modernist writers. A male-centered modernism had replaced an older suffragism. Rachel Blau Du Plessis and others have denounced Marsden's betrayal of feminism.[43] While this betrayal is undeniable, Bruce Clarke has shown that Dora Marsden's hand had not been forced by Pound and his friends; rather, she herself had engineered the change of name and even solicited an official letter from the "men of letters." In fact, it was Dora Marsden's evolution from feminism to anarchism that had led her there.

The editorial of the first issue of the *New Freewoman* does not disguise its anarchist tone. Dora Marsden writes in her leading article:

> This is the epoch of the gadding mind. The mind "not at home" but given to something else, occupied with alien "causes" is the normal order and as such

must be held accountable for that contemning [sic] of the lonely occupant of the home – the Self – which is the characteristic of the common mind. [. . .] Hence the popularity of the "Cause" which provides the Idol to which the desired self-sacrifice can be offered. The greater the sacrifice the Idol can accept the greater is it as a "Cause," whether it be liberty, equality, fraternity or what not.[44]

This attack on "Causes" is in line with the opening statement of Max Stirner's *The Ego and His Own*, which had been translated into English in 1907 by Benjamin Tucker, also a regular contributor to the *New Freewoman*. There, Stirner developed the idea that he rejected any cause not his own. He meant his rejection to be radical, not wishing to stop at a critique of religion as the other left-Hegelians had done. Unlike Bauer or Feuerbach, he wanted to destroy "the cause of mankind" as well, which entails getting rid of the "causes" of truth, freedom, humanity, justice. Stirner concluded: "Only *my* cause is never to be my concern," and refused to be shamed in the name of clichés like: "Shame on the egoist who thinks only of himself!"[45]

This philosophy of egoism allowed Marsden to repudiate the great Cause of suffragism as it had been defined by the Pankhursts. On their view, one had to be ready to give one's life for the cause, a rhetoric that was denounced as a trap by Marsden. "Mrs. Pankhurst may die and great is the Cause. What Cause? The Cause of the empty concept – the fount of all insincerity: the Cause of the Symbol – the Nothing worked upon by the Dithyramb."[46] This led Marsden to a sweeping rejection of any form of authority:

> Accurately speaking, there is no "Woman movement" . . . If primarily women are to regard themselves as Woman or as the Mother, their satisfactions as individuals would be subordinated to an external authority: the requirements of the development of Woman or Mother *as such* – Empty concepts again. [. . .] The few individual women before mentioned maintain that their only fitting description is that of Individual: Ends-in-themselves. They are Egoists.[47]

This quasi-manifesto was published in the first issue of the *New Freewoman*. From the outset, anarchism was clashing with feminism, or, more precisely was encompassing feminism: "The NEW FREEWOMAN is not for the advancement of Woman, but for the empowering of individuals."[48] Soon after, Marsden's critique of language, her new "semantics," would clash with anarchism too; in a dialogue with Tucker, who was combining Stirner and Proudhon, in November 1913, Marsden asks: "We frankly do not understand why Mr. Tucker, an egoist, and Stirner's English publisher, does not see the necessity of clearing current language of padding as a preliminary of egoistic investigation."[49] Anarchism is not enough, as Laura Riding would later write, at least if it does not begin with a critical revision of the language we use – otherwise we run the risk of being carried away by propaganda and distorted ideologies like nationalism.

No wonder that the last page of the last issue of the *New Freewoman*, published on December 15, 1913, prints side by side an advertisement for *The Divine Mystery* by Allen Upward, who had been praised by Pound as the best anthropologist of religious rituals, and an advertisement for Stirner's book, *The Ego and His Own* with the caption: "The most powerful work that has ever emerged from a single human mind."[50] Obviously, Marsden had moved from post-suffragist feminism to post-feminist anarchism, which led her to develop a systematic philosophical deconstruction of political discourse and everyday language. This she was to call her "Egoist semantics." The last issue of the *New Freewoman* contained a note explaining why it should change its name to *The Egoist* as of January 1914.[51] An open letter was signed by five men, Upward, Pound, Carter, Kauffmann and Aldington, who actually thanked Dora Marsden for her constant efforts in "establishing an organ in which men and women of intelligence can express themselves without regard to the public." They added that the title "causes it to be confounded with organs devoted solely to the advocacy of an unimportant reform in an obsolete political institution." They requested that Marsden consider "adopting another title which will mark the character of your paper as an organ of individualists of both sexes, and of the individualist principle in every department of life."[52]

The new title was supposed to be more "neutral" at a time when women were tired of strife and aspired to social recognition. There again, one senses the continuous semantic hedging that became typical of Marsden's later work, perceptible here in the way in which double quotes surround almost all the words:

The time has arrived when mentally-honest women feel that they have no use for the springing-board of large promises of powers redeemable in a distant future. Just as they feel they can be as "free" now as they have the power to be, they know that their works can give evidence now of whatever quality they are capable of giving to them. To attempt to be "freer" than their own power warrants means that curious thing – "protected freedom" and their ability, allowed credit because it is women's, is a "protected" ability. "Freedom" and ability "recognized" by permission, are privileges which they find can serve no useful purpose.[53]

The linguistics of suspicion implied by Marsden's rather embarrassed commentary deploys in parallel an ethics of autonomy (with the attendant notions of honesty, freedom, individuality and usefulness) and a new esthetic sense, geared to the direct and immediate expression of true emotions and the rejection of abstract concepts.

In his imagist manifesto Pound had urged the "direct presentation of the 'thing,' whether subjective or objective," and had instructed his disciples to "go in fear of abstractions." This fitted Marsden's political program: she was trying to destroy flabby generalities like the "Cause" and all the connected ideological constructions, and would spend another decade debunking abstract words that perpetuate oppression. One had to deconstruct them one by one, as Fritz Mauthner was doing in his monumental *Critique of Language* and his 1910–11 *Vocabulary of Philosophy*,[54] as Karl Kraus was doing, almost all by himself, in every issue of *Die Fackel*, the satirical review of Vienna of which he was, from 1911 to his death in 1936, the sole editor and contributor.

But unlike Mauthner, read avidly by Samuel Beckett for Joyce's *Work in Progress* in the late twenties, unlike Kraus, who became a visible symbol of resistance and freedom in Austria, Marsden met only indifference, incomprehension, and scorn in her country. Nobody spared her, not even the modernists whom she had sponsored, not even those who had a strong philosophical background like T. S. Eliot. In 1919, he complained that the *Egoist* had to suspend publication mostly because Marsden took the magazine as "a means for getting her philosophical articles into print," whereas the majority of the readers did not want to read them.[55] After the definitive closing of the review, Marsden isolated herself in a small cottage in the Lake District and went on with her philosophical investigations. Two volumes were produced in 1928 and 1930 by the Egoist Press, revived and funded by Harriet Weaver for the occasion, but her work remained ignored. Facing this lack of recognition, Marsden finally broke down and fell into a deep depression, spending the rest of her life from 1935 to 1960 in the Crichton Royal Hospital in Dumfries, Scotland, a hospital for the mentally ill.

In a strange parallel, for 13 years, between 1945 and 1958, Pound was interned in St. Elizabeth in Washington, DC. His depression was real, although the internment was arranged in order to find an issue to his "treason" against the United States. In spite of what both had claimed, abstract causes had the upper hand in the end. Perhaps Marsden should have paid more heed to what Rebecca West was suggesting at the time of the *New Freewoman* – that the best vehicle was not semantic analysis but the arts of fiction and especially the theater, and that plays like those of Strindberg or Shaw, especially the highly popular *Pygmalion*, permitted one to discover concretely how language, sex, and class overlap. A last coincidence of names seems to have been planned by the historical unconscious of 1913. That year saw the triumph of Shaw's play and the adoption of the label of *imagiste* by H. D. Was there such a difference between Eliza Doolittle's surprising progress when she learned to master the art of refined diction, and Hilda Doolittle's sudden adoption of a poetic persona, when she so readily identified with her pen-name, "H. D. Imagiste," generously given to her by a Pygmalion Pound?[56]

Chapter 3

Everyday Life and the New Episteme

The Scientific Spirit and its Discontents

A barometric low hung over the Atlantic. It moved eastward toward a high-pressure area over Russia without as yet showing any inclination to bypass this high in a northerly direction. The isotherms and isotheres were functioning as they should. The air temperature was appropriate relative to the annual mean temperature . . . [. . .] In a word that characterizes the facts fairly accurately, even if it is a bit old-fashioned: It was a fine day in August 1913.[1]

Here is the brilliant opening of a famous novel, in a chapter conspicuously titled "From which, remarkably enough, nothing develops." Musil's chronicle of the modern spirit, *The Man Without Qualities*, opens with a linguistic clash between a scientific account of the "normal" parameters of everyday life and an "old-fashioned" or "Romantic"[2] way of referring to a day in the calendar. The new style bears all the marks of neutral objectivity and scientific detachment; Musil chose 1913 for good reasons: this was the last year in which "Kakania" (his mocking abbreviation for the double monarchy of the Habsburgs) was still functional and stable, while portents of change and crisis were accumulating. A bolder step into technological modernity was soon to be accomplished by industrialized mass killing.

Here, modernity is signaled by precise instruments of measurement, and the scientific recalculation of all coordinates generates a universal process that impinges on everyday life, and shapes personalities, including that of the hero, Ulrich. He is too rational and skeptical to participate or act, and appears thus "without properties" or a sense of individuality. The introductory pages of *The Man Without Qualities* single out a man and a woman passing by in a Vienna street just after a car accident; the truck driver expostulates while the forgotten victim lies on the pavement, surrounded by a crowd waiting for an ambulance. This scene captures a growing concern for speeding cars in big cities at the time (the man, Arnheim, explains in a dispassionate tone, that "according to American statistics, one hundred ninety thousand people are killed every year by cars"[3]).

Automobilism was a relatively new craze in 1913, and America was leading the way. Thanks to Ford's relatively inexpensive Model T, more than half a million Americans owned a car in 1913. Ford generated profits above $20 million per year at the time. He then decided to raise the standard wage from $2 a day to $5 a day. This did not mean that horses were being retired: 20 million horses were still used for transportation in the country. In all the industrialized nations, the progression from horse-drawn carriages to automobile travel was breathtakingly exponential; for instance, France had 3,000 cars in 1900, 50,000 cars in 1909, and 100,000 cars in 1913. The young aristocrats stopped using horse-drawn carriages to go to the fashionables areas like Bois de Boulogne, and instead paraded around in Cadillac Torpedoes and Rolls Royce Phantoms. In the summer of 1913, the Paris municipal council even attempted to banish motor cars from the posh avenues, at least from 11 a.m. to 1 p.m., but the young bloods struck back by staging a procession of very noisy old carriages from Gare Saint-Lazare to Avenue des Acacias. They won the battle.[4] There was no way to stop the massive influx of cars, which were responsible for horrible accidents; this was the case when Isadora Duncan's children plunged to their death in April 1913 after their chauffeur allowed their car to fall into the Seine. Fashionable Paris paid its respects to Duncan, who never really overcame this tragedy, a dark anticipation of her demise 14 years later when her scarf got stuck in a speeding car's wheels. Speed was already a real danger in 1913, although the usual speed limit 10 or 15 miles per hour in most countries. Yet car races pitted against one another fast cars which reached amazing speeds: Fred Marriott, for instance, drove at 200 kilometers per hour in a Dion Bouton. Speed, together with light, were two new factors that changed everyday life: in cities like Paris, New York, and London, gaslight was yielding to electric light, which would be deplored by Walter Benjamin, who missed the dark recesses of the Parisian passages, suddenly exposed as tawdry by the garish electric lighting.

The process seemed irresistible and universal: distance was slowly abolished. Thus when Blériot flew over the Channel in 1909, he exclaimed that England was not an island any more. In 1913 Roland Garros flew over the Mediterranean from France to Tunisia, a record 453-mile flight. And in 1913 President Wilson was the first American president ever to be driven in an automobile for his inauguration. From this automobile revolution, Musil's character was justified in concluding that everybody's life in a modern metropolis had become cheap, chaotic, random, always at risk of being impacted by chance collisions. More dramatically, Rilke's Parisian chronicle captures a new body whose very being is traversed by new machinery: "Electric streetcars speed ringing through my room. Automobiles run over me."[5] This is the metropolitan context in which, as the sociologist Georg Simmel, who was a close friend of Rilke, had shown, people turned into anonymous counters or cogs shuttling to and fro in a monstrous engine. They tried to protect themselves from all the unexpected violent stimuli by insulating themselves within indifference. Simmel was the first to draw attention to "the calculating exactness of practical life" that results from a capitalist economy that "transforms the world into an arithmetical problem."[6] The arithmetical calculation entailed a type of scientific globalization that introduced unity in the very standards of measurement.

Measurement had to be regulated by universal criteria: the condition for the dissemination of the new world-view was not only its international character but what can be called early globalization. Globalization demanded the unification of time in most countries. This was the case with France in 1913, where, as Stephen Kern has demonstrated,[7] a major shift took place. At the end of the nineteenth century, France had had a chaotic situation: some regions had four different time zones, none of which was the standard Greenwich time. The railroads functioned on Paris time, which was nine minutes ahead of Greenwich Mean Time. In 1891, railway time became the legal time in France, but another problem arose: in order to give passengers sufficient time to board, the clocks inside the stations were five minutes ahead of those on the tracks. Finally, the French government decided to introduce order, and in 1912 President Poincaré organized an international conference on time. It determined reliable ways of sending accurate time signals through-out the world, a development which had become inevitable because of inter-national wireless transmissions. In accordance with the new protocol, at 10 o'clock on the morning of July 1, 1913, the Eiffel Tower sent the first wireless signal to be transmitted around the globe. It was not only words that could be transmitted, but images as well. In 1913, Edouard Belin invented a portable facsimile machine that scanned pictures using a photocell and sent the signals via ordinary telephone lines; soon baptized the "Belino," it was widely used by journalists, and replaced the earlier fax machine of Arthur Korn.

Cities were spreading fast as well. All of the major metropolises in the developed world had a subterranean railway, subway, or metro. Buenos Aires was the last the last big city to complete its *subte*, which opened in 1913. Building techniques were also evolving quickly. In 1913, the Woolworth

Building was completed in New York, beating the Eiffel Tower to the title of the tallest building in the world. With 60 stories, it was 792 feet high. The architect Cass Gilbert used a revolutionary steel framework to reach that height, and needed to fit the building with high-speed elevators. The same technique of using a steel framework was employed to build the Théâtre des Champs-Elysées in Paris, as we will see in the next chapter. Architecture was now dominated by new technical concerns developed by what Hermann Muthesius called *Ingenieurbau*, the strict application of rational engineering to principles of building; this was expanded into an esthetic concern for practical demands, slimness, transparency: it had to turn into an *Ingenieurästhetik* as well. The pre-war work of the Deutscher Werkbund between 1907 and 1914 was exemplary in that respect, since these artists, engineers, and architects aimed at building well, not only for the rich but for the masses. In big cities, the need to house growing numbers of often disparate populations (this was the case in Vienna, with the regular influx of *Ostjuden*) made life more chaotic. Indeed, Berlin and Vienna had more than doubled their populations in the 25 years preceding the war. Musil's evocation of everyday life in Vienna was remarkably similar to Simmel's observations about the modern metropolis:

> Like all big cities, [Vienna] was made up of irregularity, change, forward spurts, failures to keep step, collisions of objects and interests, punctuated by unfathomable silences; made up of pathways and untrodden ways, of one great rhythmic beat as well as the chronic discord and mutual displacement of all its contending rhythms. All in all, it was like a boiling bubble inside a pot made up of the durable stuff of buildings, laws, regulations, and historical traditions.[8]

Musil chose 1913 for biographical reasons as well, as this year saw the publication of two of his texts that, taken together, define the modern spirit. The first is well known, and provides a literary exemplification of the qualities of scientific detachment and precision demanded by the new spirit. It is the minute description of the agony and death throes of flies caught by fly-paper. The paper is made in Canada and aptly called "Tanglefoot"; 14 inches long and 8 inches wide, it first glues a fly by its legs. The fly is first astonished and attempts to understand, then buzzes to lift itself, in vain. The intervals between spells of frantic buzzing grow longer, and it has to rest more and more. Then it makes the momentous mistake of looking for a second point of contact, which glues it elsewhere. Finally, after more efforts, it falls exhausted, completely glued to the surface, and lies there, like a "crashed plane." The only living organ in the fly's body is an aperture near the leg-sockets that keeps opening and closing like a human eye. The two-page-long "Das Fliegenpapier"[9] was published in 1913, and develops its descriptive program while multiplying allusions to humans' desperate efforts (the fly is like a cripple pretending to be normal, like a war veteran hiding his wounds, like a mountain climber whose hand slips free and loses its grip, etc.), and alluding ominously to war: the flypaper is a subtle enemy that uses glue and "bewildering vapors" and always wins at a moment of "muddled" inattention; it seems that the whole tragedy of the impending trench warfare could be read between the lines.

The second text is more theoretical and discusses the birth of the new "Mathematical Man."[10] There again, echoes of a war in the offing can be heard. Musil begins with a critique of the view that military commanders behave like "mathematicians of the battlefield."[11] He quips that if this were the case, it would produce a catastrophe in which thousands would lose their lives – how true the prediction proved to be! If mathematics is the "economy of thinking," a triumph of intellectual organization, it should be practiced without consideration for the real world. Only when mathematics forgets pragmatic considerations can it then regulate mundane domains like engineering, architecture, or technology. Mathematics, the bold "luxury of pure reason," underpins the very stuff of human life. It helps us bake our bread, build our houses, and drive our cars. The pursuit of mathematics as such must be divorced from possible applications to everyday concerns first because the mathematical physics of the new sciences works against common-sense perception of space and time. Scientific progress shatters the world-view inherited from the Enlightenment; besides, we can no longer rely on religion or the arts to provide a totalizing synthesis. This episteme is disquieting, elusive, a-subjective, and never tallies with systems of belief. Nevertheless its progress is unstoppable – it is the root of the new spirit.

The divorce between science and subjective intuition was nowhere more visible than in the "new" mathematics. Non-Euclidian geometry had taken off with Riemann and Lobatchevsky at the end of the nineteenth century, but after 1900 the so-called "pathology of mathematics"[12] began. Cantor, Hilbert, and Dedekind had started it when discussing transfinite numbers, and soon it became obvious that mathematics should not be considered as having a real correspondence to the world. A need for new foundations was all the more acutely felt, as Henri Poincaré and Bertrand Russell knew at the turn of the century. When the new physics launched by Rutherford, Marie and Pierre Curie, and Niels Bohr needed these equations, the sense of a sudden convergence hit the scientific community as a revelation. The revelation was conveyed most explicitly by Danish scientist Bohr when, in his famous paper "On the Constitution of Atoms and Molecules," he described the structure of the atom. Bohr's model was based on the behavior of the hydrogen atom; he described it as made up of orbiting electrons which gave off or absorbed discrete and quantified amounts of energy (*quanta*); when these electrons jumped from one orbit to the other, the laws of classical mechanics did not apply but had to be relayed by Planck's quantum mechanics. Bohr's theory was the third great advance in quantum physics after Planck's in 1900 and Einstein's relativity theory in 1905. Bohr established for the first time that the atom itself was made up of parts and that each of its parts behaved discontinuously. Electrons did not spiral down, or up, they vanished from one orbital condition and reappeared instantaneously in another, according to what he called the quantum leap.

Musil's sense that scientific discoveries were ushering in a different world and a different personality calls up the Renaissance; the same enthusiasm was expressed in similar terms by Bertrand Russell as he was drawn out from the study of pure mathematical logic to the new physics of Niels Bohr, Einstein, and Max Planck. Here is what Russell wrote in the fall of 1913:

> I have been hearing more about the new physics – it is very exciting. The atmosphere of the Scientific world in this age is wonderfully exhilarating as compared to the world of culture – the people are tremendously alive, feeling that it is for them to do great things, not at all dominated by past achievements, tho' they know them thoroughly – all the best people have a tremendous sense of adventure, like the Renaissance mariners. They question everything that has been done, & are willing to pull down because they have enough energy & power to build up again. It is *the* thing in which our age excels – I am thankful to be able to have a part in it.[13]

Of course, neither Russell nor Musil was devoid of literary or artistic culture, as can be proved by Russell's futile efforts to make his gifted pupil Wittgenstein read French novels so as to "polish" him and make him abandon the obsessive ruminations about logic that threatened his sanity.

It was indeed a time when intellectual excitement seemed to be generated more from the side of the "hard" sciences than from literature or the arts. A whole world-view founded on stable substances, predictable attractions, and logical causality was being discarded and replaced by a relativistic universe ruled by Planckian and Einsteinian equations. As Einstein described the new world picture after 1915, it had to be seen as a four-dimensional entity, time being fully integrated into its reality. This evolution had been anticipated by Ernst Mach, an influential Austrian physicist and philosopher. He conceived what is still called Mach's principle, the hypothesis that, cosmologically speaking, the inertial effects of mass are not innate in a body, but are determined by the quantity and distribution of matter in the universe. Mach was the first scientist to reject Newton's concepts of absolute time and space, as Musil pointed out in his 1908 thesis.[14] We still use Mach's number when expressing the speed of matter relative to the speed of sound at a certain temperature; Mach's name still measures speed for supersonic planes. Altogether, Mach established important principles of optics, mechanics, and wave dynamics; all this was supported by a positivist conception of knowledge as a conceptual organization of the data of sensory experience.

For Mach, no statement in the natural sciences was admissible unless it was empirically verifiable. Rigorous criteria of verifiability led him to reject most common-sense notions as "metaphysical" concepts, which included absolute time and space, and thus paved the way for Einstein's relativity theory. Then, in 1886, Mach advanced the idea that all knowledge is derived from sensation. Phenomena under scientific investigation can be understood only in terms of experience since they depend upon the observer who has to be present somehow in the observation process. More than these phenomenological generalizations, it was Mach's *The Science of Mechanics* that had the strongest influence on Einstein, who said that he had been shaken out of his "dogmatic faith" by this book. Einstein met the old philosopher in 1911 and convinced him that scientific theories were not just conveniences, economic ways of describing an array of facts, but more complex truths about the world. Mach and Einstein would unite to reject the fictionalist position of neo-Kantian philosophers such as Hans Vaihinger, whose influential *Philosophy of "As If"* (first published in 1911) stated that terms such as electrons, atoms, and electronic magnetic waves were hypothetical constructs, useful fictions whose reality we had to assume but could never verify. Thus Einstein was overjoyed when he thought he had dragged the old philosopher into his camp, and when Mach died in 1916 he composed a vibrant eulogy, pointing to the visionary aspect of his scientific views.

Alas, in June 1913, just before his death, Mach wrote a new preface to his *Principles of Physical Optics*. There, he publicly disavowed relativity theory, and went back to his conceptions about the physiology of the senses.[15] Mach's effort at rejecting the neo-Kantian idealism that dominated in Germany had brought him too deeply into a subjective relativism that could not accept a shattering revolution in scientific and cosmological paradigms. Philosophical content was for him bounded by sense-data, and science only provided interpretations of sense-data. Like William James' later atomistic pragmatism, Mach's idea of the self was fundamentally sensualist: the self was a bundle of perceptions not necessarily unified by a stable subject. Thus, for Mach, the old "I" was nevertheless "unsaveable," or, in his famous phrase, "das Ich ist unrettbar." Subjectivity was unified only through projective empathy with or deductive abstraction from appearances. As was the case in Berkeley's idealism, the self dissolved into visible, audible, touchable, and sensible series of sensations. This point was attacked by Lenin, who wrote a book to refute Mach. In *Materialism and Empirio-Criticism* (1909), Lenin refused any compromise between dialectical materialism and Mach's reduction of matter to sensory elements. Phenomenalism could not allow one to understand how the economic basis determines material life. This was not the route followed by Musil in his dissertation on Mach's philosophy. Closer to neo-Kantian critics like Stumpf, Musil saw in Mach's skepticism, in his endless decomposition of abstract entities, a series of contradictions that could be refuted as skepticism generally is: if only experience teaches us to observe regularities, how can we know that these are regularities without having a prior concept of truth? It is true that Musil had been forced by Stumpf to sharpen his critique of Mach and to rewrite parts of the dissertation.[16] In the end, Musil was groping toward a position that was both logicist and phenomenological, although he refused Mach's phenomenalist utilitarianism in the sciences. This brought him closer to problems treated at that time by Husserl, as we will see. However, the diffuse Machian positivism of the Viennese favored a rapid development of the sciences in optics, physics, cosmological observations, and engineering.

Even if there was some resistance to what was called Einstein's "Jewish" physics among various nationalist circles and in broader public opinion, Einstein and fellow discoverers like Marie Curie were distinguished. Curie received the Nobel Prize twice, once in physics in 1903, and once in chemistry in 1911. The scandal that engulfed her when she admitted to living openly with a married scientist, Paul Langevin, an early popularizer of Einstein's relativity theory, had very little impact on her brilliant scientific career. On his side, in 1913 Einstein was being recognized as a leading scientist in most parts of the scientific community: he was elected to the Prussian Academy of Sciences and was offered a research professorship at the University of Berlin, to become director of the Kaiser Wilhelm Institute of Physics. He was at the time working on "general relativity," the fully generalized equations of space, time, and motion that would include his uniform-motion relativity of 1905 as a special case. He published his *Outline of a Generalized Theory of Relativity and of a Theory of Gravitation*, co-authored with Marcel Grossmann, in 1913. There, Einstein provided the physics, Grossmann the mathematics, but he soon guessed that something was missing to create a complete picture: gravitational field equations in cases of non-covariance. The last difficulty would soon be overcome in 1915, when Einstein completed his generalized theory of gravitation.[17]

The vital intermeshing of technological revolutions and changes in everyday life conforms to Michel Foucault's concept of the *episteme*, a concept meant to describe the system of positive knowledge that underpins a whole epoch. This notion is usually derived from a synchronic view over a long period like a century. It is the object of what he calls an "archeology": "archeology, addressing itself to the general space of knowledge, to its configurations, and to the mode of being of the things that appear in it, defines systems of simultaneity, as well as the series of mutations necessary and sufficient to circumscribe the threshold of a new positivity."[18] As we have seen, the enforced simultaneism generated by the focus on one single year draws more attention to the emergence of the new, especially when crucial years like 1913 seem to have precipitated the slow evolution of mentalities into a single moment of crisis. And in 1913 this was felt nowhere more acutely than in the domains of fashion and theories of gender.

Figure 6   Marie Curie and Albert Einstein, 1913, Engadine, Switzerland.
Photograph Aip Neils Bohr Library

New Women and New Sexualities

An anonymous correspondent of the *Times* denounced the "Bacchanal rage" of current fashion – inspired by the French – on 16 July 1913:

> It is no exaggeration to say that we are in the height of a revolution in feminine clothes, such as has not been seen since that other revolution gave sanction to the excesses of women in the Directoire and the Empire. [. . .] Nowadays women wear almost nothing under their gowns even in the daytime.
>
> Petticoats went some time back and were replaced by tights – or not replaced at all. The stockings are of such diaphanous silk as to embarrass the beholder who sees, even in the street, so much of them, and they are not covered by any but court shoes. So much for the foundation. Over this is worn a filmy sheath of half-transparent material, cut almost as low by day as by night, and with such slashings and liftings in the skirt as may fully display the leg half-way to the knee and which show every movement of the limbs – almost to the muscles.[19]

The anonymous writer links this new tendency with a general restlessness in society – of course, only to condemn it as mere "anarchy":

> It is interesting to note that the Bacchanal rage has fallen upon women at a time when much is in the melting-pot, at a time of world restlessness, of war abroad, of constitutional crisis at home, of social misery everywhere. It is difficult to see the connection between fashions and such things, or to say which is cause and what effect, or to determine how much our almost bare feet and quite bare arms and neck owe to Mr. Asquith's indifference to stable government or to the anarchy in the political and artistic world.[20]

This inflamed rhetoric captures well the new rage for fresh sensations that seemed to spread in 1913, as if at last remnants of Victorian prudery were being discarded. Paris was setting the example of emancipation by rejecting the old corset, the armor of textile and whalebone that had imprisoned women; pre-1914 haute couture displayed loose and flowing dresses that let bodies move freely in very thin fabrics, soft and sheer materials like satin, tulle, or light silk, while clothing for sports like skiing and tennis lent more freedom to the limbs. Already the corset was giving way to the brassiere, which offered more flexible support.[21] And in February 1913 the French actress Réjane created a scandal when she appeared on a stage with a skirt slit to the knee, letting a gold knee-bangle shine underneath. The new dresses

81

of couturiers like Poiret, Worth, Paquin, Lanvin, and Cheruit were also deemed scandalous because they were low-cut and tight-fitting, afternoon dresses being as low as evening gowns, skirts cut so close to the body that they showed the outline of the thighs. American reporters described these as "peek-a-boo blouses" and "X-ray skirts."[22] Some revealed half the leg, which would have been unthinkable a few years before, and the colors were as bright and jarring as possible, as if Delaunay's prismatic colors had been an inspiration. Women from London to New York often copied these models, at a time when it was easy to find competent and cheap seamstresses, and thus the new fashions were disseminated more quickly.

To these insults to good taste was added injury to the ears: 1913 saw the arrival of the tango in most European capitals. The dance had disreputable origins, as it came from the brothels and immigrant working-class sections of Buenos Aires such as La Boca, but the furor was undiminished throughout the whole year. London, Berlin, Paris, Florence, and Rome had gone tango-crazy. Tango was a sudden obsession just as waltzes and polkas had been in the past. There were tango suppers in chic hotels like the Trocadero in London, and everywhere in Paris restaurants. Even though it was decried as immodest and exotic, it found a vocal defender in the former anarchist poet, recently elected to the French Academy, Jean Richepin.[23] In Berlin, the Kaiser was outraged when he learned that the Countess Schwerin-Löwitz had organized a tango-tea in the official parliamentary rooms, and he published an edict forbidding any man in uniform to dance the tango, or even to be seen in a house where guests danced it. Hobble skirts that revealed too much of the leg would be banned from the streets or their wearers fined. In American cities, however, the new fashion was not tango but jazz dances. The syncopated rhythms of ragtime had been adopted by New York and Chicago as early as 1912, and by 1913 the craze was general: Manhattan had indeed gone dance-mad.[24] As usual dance halls, clubs, and bars did not suffice; eager dancers flocked to hotels, lounges, and restaurants where one could have a tea-dance in the afternoon, or a dinner-dance in which food was served as a pretext only. New dances were launched in a bewildering succession of quirky appellations: the Turkey Trot, the Grizzly Bear, the Bunny Hug, the Kangaroo Dip, the Chicken Scratch, and the Crab Step offered a whole menagerie of syncopated steps for the younger generation. Ragtime dances were thought to be grossly indecent, however, and many typists, secretaries, and clerks were sacked by their Manhattan bosses when they found out that they used their lunch-breaks to dance the Turkey Trot, the ancestor of the foxtrot. The mayor of New York sent plain-clothes policemen to report on the dance-hall situation, and they reported that women would unbutton the slashes of their skirts to whirl more freely and that gin-fizzes were consumed by men *and* women. Public dance-halls had to close at 1 a.m., but hotels and restaurants were untouchable because they were private premises.

This radical change in public mores corresponds to the rise of the "new woman," or to the emancipation of one-half of the population, kept until the end of the nineteenth century in conditions that were not very far from those of the Middle Ages. It may also have come from an "Americanization" of women in big cities – since just before the war, most European visitors to New York expressed their astonishment facing American girls: they were thought to be "brusque, jerky and full of nervous energy,"[25] over-assertive and opinionated, allowed to lunch and dine in groups of peers, and above all meaning to enjoy themselves. While this shocked foreign visitors, this liberated air was praised by the radical journalist Floyd Dell in his groundbreaking *Women as World Builders: Studies in Modern Feminism* (1913). He expressed his sympathy for the "young woman of the leisure class" who endeavors to "create a livelier, a more hilarious and human morale"; even in her "hell raising tendency," she achieves a necessary emancipation from dull middle-class morality.[26] Dell, who was to found the radical journal *The Masses* in 1914, devoted his *Women as World Builders* to biographical sketches of ten emblematic women: Charlotte Perkins Gilman, Emmeline Pankhurst and Jane Addams, Olive Schreiner and Isadora Duncan, Beatrice Webb and Emma Goldmann, Margaret Dreier Robins, Ellen Key, and Dora Marsden. This had been prepared by public shows like the Anglo-French International Exhibition of 1908 which granted a central place to women when it displayed in a centrally located Palace of Women's Work an exhibit of distinguished women's work, from young Victoria to the Brontë sisters, from anonymous needlework to Florence Nightingale's carriage.[27] It looked as if the movement of opinion launched by visionaries like Mary Wollstonecraft and Ibsen in plays and essays had finally come to fruition in the first decade of the century, and it was made more visible by the concerted agitation of the suffragettes in England and America.

The British suffragettes were the most radical of all; led by the Pankhurst sisters, they had moved on to a revolutionary feminism marked by direct action. After 1911, as we have seen, active militancy had become a watchword, and in the first months of 1913 British suffragettes smashed shop windows in the West End with hammers hidden in their muffs, destroyed golf courses with acid, burned mailboxes, cut telegraph and telephone wires, broke into the royal greenhouses, posted pungent snuff to Members of Parliament, slashed several paintings in the Manchester Art Gallery, and set fire to empty trains. Then, on June 4, Emily Davidson ran on the tracks at the Epsom Derby toward the galloping horses, grabbed the reins of the king's horse, and brought it down as it trampled her. She died a few days later, and the outrage was enormous. Davidson had been a militant suffragette just like Marsden before 1911; like her and many other suffragettes she had been jailed several times and forcibly fed through the nose. Her suicidal action captured headlines, and a huge funeral was organized in her honor. The American supporters of votes for women, coming from prosperous bourgeois families, were less militant, although they organized huge parades, demonstrations, and letter campaigns. They had arranged a big parade converging on Washington, DC, at the time of President Wilson's inaugural. It was a partial failure, as the police refused to provide protection and the marching groups were jeered at and even physically harassed by rough men and boys. A group left New York for a march on Washington on February 12. The "crusade" failed to gain massive support as they passed through Newark, Camden, Philadelphia, and Wilmington, but the press nevertheless gave a broad coverage to their efforts.[28]

The social unrest and need to redefine age-old relationships between the sexes was not limited to political agitation and rampant feminism. It had a scientific (or at times pseudo-scientific) component, marked by the emergence of endocrinology, sexology, and eugenics. As Allen G. Roper put it,[29] eugenics had always existed in ancient societies, from archaic barbarism with the killing of sickly infants to the practices of death by exposure in Sparta or Rome and the smothering at birth of supernumerary female babies in China, but it had taken a scientific turn in the nineteenth century, with the increasing use of statistics in Malthusian accounts of decreasing or rising birth-rates, and post-Darwinian concerns for natural or institutionalized selection in a given population. The question was to know whether population control should be left to scientists and politicians or to be decided by the regular blood-letting of war.[30] Eugenics had a scientific basis in Mendel's laws of hybridity and heredity, that had been defined more accurately in 1909 when the Danish biologist Wilhelm Johannsen identified genes as particular units of heredity and distinguished between the "genotype" (the genetic constitution of an organism) and the "phenotype" (the characteristics inherited by this organism), and in 1913 when Alfred H. Sturtevant created the first gene maps.

Eugenics, in spite of its strong ideological component, was not then defended by right-wingers and proto-Nazis only; most Fabians and socialists believed in eugenics before the war, and were hoping to create a better race of workers in the future. Shaw, Wells, Bertrand Russell, and Lady Ottoline

Morrell were all for eugenics, as were the more conservative Winston Churchill and D. H. Lawrence. In England, the Eugenics Education Society came into being in 1907, and already "eugenics had infiltrated more or less every aspect of intellectual and public life in Britain."[31] In America, the Eugenics Record Office was founded in Cold Springs, New York, in 1910, and its director was Charles B. Davenport, who published in 1913 the influential *Heredity in Relation to Eugenics*. The society debated issues such as "state laws limiting marriage selection" and the treatment that ought to be meted to subjects whose mental deficiency was attested. As Davenport wrote with involuntary humor, "human matings could be placed upon the same high plane as that of horse breeding," and it was crucial to prevent the propagation of the weak and the mad. His colleague Henry H. Goddard was multiplying case studies of "feeblemindedness."[32] This issue surfaced in one of the most embattled legal controversies of pre-war Britain, when Churchill, then Home Secretary, introduced in 1913 the Mental Deficiency Act. It distinguished four categories of subjects at risk, the "idiots," the "imbeciles," the "feeble-minded," and the "moral defectives" (which included unmarried mothers). The bill aimed at compulsory certification for all those whose were admitted to mental institutions and planned the enforced sterilization of the first three categories. A Board of Control would be under the responsibility of hand-picked specialists, the "lunacy commissioners." The project of enforced sterilization was defeated after the writer G. K. Chesterton denounced it publicly, but the rest of the bill was adopted, and was only revoked after the war.

The year 1913 also saw the unlikely combination of sexology and eugenics. One pioneer had been Magnus Hirschfeld, who in 1912 operated on a 20-year-old woman in Berlin and transformed her into a man, the first case of sex change ever recorded. His disciple Eugen Steinach, an endocrinologist from Vienna, started experimenting on guinea pigs' gonads in 1912. In 1913, he published the result of his investigations in *Feminization of Males and Masculinization of Females*, showing how, after having neutralized a previously female animal and injected male gonads into it, the masculinized guinea pig started mounting unaltered females. Conversely, the injection of female gonads into previously male pigs changed their behavior, making them offer their genitals to male partners exactly as females would. Later made notorious by experiments on homosexuals who were castrated and injected with a "normal" man's testicular tissue, which all "failed," he had more luck with the "Steinach operation," a simple vasectomy that was supposed to let interstitial tissue proliferate and release male hormones into the blood, thus "rejuvenating" men, or at least halting the aging process. It worked wonders for Yeats in 1934, although it failed to have any effect on Freud in 1923.[33] The man who would become Steinach's disciple in the US was Harry Benjamin, who went to Columbia University in 1913, was prevented from returning to Europe because of the war, and stayed in America, disseminating Steinach's theories. Meanwhile, Magnus Hirschfeld, who had been called the "Einstein of sex," had founded with Iwan Bloch the first sexological institution, called the Medical Society for Sexology and Eugenics, which was launched in 1913. Their arch-rival was Albert Moll, who in 1913 started the International Society for Sex Research in Berlin; he invited Freud to join, but the founder of psychoanalysis was reluctant, given the physiological standpoint of the first sexologists. Hirschfeld had started publishing widely on issues such as bisexuality (1906), transvestites (1910), and sexual transformations from male to female and vice versa (1912). Is was Havelock Ellis who defended a psychological standpoint when he argued against Hirschfeld that transvestism had nothing to do with misplaced hormones, but depended upon "inverted" identification with the other sex.[34] Meanwhile Walter Heape, a groundbreaking British biologist who had managed to transfer rabbit embryos from one mother to another in 1890, was raising the specter of sexual war in a notorious book entitled *Sex Antagonism*, to which I will return.[35] After a survey of exogamy defined as a "natural law" in all cultures since it is founded on sexual difference, Heape systematized the biological conception of sexuality based on hormone theory. The radical difference between male and female sexuality depended on physical differences like the "soul-wrenching trauma" caused by menstruation that rendered women physiologically unable to be rational and therefore unfit to vote.

In a related domain, but with a different animus, Karl Jaspers published his huge *Nature of Psychotherapy* (*Allegemeine Psychopathologie*) in 1913 in an effort to establish a bridge between critical philosophy and conventional psychiatry. Jaspers had graduated from medical school in 1909 and worked in the psychiatric hospital of Heidelberg where Emil Kraepelin, the main theoretician of paranoia in the nineteenth century, had worked earlier. In 1910 Jaspers published a paper questioning the relevance of the diagnosis of "paranoia." Soon he became dissatisfied with the repressive manner in which doctors treated patients and he attempted to improve the psychiatric approach. His dissatisfaction with the institutional treatment of mental disease led him to question both diagnostic criteria and the relational methods of clinical psychiatry. He studied patients by quoting them abundantly, letting all the details of their biographical background establish a varied symptomatology before offering a diagnosis. This launched the biographical method, now standard psychiatric practice. *Nature of Psychotherapy*, a classic of psychiatric literature, promotes a "phenomenological" method and states that a diagnosis should focus on the form of symptom, especially in cases of psychosis, and not on its content. Thus, a hallucination means something less by what it explicitly conjures up than by the fact that it chooses a certain medium to express itself, such as vision, sounds, dreams, voices, and so on. The theory that a symptom will be understood by paying attention to details of style and not to the ideated content is very Freudian, and leads to Jacques Lacan's psychiatric work with paranoia in the thirties. Like Jaspers, Lacan brought Freud's teachings to bear on psychiatry, and would take seriously a book like *Totem and Taboo*, although it had been immediately discredited as a post-Darwinian fantasy.

Totem and Taboo was published in 1913 and goes back to 1911, when Freud announced that he was working on the "psychology of religious faith and ties."[36] It seems that Freud's interest had been awoken by Carl Gustav Jung's own investigations in the domains of myth and ritual. It was not so much that Freud wanted to emulate his chosen heir – Jung had been installed president of the International Psychoanalytical Association in 1910 at Freud's insistence – as that he wished to correct what he saw as looming theoretical deviation. Jung, who had been chosen as Freud's "crown prince" mostly because he was not Jewish, and would thus contradict the accusation that psychoanalysis was a disreputable Jewish science, had chosen the myths and symbols of a wide variety of religions with the aim of softening the psychoanalytic dogma on incest repression, the Oedipus complex, and early infantile sexuality. By stepping on his domain, Freud meant to show that the theory of the libido was actively verifiable there as well. Jung's analysis of primitive religions and anthropological accounts of rituals found a perfect expression in *Metamorphoses and Symbols of the Libido* (*Wandlungen und Symbole der Libido*) published in 1911–12. The theoretical disagreement focused on the issue of the term "libido," which Jung was often using in a non-sexual sense, so as to be more "energetic" or "dynamic," as if sexuality implied too regressive a return to the most archaic determinations of the patient. At the same time, Jung was reducing the incest taboo to a mere fantasy, whereas for Freud it was a cornerstone of his doctrine.

In a letter, Jung confided to Freud that his conferences in the United States of September 1912 had gone smoothly because he had downplayed sexual issues that created discomfort over there. Freud was understandably annoyed. In November 1912 Freud, Jones, Abraham, Jung, and a few Zurich psychoanalysts met in Munich to try and sort out their differences. The atmosphere was relaxed. Freud and Jung had apologized to each other for real or imagined slights, when Freud had a fainting attack. In the aftermath,

Jung became at once more friendly and all too paternalistic. He reminded Freud that earlier, in 1909, he had refused to disclose personal information about a dream that Jung was analyzing because Freud did not want to lose his authority. In several letters, Jung pointed to the neurotic element in Freud's personality, and Freud concurred but reassured Jung that his neurosis never injured him. A truce was in place until December 14, 1912. On that day, Jung concludes a letter with a slip of the pen, writing: "Even Adler's cronies do not regard me as one of *yours*," when he meant obviously: "one of theirs." Freud wrote back, pointing out the slip, asking whether Jung could be "objective enough" when he allowed such admissions of ambivalence to pass. Jung exploded in the following letter dated December 18, 1912:

> I am objective enough to see through your little trick. You go around sniffing out all the symptomatic actions in your vicinity, thus reducing everyone to the level of sons and daughters who blushingly admit the existence of their faults. Meanwhile you remain on top as the father, sitting pretty. For sheer obsequiousness nobody dares pluck the beard of the prophet and to inquire for once what you should say to a patient with a tendency to analyze the analyst instead of himself. You would certainly ask him, "Who's got the neurosis?"[37]

And then Jung adds: "I am not in the least neurotic – touch wood!"[38] In the following exchange, Freud controls his anger and tries to remain above the fray, but suggests that they abandon all personal relations entirely, adding a last shaft: "But one who while behaving abnormally keeps shouting that he is normal gives ground for the suspicion that he lacks insight into his own illness."[39] This was written on January 3, 1913, and marked the end of their personal friendship while allowing for a more distant collaboration.

Freud tried to be aware of his own neurotic features whereas Jung denied them vehemently. Jung was often brutally frank while Freud appeared more political, but fundamentally unwilling to yield anything about doctrinal points. Freud thus wrote: "Believe me, it was not easy for me to moderate my demands on you; but once I had succeeded in doing so, the swing in the other directions was not too severe . . . I believe we shall have to lay by a fresh store of benevolence towards one another."[40] This conciliatory attitude was to work for a while, and Freud hoped that by having invaded Jung's secessionist territory, he had brought some peace to the increasingly fractious and divided kingdom of psychoanalysis. *Totem and Taboo* would fulfill this function, and "serve to make a sharp division between us [Jews] and all Aryan religiosity."[41] The book would "come at the right time to divide us as an acid does a salt."[42] Freud told all his friends that he had never been as elated writing a book since his masterpiece, *The Interpretation of Dreams*. But once *Totem and Taboo* was published, he was full of doubts. He explained this to Jones, who was wondering about his diffidence: "Then I described the wish to kill one's father, and now I have been describing the actual killing; after all it is a big step from a wish to a deed."[43] This ritual killing explains the creation of religions: for Freud, the founding father or the leader of the primitive horde was to keep all the women for him, until the sons united and murdered him. Soon after, their guilt would find an outlet in the divinization of the murdered king. Moses was a good example of this metamorphosis: according to Freud's later book on monotheism, he had been killed by the rebellious Hebrews and then turned into a holy intermediary with God's word.

This insight found an outlet in Freud's essay on the Moses of Michelangelo, obviously marked by the struggle with Jung and the Zurich group. First published anonymously in 1914 as "The Moses of Michelangelo," it concludes a long hermeneutical effort that went back at least to 1901, when Freud discovered a monumental statue of Moses that he visited repeatedly. In 1912, when in Rome, he took notes and compared interpretations, and in September 1913, Freud stayed alone for three weeks in Rome, lost in contemplation in front of Moses' statue every day.[44] When he thought that he had guessed the secret of the statue, he wrote his essay, no doubt thinking of Jung as well. His ambivalence about his rival stemmed from his own sense of kinship with the rabble of unbelievers whose idolatry triggered the fury of the prophet. "How often have I mounted the steep steps from the unlovely Corso Cavour to the lonely piazza where the deserted church stands, and have essayed to support the angry scorn of the hero's glance!"[45] In a narrative that explains the awe created by the stone effigy, Freud exposes both his wish for intellectual control and his empathy with the rebellious and ultimately murderous rabble. He is helped by the fact that he has already elaborated the theory of the "murder of the father" in *Totem and Taboo*.

Freud listed all the previous interpretations of the statue and concluded that they were contradictory and could not explain the peculiar attitude of the prophet. By narrowing his gaze to Moses' right hand, Freud perceived that Moses' thumb was hidden while the index finger presses the beard. Then, curiously, he did exactly what Jung threatened to do to him, that is to "pluck the beard of the prophet." This time the prophet is Moses, and his lengthy analysis of Moses' beard yields a series of movements from which he deduces a whole inner drama. Moses was resting on his throne with the tables of the law when he was startled by the screams of the crowd carrying the Golden Calf. Seized by indignation, he was going to destroy the idolaters and the tables, then mastered himself and decided not to annihilate them but to give the law instead. This interpretation fits with Michelangelo's conflicted relationship with Pope Julius II, whose tomb the statue was to adorn. Both the Pope and the artist had a violent temperament, and Michelangelo carved his Moses "as a warning to himself, thus rising in self-criticism superior to his own nature."[46] However, the calm following a storm hid a calm preparing another storm. In 1914, Freud would reiterate that Jung's theories were incompatible with his, and recommended that the Viennese group and the Zurich group should part ways: the contested libido had reached the end of its "metamorphoses" and other distorted symbols.

New Foundations in Philosophy and Esthetics

One of the most astute observers of the philosophical scene in 1913 was George Santayana, who published *Winds of Doctrine: Studies in Contemporary Opinion* in 1913. The book concluded with an often quoted lecture that he had given in California in 1911, "The Genteel Tradition in American Philosophy," in which he tried to take stock of the ending of an earlier and more intellectual pragmatism with the demise in 1910 of William James (Charles S. Pierce, who launched "pragmatism" didn't die until 1914), to whom the lecture was a sort of homage. In 1913, Santayana saw the world of ideas dominated by two thinkers, Henri Bergson and Bertrand Russell. He reproached James for having been too generous with Bergson (as just then James was attempting a fusion between pragmatism and Bergsonian intuitionism). Thus Santayana devotes a long and critical chapter to Bergson and Russell before returning to his own favorite writers: Shelley, for the praise of human and divine inspiration, and Emerson, for making transcendentalism the rightful heir of German idealism. His own mixture of sensualism, skepticism, and crypto-Catholicism explains why Santayana did not feel at home at Harvard. In 1912, he decided to leave America for good and spend all his time writing in Europe.

Indeed, the popularity of Bergson was at its peak in 1913. There had been an English translation of the *Essai sur les données immédiates de la conscience* in 1910 (titled *Time and Free Will*), and his books were being discussed in the most important English, French, American, German, Austrian, Italian, Polish, Dutch, Spanish, Rumanian, Swedish, Russian, and Hungarian reviews. In 1911 Bergson started traveling widely, first to Italy and England (he was bilingual, his mother being English), and then in 1913 to visit the United States at the invitation of Columbia University. He lectured in several American cities, where he was welcomed by very large audiences, and spoke in both French and English on spirituality, freedom, intuition, time, and related topics of his philosophy. In 1914 Bergson's recognition became official when he was elected to the Académie française.

Bergson's rival was Bertrand Russell, who had heard Bergson lecture at the Aristotelian Society in 1911 and then read a paper on his work. He had little patience with Bergson's philosophy of intuition, and disparagingly referred to him as a "company-promoter" rather than a philosopher. For Russell, Bergson's anti-intellectualism was "merely traditional mysticism expressed in a slightly novel language."[47] Yet he was ready to give some credit to Bergson's theories of the image and cinema: in order to test them out, in 1912 he went with a friend to see a film, and decided that their experience bore out Bergson's analysis of the filmic image as condensing either time or movement.[48] For Russell, whose major work in the philosophy of mathematics was now behind him, the issues were the ways in which one could resolve the paradoxes that he had sprung on Frege as early as June 1902, as he was completing his own *Principles of Mathematics*. Frege accepted stoically that all his earlier efforts at building a systematic mathematical logic had been vain, killed at one blow by Russell's paradox of the "class of the classes which do not belong to themselves," a class which cannot be a member of itself. The paradox had opened a gap in strict mathematical axiomatics. Between 1902 and 1910 Russell toiled at a great synthesis of logic and mathematics with the help of Alfred North Whitehead. The result was the magnum opus *Principia Mathematica*, published in three volumes between 1910 and 1913. It generalized the conclusions of the *Principles of Mathematics* by demonstrating that pure mathematics deal with concepts that can be defined by logic, and that its propositions can be deduced from a limited number of fundamental logical postulates. The collaboration went smoothly enough, even if, as they progressed, they met new difficulties, Whitehead being responsible for the technical mathematical demonstrations, Russell for the philosophical speculations that accompanied them. They were reaching completion of the enormous project (in total more than 2,000 dense pages) when an unknown Austrian student arrived upon the scene.

This was none other than Ludwig Wittgenstein. He had left Vienna to study engineering in Manchester where he came under the spell of Russell's mathematical philosophy. He went to Cambridge with the intention of studying with Russell, and the student was soon designated as Russell's "successor." Their first meeting took place in October 1911. At first Russell was impressed by his student's intellectual passion but put off by his moodiness, his obstinacy, his gruff rebuttals. Russell became Wittgenstein's official supervisor in June 1912, but it was less to lead him to a PhD than to leave him to finish a job that he could not complete himself. In March 1912, Wittgenstein, who was leaving Cambridge to go to Vienna, told Russell that the hours spent discussing philosophy in his rooms had been the "happiest of his life." Russell later mused openly to his lover Lady Ottoline Morrell: "I love him & feel he will solve the problems that I am too old to solve – all kinds of vital problems that are raised by my work, but want a fresh mind and the vigour of youth."[49] However, Wittgenstein did not exactly fit that role, and instead pushed Russell to a new skepticism regarding his concepts and methods. Russell was trying to recover from the strain of thinking through the last volume of *Principia Mathematica*, saying that he had been drained intellectually by the effort. In the autumn of 1912, Wittgenstein read a paper to the Moral Science Club on "What Is Philosophy?" and broke all the records by speaking for less than four minutes. He defined philosophy as the set of primitive propositions assumed to be true without any proof by various sciences.[50] Wittgenstein's abrasive skepticism was gnawing at the remains of Platonism in Russell's philosophy of mind.

Their divergence led to a momentous clash in 1913, while Russell was writing the Lowell lectures for his forthcoming trip to America, which forced him to revise his theory of judgment. Wittgenstein tried to voice his objections, but more and more fell into stubborn, oppositional silences or incomprehensible rhapsodies. Russell had to ask him to leave once or twice, although fearful that his disciple would either go mad or commit suicide. Wittgenstein perceived the flaw in Russell's reasoning but seemed unable or unwilling to explain what it was. Russell was paralyzed, Wittgenstein more and more frantic. Russell was groping for something that announced logical atomism, when he tried to distinguish "Atomic Propositional Thought" and "Molecular Propositional Thought." Wittgenstein left for Norway, and when he returned to Cambridge, announced that he would stay in Norway until he had solved all the problems of logic. He offered to write down what he had found, but was unable to do so, and Russell had to ask a shorthand writer to take notes on their discussions. These notes were decisive, and condense Wittgenstein's program for his *Tractatus Logico-Philosophicus* while orienting Russell's work on logical atomism after the war. Wittgenstein had concluded that Russell was too old to be helpful or helped, while Russell has been persuaded to abandon his previous efforts to expand logical analysis into epistemology; instead, he would realize that truth was divisible into irreducible "atomic propositions." The dispute provided the steppingstone for Wittgenstein's *Tractatus Logico-Philosophicus* in which he showed that no proposition could be forced by logic to produce a new truth, that mathematics was a string of tautologies and that only by a careful analysis of language would one avoid making philosophical mistakes. All this was still unclear to Russell, who, both fortified and mortified by Wittgenstein, put the manuscript of the third section of the *Principia Mathematica* into press in 1913 and prepared to go to America.

Another serious attempt at establishing new foundations for philosophy was under way in Germany and came from the phenomenology associated with Husserl. Like Russell, Husserl refused psychologism, a term which encompassed Bergson's intuitionism and William James' pragmatism. Husserl published *Ideen I* in his *Jahrbuch* in 1913, describing the book as his "breakthrough to pure phenomenology." Already, in his *Logical Investigations* from 1900–1, he had shown that phenomenology was the basis of all sciences without being a psychology, whereas Mach took phenomenology to be part of psychology. In 1913, Husserl advanced that the ground of logic was phenomenology. This launched his "transcendental idealism," which surprised and chagrined some of his students at Göttingen University. In *Ideas I* Husserl showed that it is necessary to suspend the natural attitude in order to describe the structure of consciousness, in which he discovers the *cogito* as a pure act. Absolute consciousness is posited after the world has been nullified or bracketed off. Husserl avoids the trap of subjective idealism by leading back to science, the basis of which is a fundamental noetic–noematic interaction. This allows him to analyze objects split up into various *Abschattungen* (shadings) thanks to the tool provided by transcendental reduction or *epoché*. All the abstractions of science will be grounded in an absolutely pure "transcendental ego," isolated from stream-of-consciousness perception and the objects in the world, and thus offering the guarantee of scientific rigor. Husserl hoped he had bridged the divide between idealism and realism, although new "reductions" would be necessary to progress toward the world of culture, history, and intersubjectivity.

Martin Heidegger was to become Husserl's disciple in the post-war years, and his point of departure was the same as Husserl's in the *Logical Investigations*. He defended his thesis in 1913, and focused on "psychologism" to demonstrate that logic had nothing to do with psychology. He examined the theories of Wilhelm Wundt, Heinrich Maier, Franz Brentano, Anton Marty, and Theodor Lipps in *The Lesson of Judgment in Psychologism*, which is a juvenile work to be sure, but which testifies to an engagement with epistemology before moving on to the plane of pure ontology. In an interesting footnote, Heidegger refers to Russell's *Principles of Mathematics*, suggesting that mathematical logic should be criticized for having forgotten the problem of meaning and sense-giving. This was, by a totally different route, the objection of Wittgenstein to Russell: before we start calculating, we need to question the meaning of meaning. For Wittgenstein it would lie in language; for Heidegger, at this point in his philosophical journey, it resided in the structure of consciousness.

It would take a second world war and a *Kehre* (turning point) for Heidegger to reach the view that the question of being hinges around language, especially poetic language. This position had already been defended by the Italian philosopher Benedetto Croce. Croce had attained visibility in Italy at the end of the nineteenth century in debates over the scientific status of historical knowledge. His idiosyncratic criticism of Hegelianism and enthusiastic endorsement of Giambattista Vico's *New Science* mixing up "poetic wisdom," proto-historicism, and linguistic investigations led him to an estheticist theory of knowledge. This was outlined in the celebrated *Aesthetic* of 1902. With Giovanni Gentile as his junior partner, Croce launched *La Critica* the next year, a review that was the focal point for young artists of the emerging avant-garde. They were lumped together as neo-Hegelians, although they fell out over philosophical matters in 1913. Gentile adhered to Hegel's idealism before converting to fascism, while Croce rejected systems of philosophy just as he had done in 1906, in a book that asked provocatively *What Is Living and What Is Dead in Hegel's Philosophy?* Croce, a devoted pacifist, became a senator in the Italian parliament in 1912. A clear synthesis of his esthetic views appeared in the 1912 lecture for the inauguration of the Rice Institute in Houston, Texas, published in 1913 as *Breviario di estetica* ("Breviary of Aesthetics"). There, Croce insisted upon the primacy of art over science or metaphysics; for him, only art could edify people while giving birth to the new.

Such a point of view was shared by Miguel de Unamuno, who had started a correspondence with Croce in 1911, and whose pre-existentialist philosophy similarly rejects Kant, Hegel, and Bergson and leads to an inconclusive personal wisdom. In the struggle with faith memorialized by *The Tragic Sense of Life in Men and Nations* (first published as a book in 1913), he finds precursors in Pascal, Kierkegaard, and Nietzsche. Like Croce, he shows great respect for Vico's poetic historicism but prefers Giordano Bruno, who died burnt at the stake by the Inquisition for his revolutionary scientific ideas. Following Bruno, who set aside all caution for the furthering of progress, de Unamuno identified wholly with Don Quixote, the Spanish emblem of the questing soul, and spurned the illusory comfort of rationality (he derides Jules de Gaultier who had claimed that it was the privilege of the French never to be taken in, *de n'être pas dupe*, a "sorry privilege"[51] indeed for the resilient Basque thinker). The comic quester will always find tragedy as the inevitable limit of human endeavors. This wide-ranging, well-written, and learned book was admired by personalities as different as Ezra Pound and Jorge Luis Borges. De Unamuno criticized both *modernismo*, the Hispanic version of symbolism launched by Ruben Dario, and theological modernism, the attempt by Catholic thinkers to reconcile faith and reason, but refused to give an easy answer. In his conclusion, he announced that he planned to meet his readers between the acts of the ongoing tragedy (it peaked in 1936, during the Spanish Civil War, when de Unamuno, the rector of the university of Salamanca, courageously opposed Franco's fascism), sticking to his quixotic belief that neither scientific progress nor grand political triumphs would ever be spared by ridicule.

Chapter 4

Learning to be Modern in 1913

The Modernizing Effort

Ridicule was a weapon loved by most modernists, and conspicuously displayed, although with a reflexive intent, by Eliot's early poems. Just after having received Eliot's ironical and pathetic "Love Song of J. Alfred Prufrock," whose first version had been written in 1911 in Paris,[1] when Eliot was still under the influence of Bergson, Pound wrote to Harriet Monroe that he had at last discovered a poet who had "actually trained himself *and* modernized himself *on his own.*" He added: "It is such a comfort to meet a man and not have to tell him to wash his face, wipe his feet, and remember the date (1914) on the calendar."[2] This exuberant praise highlights Eliot's attunement to a sharper sense of the modern than Pound's inveterate archaism in spite of the movements that he launched in London, such as imagism and vorticism. As he was made aware, Eliot's modernity was not innate. Rather, it was the result of hard work and concerted action, something that can be documented with precision. In December 1912 Eliot wrote to his friend Jean Verdenal and outlined his program of "self-modernization": "I propose to give myself an organized scheme of literary and philosophical study. Forgive my ambition, but I detest amateurs."[3] The letter offers season's greetings to his French correspondent, who, like him, favors discipline and strict method. The coherent building of the self is an inner effort that has little to do with launching new schools, as Eliot observes, mocking the way futurism was just then burying cubism. The fashionable manifestos exhibit a "mixture of violence and lack of strength" which boils down to an admission of weakness.[4] Eliot's resolve, on the other hand, aimed at combining a "new sensibility" with an intellectual program straddling philosophy and literature.

This resolve has to do with his progressive dissatisfaction with Bergson, whose famous and crowded lectures Eliot religiously attended in 1910–11. His distance was achieved by way of irony, through which he could stage and deflate Bergson's theses about time, intuition, and creative *élan*, adapting the strategy of polite humor invented by Jules Laforgue in his wry autobiographical "songs" or "complaints." Back in Harvard in 1911 as a graduate student, Eliot was tempted by another synthesis, the neo-Hegelian system that he found in 1913 via Bradley's philosophy. In Harvard he soon settled on a PhD devoted to analyzing Bradley's philosophy, a thesis resembling in many respects Musil's doctoral thesis on Mach. Both Musil and Eliot concluded that their authors' doctrines were muddled and full of deep rifts; both finally abandoned the specialized study of philosophy to devote their free time to creative writing. The difference was that Eliot's very philosophy led to its own demise as it concluded that it should be replaced by something else – literature in the first place, to be followed by religious mysticism – whereas Musil stuck to the firm belief that it was possible for an exact philosophy to coexist with literature.

It is in this context that I would like to examine the various modalities taken by the wish to be "modern" in 1913. Pound recognized in Eliot a poet and thinker, who, if he was not a systematic philosopher, allied careful conceptual discrimination with the idea that writing was a skill that should be developed by training and exercise. The collaboration of Pound and Eliot led to a mixture of the classicism and modernism that they promoted after the war. As we have seen, this was by no means the whole picture of modernism. But they define precisely an essential component of all modernisms: modernism never abandons the "historical sense" that Eliot described in 1919. It strives for an active synthesis of the past and the present which can only be obtained by "great labor." The novelty claimed by modernism emerges from the consciousness of a past heritage. In other words, History is inevitably part of the Absolute, a move that was allowed by Hegel himself but forgotten in the ahistoricism of later Hegelian thinkers like Bradley.

In September 1913 Eliot enrolled in Josiah Royce's seminar devoted to a "Comparative Study of Various Types of Scientific Method," and it is likely, as Piers Gray has shown,[5] that he was drawn to F. H. Bradley because the Oxford philosopher had engaged in a critical debate with Royce, soon to become Eliot's thesis supervisor, about the nature of proof in historical facts. Royce, who had just published *The Problem of Christianity* in 1913, stated that the "proofs" brought by the testimony of the apostles about the existence of a historical Jesus depended upon the trust and loyalty of a community of men. Bradley questioned the very concept of history in "The Presuppositions of Critical History." As Gray surmises, this paper attracted Eliot to Bradley in the first place because Bradley questions the existence of "historical facts" and of a "true interpretation" of the world, which were central tenets in Royce's philosophy; instead, Bradley saw "facts" as created by theories, stating that no fact would be independent of a certain discourse. Thus the "proofs" brought by the sciences were of an altogether different nature from the proofs needed for historical facts, which are contingent upon the whole "human tradition," not just a group of devoted apostles, from which history is created by refinement and extrapolation.

Just a little later, Eliot rejected both Bradley's Absolute and Bergson's *durée*. He criticized them together in a paper on Bergson and vitalism written in 1913 at Harvard. For him, the central problem was that in Bergson's vision as in Bradley's system "nothing *essentially* new can ever happen; the absolute, as Bradley says, bears buds and flowers and fruit at once."[6] Already Eliot wanted to appreciate the irruption of novelty without having to fall into mystical communion with an impersonal *élan vital*, or trusting that the "Absolute" would be mysteriously connected with the atomized "finite centers" of individual consciousnesses. Eliot was impressed by Bertrand Russell when he visited Harvard in 1914. Perhaps Russell would provide an answer to the idealist dichotomies of Bergson and Bradley. For Russell, time and space do not exist in our minds only; they are physical facts in the world. Our knowledge of the external world is built upon a sequence of rigorous logical propositions and not on pragmatist experience or a mystical inner duration. Only logical forms lead thought back to the external world, which meant for instance that time could be split up in infinitely divisible units, each one endowed with mathematical properties. This was the exact opposite of Bergson's philosophy. When Eliot returned to England to marry and find Russell turned into too close a friend of his wife, he could not choose between the two main trends of philosophy – Oxford idealism with Bradley, or Cambridge realism with Russell. Bradley postulated a subject of absolute knowledge while offering fractured subjectivities split up between psychological and epistemological centers. Thus for a while, between 1913 and 1916, Eliot tried hard to bridge the gap between the "finite centers," the monadic bases of experience linked to the Absolute, and Russell's logical anti-subjectivism. He was groping for an empathic "feeling" capable of underpinning the historical sense, which would allow the integration of experience into new wholes; not surprisingly, only poetry could provide it.

Accelerated Aging Processes

Thus, beyond the complexity of the philosophical debate in 1913–16, Eliot's test of modernity triggered a new awareness of aging. Eliot's first recipe was to play at becoming older: "I grow old . . . I grow old," is Prufrock's refrain, even though he is probably not more than 30. This inner sense of time does not open up to inner duration but to an aging process compounded by social embarrassment: "I grow old . . . I grow old . . . / I shall wear the bottoms of my trousers rolled."[7] The calculated obsolescence of the lyrical voice gathers speed with "Gerontion" in which the speaker, literally "a little old man," is waiting for nothing, being read to by a boy while spinning out "thoughts of a dry brain in a dry season."[8] A similar evolution is perceptible with James Joyce and D. H. Lawrence. When Joyce rewrote his juvenile autobiography, *Stephen Hero*, as *A Portrait of the Artist as a Young Man*, which he did between 1908 and 1913, he replaced an earlier youthful heroism by an honest admission that his mouthpiece Stephen is, after all, still very "young" when the book ends. Less than a classical *Künstlerroman* in which we follow the itinerary of a soul reaching, step by step, artistic creativity, irony, stylistic revisions and historical contextualizations provide another frame in which we can assess Stephen's immaturity, much as Flaubert did when he revised his *Sentimental Education*. This stress on immaturity can be interpreted as a sign that Joyce himself had matured in between, and that there was a pressing need for an "older" point of view. This would be the main impact of Bloom's invention, since the last story of *Dubliners* still leaves us with a grown up, Gabriel Conroy, who discovers in the last pages the troubling signs of a hitherto well concealed immaturity. The fact that Stephen is shown as less than heroic and very priggish does not mean that he is a simple caricature, however, as Hugh Kenner and other critics have argued; it just confirms that we must take his pronouncements with a pinch of salt – which remains true in *Ulysses*.

In the same way, the very title of *Sons and Lovers* (published in 1913) foregrounds the sexual and emotional immaturity of Paul Morel. The title could be easily rephrased as "*Either* Sons *or* Lovers," since the novel shows that Paul cannot love Miriam not only because she is a little frigid and "hysterical" but above all because he is still too attached to his own mother. Paul remains a virgin until quite late because, as he explains, "Being the sons of mothers whose husbands had blundered rather brutally through their feminine sanctities, they were themselves too diffident and shy. [. . .] for a woman was like their mother, and they were full of the sense of their mother."[9] When, after eight years of intense courtship and passionate declarations of mutual love, Paul breaks off with Miriam at last so as to be free with Clara, she accuses him of being a child of 4; he replies that if this is the case he does not need another mother. He condenses the whole affair cynically: "All these years she had treated him as if he were a hero, and thought of him secretly as an infant, a foolish child."[10] The diagnosis is accurate: Paul cannot love any woman because he is too much of a "son," which is why he rushes into another Oedipal pattern when he meets Clara. The fact that she is freer, articulate, sensual and beautiful, a feminist "suffragette," married but separated from her husband, who takes the initiative in the seduction, renders her sexually desirable – until Paul feels a deeper need to reunite her with her estranged husband. When his own mother dies he definitively refuses Miriam's renewed offer of marriage. She seems to have aged prematurely, while Paul is still very young at heart, and, having worked through his Oedipal hangover, ready for a real adventure.

The division of women into two roles, the sacred mother one can "love," and the libertine who is desirable but degraded, follows a typical Freudian pattern, and Lawrence had been made aware of his Oedipal plight by Frieda, who was an avid reader of Freud.[11] A similar split occurs in *Exiles*, Joyce's play, begun in 1912, continued throughout 1913 and completed in 1914. The plot opposes Richard and Robert: the latter is an outgoing journalist who tries to seduce Bertha, Richard's common law wife, while the introspective writer Richard, just back in Dublin from "exile" in Rome, feels attracted by the intellectual sympathy of Beatrice, Robert's cousin. The key issue is whether Bertha remains faithful or not after having followed Robert, a dilemma which has lost much of its pathos given today's permissive morality. In fact, it is not an exaggeration to say that the play is more interesting for the extensive notes taken by Joyce in 1913 as he was moving from Act I to the rest, than for its languid post-Ibsenian staging of marital dilemmas. It took no less that Harold Pinter to downsize it in 1970 when he cut long passages and rendered it actually performable on a stage (but then it sounded like a Pinter play).

The notes for *Exiles* drafted in 1913 reveal that Joyce was fascinated by his life-long companion Nora's dreams and analyzed them exactly as a psychoanalyst would, with the difference that his associations follow from hers. In a dream of November 13, 1913, Nora saw Shelley's grave in Rome and the poet rising from it. Joyce immediately interpreted this as a memory of the sickly adolescent who had "died" for her by catching cold under her windows when she was a young woman. In anticipation of Molly Bloom, Nora turns into the earth or Gea Tellus, as Joyce freely associates with the plot of the play:

She is the earth, dark, formless, mother, made beautiful by the moonlit night, darkly conscious of her instincts. Shelley whom she has held in her womb or grave rises: the part of Richard which neither love nor life can do away with: the part for which she loves him: the part she must try to kill, never be able to kill, and rejoice at her impotence. [. . .] She weeps over Rahoon too, over him whom her love has killed, the dark boy whom, as the earth, she embraces in death and disintegration.[12]

The fragment generated a poem entitled "She weeps over Rahoon"[13] (dated Trieste, 1913), in which a feminine voice laments the death of her lover. The stage notes document Joyce's hesitations, especially when he could not see how the play would end, and this hesitation facing his plot duplicates the uncertainty from which Richard refuses to be shaken at the end.[14]

A similar rapport can be observed in Lawrence's poetry: the poems written in 1913 could go directly to sections of *Sons and Lovers*. Some, such as "The Collier's Wife,"[15] narrate dramatic situations via the diction of Nottinghamshire working-class people, and could be attached to the cycle of Paul Morel's father. Others explore the analysis of love understood as a physical or physiological passion. This is the case with "Lightning" (also from *Love Poems and Others*, 1913), which ends on a frank admission of ambivalence in the mist of shared sexual bliss:

> I heard the thunder, and felt the rain,
>   And my arms fell loose, and I was dumb.
>   Almost I hated her, she was so good,
> Hated myself, and the place, and my blood,
>   Which burned with rage, as I bade her come
> Home, away home, ere the lightning floated forth again.[16]

This almost sounds like a parody of certain scenes in the novel, yet it contains the gist of Lawrence's complex sexual dialectics as developed in *Sons in Lovers*, and later in *Women in Love*. Love is not the opposite of hatred, on the contrary, and in order for a "son" to become a "lover," he or she just needs to make room for ambivalence in libidinal investments.

It is on the issue of revision that Lawrence and Joyce are diverging; for Joyce, the secret was to re-read his first drafts critically enough so as to revise what was already written and bring it to a new level of stylistic perfection. Style and craft brought along the very openness and psychological over-determination necessary for a fuller, denser, and more focused psychological portrait. Lawrence took the opposite direction, and thus it is revealing that it was not him but his editor who cut a good percentage of *Sons and Lovers'* original draft, something that Joyce would never have accepted. In all of his subsequent novels, and in the poems whose genesis is obscured by endless rewritings, we see Lawrence continually revising drafts but never cutting anything, only adding and developing new motives and variations. In fact, Lawrence never abandoned his initial heroic posture but learned to relativize it; for instance, in the debate between Paul and Miriam, the male protagonist accepts the accusation that he is a baby, enjoying the privilege of that regressive stage, and later empathizes with different points of view, especially feminine ones, until he outgrows even these. Lawrence became modern through a dialogical empathy that projected different selves and points of view, a projection that would need *Women in Love* to be complete, while Joyce concentrated everything in the subjectivity of the "artist," more and more identified with language alone. The result is that *Sons and Lovers* is a very good nineteenth-century novel while *A Portrait of the Artist as a Young Man*, admittedly not so successful in parts, definitely belongs to the twentieth century.

Another modernizing strategy consisted in constituting a couple in which the "older" and the "younger" partners exchange their positions and prerogatives. This is what happened in the productive interaction between Yeats and Pound in 1912–13. Pound, who was 20 years Yeats' junior, had come to London in the hope of meeting him, and this he did in 1909. Even before he had actually met him, he was imitating his Irish accent and poet's garb; he soon became indispensable to Yeats, whom he would at times frighten with his violence and arrogance, though he also flattered him with his unstinting devotion.[17] It is usually believed that the raw energy of the young American poet pushed Yeats out of the "nineties" and destroyed his mentor's complacency with Celtic twilights, theosophic séances, and hazy dreams of a Romantic Ireland. Pound would have pushed the older poet forward when they collaborated in the winter of 1913 as they worked together in Stone Cottage. However, it seems truer to say that Yeats' modernization pre-dated Pound's impact; at least, this was Pound's own view, since he wrote that the Irish poet's modernization was due to Synge's example much more than to his own influence. Pound wrote in 1915 that the "adorers of the Celtic twilight" were "disturbed" by Yeats' "gain in hardness" in the years 1910–13. Pound alluded to poems like "The Magi," "The Scholars," and "No Second Troy," adding: "There is a new strength in the later Yeats on which he & Synge may have agreed."[18] The reference to Synge is crucial – he had died in 1909, leaving Yeats bereft, deprived of a friend and ally, a most important Irish voice. Much has been made of Pound's minor revisions of Yeats' poems that were sent to *Poetry* magazine in 1912. Yeats first dismissed them as mere "misprints," but he came to accept Pound's suggestions. In January 1913 Yeats acted rather generously, writing that Pound's revisions were helpful. However, his careful word choice emphasizes the archaism of the young American poet:

> He is full of the middle ages and helps me get back to the definite and the concrete away from modern abstraction. To talk over a poem with him is like getting you to put it into dialect. All becomes clear and natural. Yet in his own work he is very uncertain, often very bad though very interesting sometimes. He spoils everything by too many experiments and has more sound principles than taste.[19]

The sharpness and the pertinence of the diagnosis prove that Yeats had kept his critical faculties intact. For him, taking Pound's advice and returning to the medieval or Renaissance virtues extolled by Pound, whose troubadours were the models of a simple, direct, and musical expression, was a paradoxical way of modernizing himself.

Yeats' new tone came to the fore in *Responsibilities* (1914). Its poems have noticeably gained in strength: they are pared down, often colloquial, at times truculently topical or violently political. For all that, the new tone is not necessarily "modernist" yet, since in "September 1913" Yeats laments the passing of "Romantic Ireland" ("Romantic Ireland's dead and gone / It's with O'Leary in the grave"[20]) as he denounces the rejection of Sir Hugh Lane's gift to the Municipal Gallery. His models are to be found in the Italian Renaissance and the nineteenth-century Irish patriots who sacrificed their lives for the nationalist cause. Yeats attacks the materialism of the middle class, and suggests that the new heroes of Irish nationalism should not be miserly but spendthrift and sacrificial. In brief, it was under the pressure of burning Irish issues like Parnell's legacy, the controversy triggered by Synge's *Playboy of the Western World*, and the scandal surrounding Lane's bequest, that Yeats was pushed forward.

The "Frisson of the New" in the Wilderness of the Present

Pound appeared more as a trained listener and eager disciple, a perfect critic for others but full of blind spots for his own works. Eliot called him a perfect *"sage-homme"* for his productive mediation in the "birth" of *The Waste Land*. It was Pound who discerned in his friend William Carlos Williams' first collection, *The Tempers* (1913), one poem at least in which the note of youthful freshness and restlessness pierces through layers of secondary influences. At that time, indeed, Williams was trying to break free from the obsessive eye-rhyme that conflated a mature Keats with a younger Yeats, as he struggled with the "rarefied atmosphere of the Pre-Raphaelite Brotherhood." Much later, Williams commented: "I knew nothing of language except what I'd heard in Keats or the Pre-Raphaelite Brotherhood."[21] Yet Pound's unfailing ear had detected the *frisson* of the new in "HIC JACET":

> The coroner's merry little children
>> Have such twinkling brown eyes.
> Their father is not of gay men
>> And their mother jocular in no wise,
> Yet the coroner's merry little children
>> Laugh so easily.
>
> They laugh because they prosper
>> Fruit for them is upon all branches.
> Lo! How they jibe at loss, for
>> Kind heaven fills their little paunches!
> It's the coroner's merry, merry children
>> Who laugh so easily.[22]

The irreverent laugh at death that feeds new life for happy children allegorizes the position of emerging modernists who feast merrily and "prosper" on the decaying corpses of late Victorian predecessors.

Pound similarly acknowledged D. H. Lawrence's *Love Poems and Others* and Robert Frost's *A Boy's Will*, both published in 1913. Pointing to some infelicities in their collections, Pound nevertheless insists on their honesty and sincerity. Frost appears almost as autonomous as the young Eliot, and he brings with him the fresh scent of New Hampshire woods. He is definitively "not post-Miltonic or post-Swinburnian or post-Kiplonian,"[23] and triggers personal associations with Pound's American past. He quotes from "The Tuft of Flowers," the poem in Frost's first collection that then generates the famous "Mending Wall" of *North of Boston* (1914), as it best conveys Frost's anguished awareness of solitude in nature, mitigated by a deeper consciousness that no one is ever alone: a "brotherly speech" connecting all humanity is always possible with the other whom one "had not hoped to reach."[24] Lawrence, who shocked Pound with his erotic "slush," nevertheless is commended for having "brought contemporary verse up to the level of contemporary prose," no mean achievement by the exacting standards set by Joyce and Ford Hueffer.[25] Pound did not mention another American writer who was then coming into her own because she was still under the radar of international visibility, someone of whom one can also say that she pushes prose to the level of poetry, Willa Cather. With the publication of *O Pioneers!*, Cather combined a purely American lyricism of place with a novelistic plot that transformed its traditional elements.

The first American reviewers had not missed this feature: a favorable review published in the *Philadelphia Inquirer* on August 10, 1913, mentions Walt Whitman not only as a source for the title but as a pervasive inspiration in the theme of the novel. Willa Cather is quoted at length, and she gives as her artistic credo a combination of tips that are very close to Pound's own admonitions. One should always remain "honest" when writing, good style comes from the depth of personal feelings, one should aim at simplifying from many sketches. As her literary mentor Sarah Orne Jewett had advised her, "Write the truth," and then readers will have to adapt to it.[26] In a moving autobiographical account of how she settled in the relative wilderness of Nebraska as a child, Cather speaks of the "erasure of personality"[27] that accompanied such a dislocation, adding that she needed those infinite spaces to find a perfect community made up of immigrants, those Swedish, Danish, Norwegian, and Bohemian mothers who taught her the art of storytelling and the gift of empathic identification with other people. If Cather's *O Pioneers!* manages so successfully to blur the boundaries between poetry and prose it is because the plot, loose, broken, chaotic as it is, remains accessory to a sense of the land itself through Cather's mythical treatment of characters who embody primary drives. The unforgettable Alexandra Bergson embodies sheer resilience and a feminine strength that opposes both natural and human destruction because it is attuned to natural rhythms. Like Frost, Cather sings of the reconciliation between a small community and strong individuals. Death is not to be feared since it accomplishes a literal communion between humans to be born and the cyclical realm of natural production: "Fortunate country, that is one day to receive hearts like Alexandra's into its bosom, to give them out again in the yellow wheat, in the rustling corn, in the shining eyes of youth!"[28]

A similar sense of repetition linked with the postulation of an "eternal present" contained in the act of writing underpins Gertrude Stein's work in 1913. By comparison with her fellow modernists, whether poets or novelists, her advance and the new ground covered are staggering. In 1903, when she began her long novel *The Making of Americans*, she learned to spatialize literature by treating the page as a blank canvas. The novel was completed in October 1911. In between, she had met and befriended Matisse and

Picasso, preferred the latter to the former, and in 1908 declared that there were only two geniuses alive, both male, Picasso and herself. The cubist portraits "Matisse" and "Picasso," published by Stieglitz in *Camera Work* in August 1912, which officially consecrated her status as an icon of the American avant-garde, have been much admired and denigrated. In 1913, the final break with her brother Leo over the value of cubism in art and literature forced them to divide up their extensive collection of paintings, after which Gertrude could feel safely "married" to Alice Toklas. It would take too long to analyze crucial 1913 pieces like "Susie Asado," "Americans," or "Guillaume Apollinaire."[29] Instead I will focus on one famous example from "Sacred Emily," the sentence "Rose is a rose is a rose." Here is how it appears close to the end of "Sacred Emily," as part of a long litany of disjointed sentences:

> Color mahogany.
> Color mahogany center.
> Rose is a rose is a rose is a rose.
> Loveliness extreme.
> Extra gaiters.
> Loveliness extreme.
> (*Writings* 1, p. 395)

Let us note that Stein wrote: "Rose is a rose is a rose is a rose." She added a period at the end of the line and capitalized "Rose" at the beginning. One particularity of "Sacred Emily" is that it abolishes the distinction between proper names and common nouns. It would be idle to ask: "Who is Rose?" or "Who is Emily?" Who are the Willie and Henry of "A hand is Willie. / Henry Henry Henry. / A hand is Henry. / Henry Henry Henry. / A hand is Willie. / Henry Henry Henry" (*Writings* 1, p. 389)? Is "Rose" capitalized because it is a woman's name or because it is the beginning of the line? Other names are written with a lower-case letter, as we see in the third line: "Come go stay philip philip" (*Writings* 1, p. 387). Because thinking is writing and both are processes in the present tense, this undoes the fetish of proper names. A playful echolalia rifles dictionaries and common idioms without paying heed to grammatical distinctions. The musical or painterly arrangement of words on the page dislodges an old-fashioned "reason": "Please repeat. / Please repeat for. / Please repeat. / This is a name to Anna. / Cushions and pears. / Reason purses. / Reason purses to relay to relay carpets" (*Writings* 1, p. 394) Could the initial sentence have been uttered by a little girl, the main character of *The World is Round* who sings her song: "*I am a little girl and my name is Rose, Rose is my name*" in a chapter entitled "Rose Is a Rose"?[30] *How To Write* teaches us that "a noun is a name of anything,"[31] making her post-Russellian tautologies into an original "theory of descriptions" thanks to which poetic language becomes completely performative and dynamic, creative and intransitive at once.

In fact, Stein also wrote "a rose is a rose is a rose is a rose," although it was then relayed by another voice, that of Alice Toklas. The capital disappears as the line becomes endless: it is used for decorative motifs adorning towels and letter-heads. As *The Autobiography of Alice B. Toklas* (1932) has it, Alice Toklas picked up the sentence in the manuscript of "Sacred Emily" and made it into an emblem. Once more, the couple was needed, as had been the case with the typing of *The Making of Americans*, a novel that owes its length and repetitiveness to the refusal by Stein and Toklas to set a limit to the process of textual and sexual fusion. Stein explains via Toklas that her friendship with Carl Van Vechten led to his having printed this "*device*" on his letter paper. Carl Van Vechten printed in one of his books "the device on Gertrude Stein's notepaper, a rose is a rose is a rose" which became a motto. On the same page, "Toklas" adds: "Speaking of the device of rose is a rose is a rose is a rose, it was I who found it in one of Gertrude Stein's manuscripts and insisted upon putting it as a device on the letter paper, on the table linen and anywhere that she would permit that I would put it. I am very pleased with myself for having done so."[32] This corresponds to Stein's increasing visibility and popularity in the thirties. "Rose" turned into an emblem of rebirth, the key to resurrection in a process blending abstraction and singularities. Stein had started her investigations alone, but she could not have gone on for so long without meeting in the flesh other geniuses like Matisse and Picasso, and also without having been "married" to Alice. She was not only the "first modernist" but also perhaps the last – and in that sense, Stein has as many affinities with Stravinsky as with Picasso. As we saw in chapter 1, Toklas' imitable voice (at least for her partner) was best equipped to describe what it felt like to be in the Théâtre des Champs-Elysées during the fracas caused by the *Rite of Spring*. Symptomatically, "she" narrates this on the same page on which she mentions the invention of the device "rose is a rose is a rose" (*Writings* 1, p. 798). Stein wished to link these two watersheds, the two main modernist "inventions." This will bring us to a different medium, architecture, which is also, almost by definition a collective enterprise, in order to ask the same question: how can one learn to be modern?

How Modernism was Created in Architecture

The Théâtre des Champs-Elysées that opened on March 30, 1913, for a relatively conventional performance of Hector Berlioz's *Benvenuto Cellini* and Weber's *Freischütz*, was immediately remarkable for its white lines, its grandiose simplicity, and the novelty of its design. Even if stray visitors derided it for being "neo-classical German," or just "Belgian" (always an insult in France), or even close to "a Theosophist temple," all agreed that it was an important avant-gardist landmark, a new temple of the arts for Paris. A fit setting for the première of *Rite of Spring*, this was the monument to contemporary dance, music, and theater that Gabriel Astruc had been dreaming of for some time. Gabriel Astruc came from an old Sephardi family of Bordeaux, and his father, a rabbi in Bordeaux, Brussels, and Paris, had many contacts with the rich and assimilated Jewish families of the belle époque. Astruc began his career as an editor with a good press, Ollendorf, then through his marriage found a connection with the music publisher Enoch, for which he worked tirelessly. It gave him a serious musical education and brought him into contact with all the important musicians and composers of the times. Astruc then launched the Musical Society, and after a few years of successful concerts found that he needed a separate venue, as symphonic and philharmonic halls were scarce in Paris. He wanted a building capable of housing three halls at once. His "Palais Philharmonique" was to offer to the public the latest inventions in matters of acoustics, security, and comfort. He decided to situate it in the Champs-Elysées, where upper-class luxury and modern mass entertainment met, as the old boulevards had become too proletarian. The old Cirque d'Eté had been demolished and its site was available, and with the support of leading capitalists including Isaac de Camondo, the Rothschilds, Pierpont Morgan, Vanderbilt, and even Otto Kahn, the president of the New York opera, Astruc was able to raise adequate funding. The Countess Greffuhle, Proust's friend and a model for Oriane de Guermantes, as well as noted politicians such as the minister Louis Barthou, lent a hand in the campaign for the new hall, while the right-wing press attacked Astruc violently, which triggered a second Dreyfus campaign since the accusations were clearly anti-semitic and chauvinist. The debate even reached the National Assembly in 1909, when two members of parliament discussed it and Clemenceau opposed the project. The promised concession near the Rond-point des Champs-Elysées was refused, and Astruc had to let Gabriel Thomas become the official director of the project.

Since the Théâtre des Champs-Elysées is a building that has been variously described as neo-classical, modernist. or a French variation on *Ingenieurästhetik*,

Figure 7   Léon Gimpel: Le Chantier du Théâtre des Champs Elysées, January 1912. (Paris, collection particulière) Paru dans Gil blas, 20 janvier 1912

it is worth studying it in order to understand the mixture of audacity and conservatism that is found in most of the landmarks of 1913 modernism. The building was the result of conflicted collaborations, as was most often the case in poetry and the arts. Its complex genesis entailed no fewer than four architects, who worked in succession from 1907 to 1913. The first architect who had been asked to work on a preliminary draft was Henri Fivaz, a rationalist and eclectic architect, who was rather conventional. He was helped by Roger Bouvard, whose father was the director of Paris's architectural services. The young Bouvard was a staunch defender of classicism and hated rationalism and "art nouveau." The first series of plans given to the official services were the work of both men, and what they envisaged resembles the Grand Palais or the Petit Palais, still visible not far away to the east:[33] a glorious combination of ancient styles typical of the "Beaux Arts" style. Happily, given the political struggles, Fivaz left and Bouvard was left to continue the drafting alone. He presented a purely neo-classical building that calls up Schinkel's work in Berlin or Odessa. He reserved all his novelties for the interior decoration, which was to be stunning and radically up to date.

109

Again, the municipal opposition to the project multiplied difficulties, and Bouvard had to keep modifying his plans to meet new criteria. His efforts were in vain. Even the site had to be abandoned. Fortunately, Gabriel Thomas found another site, not far from the first, the former hotel of the Marquis de Lillers at 13–15 avenue Montaigne. The terrain was larger, and the municipal requirements easier to satisfy. Bouvard adapted his previous drafts, and produced a plan in a pure Louis XVI style, which achieved its aim: in spite of formal innovations inside the building, it was accepted by the conservative municipal committee. It was only because of discrepancies in the inner decoration, which pleased no one, that Henry Van de Velde was called upon in May 1910.

Van de Velde was introduced by Gabriel Thomas when he started wondering whether Bouvard could realize such a complex project alone. Van de Velde was the exact antithesis of Bouvard: one of the most famous art nouveau architects of the period, he had designed original furniture, had published widely, and had worked on the interior decoration of several museums in Germany. He did not reject ornaments as Loos did, but like Gaudi wanted lines and shapes to express life organically, fluidly. He had worked with Max Reinhardt and Cordon Craig and had original ideas about theaters and opera houses. Van de Velde worked on the dress circle and upper circles as opposed to the stage and the stalls, and on the columns and the orchestra pit. His main hall managed to integrate the expansiveness of a Wagnerian sensibility with a symbolist concern for meditation as the main hall was organized in a discreet harmony of curves. All the modifications were accepted, and Bouvard continued to deal with the administrative issues while Van de Velde started modifying the previous plan in 1911. It was Van de Velde who let the enemy in when he recommended the use of reinforced concrete instead of brick or stone so as to achieve a less costly and also freer structure. Van de Velde himself asked the brothers Auguste and Gustave Perret to give an estimate. They answered that his plan was unbuildable and suggested important structural modifications. Their insistence on low costs (reinforced concrete was much cheaper and more reliable) was accompanied by demands for transformations in the Van de Velde–Bouvard project, until Van de Velde, finding that his plans were constantly modified, decided to leave in his turn.

Auguste and Gustave Perret were the equivalents of Muthesius in Germany: they believed in honesty and simplicity, and they hated the mannerism of art nouveau with its fluid undulations and floral rhythms. They argued for clear, straight, transparent lines and simple volumes. They believed that materials should remain visible ("Make materials visible, there's nothing better" was their motto) and that "truth alone was beautiful."[34] For Auguste Perret, who had written a *Theory of Architecture*, reinforced concrete offered a revolutionary way of returning to classical concepts such as harmony, scale, symmetry, and proportion. Good engineering would generate beauty and art effortlessly, as it were. Perret had made, he claimed, the first step ever in the direction of a reinforced concrete esthetic with his 1905 garage, situated on the rue de Ponthieu in Paris. The façade had a rhythmical span of 3:5:5, and managed to translate Beaux Arts esthetics into a simple structure of concrete. Earlier, in 1902–3, his rue Franklin buildings were constructed with bay windows on eight stories that seemed to be suspended without support. For Auguste Perret, a building consisted only of the structural frame and infillings; ornament was not permitted, since the function of ornament would be taken over by the structural elements.[35] It is worth noting that a young Swiss architect had just been working for the Perrets in 1908–9: Charles-Edouard Jeanneret, who would later adopt the name of Le Corbusier, learned the basics of his craft from this combination of revolutionary techniques using ferro-concrete as a ductile material that could be coupled with such a rigorously functionalist neo-classicism that it turned modernist by itself.

Thus, despite the beautiful plans provided by Van de Velde for his stone façade, the Perrets used the argument of technology to reject his subtle decorative rhythms. After July 1911, the Perret studio took over completely, which triggered a legal suit with Van de Velde, who accused them of having stolen all his good ideas (which they did). The Perrets retaliated by saying that he was only a fancy decorator who had no idea of building technology. Only the war put an end to the bitter polemic. However, the Perrets managed to reconcile everyone: not only were they French, they had the necessary solid technical credentials, their building pace was fast, the building was cheaper than if traditional materials had been used, and it was solid, elegant, classical, and modern at the same time. In order to make the audience accept the formal audacity and stark austerity of the façade, the interior decoration remained extremely traditional: the main auditorium was decorated with frescoes painted by Maurice Denis, a late symbolist close in spirit to Puvis de Chavanne, and the foyers were decorated by Edouard Vuillard, one of the Nabis. It was richly painted in gold and amaranth, gleaming white marble was used abundantly in the entrance, while the only decoration on the exterior was provided by Bourdelle's sculptured high reliefs representing the main arts. Dance was illustrated by Isadora Duncan. The result was exactly the inverse of the initial project: whereas originally modernity was to be reserved for the interior and hidden behind a neo-classical façade, the final project put tradition inside the building while flaunting the pure, rigorous lines that testified to an undeniable modernity.

The successive layers of neo-classicism, historicism, Beaux Arts, modern style, art nouveau, post-symbolism, and technological modernism had created a rare synthesis, a building that could be seen as either progressive, archaic, or neo-classical depending on one's point of view. It was at any rate a fit setting for the energies released all at once by the *Rite of Spring* in the spring of 1913. Unhappily, the instrument of Astruc's triumph, the reason why he is remembered in the chronicles of modern art, also proved to be the cause of his commercial failure. First, Diaghilev had been greedy, asking Astruc to pay double the fee charged by the Opera for his Ballets Russes; second, the rent was exorbitant. Thus tickets were more expensive, but their sale failed to recoup the financial outlay involved in staging the concerts and ballets. There was no state or municipal funding available. Astruc royally, prodigally, spent all his reserves until the end came early, as he was forced to close the Théâtre des Champs-Elysées in October 1913, in spite of last-minute help from bankers like Rothschild, Camondo, and Menier. In November the theater property was seized, the magnificent costumes and sets for *Boris Godunov* (there was a last performance, a single one, before the closure) and *Khovantchina* just brought in from Ukraine were auctioned off. The French press was unsparing, applauding Astruc's fall in crudely anti-semitic terms, while Proust wrote a beautiful letter praising his devotion to the noble cause of art.

This example shows concretely how modernism was the result of collaborations that would deflect the original intentions of the creators, how it freely mixed forms taken from various vocabularies, and how it ended up reconciling tradition and modernity. The furor surrounding the Théâtre des Champs-Elysées was the last society "event" of the pre-war years: passions flared, opinions diverged, and esthetic doctrines were brandished in good or bad faith. The agonistic process reminds us as well that the artistic achievements of the belle époque did not come into being as peacefully as is commonly believed. There are many different ways of being modern, which is why they cannot be reduced to formal criteria. I will now take the example of painting to probe the issue further. The years around 1913 saw the invention of painterly abstraction, a new departure often thought to be typically modernist. The invention of abstraction was not just a stylization of certain features of painting, but a decision to paint abstract pictures that did not represent any object. This signaled a resolute break with the world of visual appearances, akin to Schoenberg's rejection of the world of tonality (Kandinsky was to write to Schoenberg in admiration, stating the similarity of their purposes).

Myth or Abstraction

The four historical pioneers of abstraction were Frantisek Kupka, Vassily Kandinsky, Kasimir Malevitch, and Piet Mondrian. Each of them followed an individual evolution that was not influenced by the others. Each evolution took place more or less at the same time, between 1911 and 1914, a simultaneity which can be accounted for by common preoccupations: all four had marked esoteric leanings, believed in a global system of the arts in which music was a model, and were aware of the new scientific model of the world in which invisible forces had exploded the certainties offered by simple vision. Vassily Kandinsky signed and dated a watercolor from 1910 which is often considered the first abstract painting. After 1911, he composed rhythmic and musical interactions of color blots that float in an indeterminate background. Frantisek Kupka's *Vertical Planes I* is dated 1912–13 and shows a concern for verticality that corresponded to his notion of an arrested dynamism through which time would appear as the fourth dimension. Kupka had settled in Puteaux, where he was in touch with the three Duchamp brothers. Like them, he passed rapidly though cubism before moving to a more conceptual mode of abstraction. Kupka exhibited his first abstract works at the Salon des Indépendants in 1913. And as we have seen, it was also in 1913 that Malevitch painted the stage sets and the costumes of the postfuturist opera *Victory over the Sun*, which led him to simple black and white squares. At the same time, Kandinsky's single painting shown and bought at the New York Armory Show was *Improvisation no. 27*, an abstract picture.

It is against this background that I will focus on the evolution of two influential painters in 1913, Piet Mondrian and Giorgio de Chirico, trying to understand what made the former opt for abstraction and the latter for representation. Pieter Mondriaan (as his name was originally spelled) had always wanted to follow the example of an uncle who was a painter, and he financed his studies by teaching in various schools in the Netherlands. He mastered many styles, from classicism to Fauvism, symbolism, impressionism, and pointillism, while painting esoteric topics that illustrated his theosophical tenets. Simplifying the spelling of his own name, he settled in Paris in 1912 with the aim of understanding cubism and of meeting the French members of the Theosophical Society. He did meet Fernand Léger, Diego Rivera, and Gino Severini, but was relatively isolated. It was in Paris that Mondrian produced the series of "trees" paintings, achieving a sort of simplified allegorical language in which upright trees would embody the male principle, while the feminine element tended to be represented by the horizontal line of the sea. These stylized naturalistic motifs led to a sort of elongated cubism. As he wrote repeatedly in 1912 and 1913, one had to reach the spiritual by diminishing reality, making as little use of it as possible, until its shapes and colors became a simple pretext. In the "trees" painted in 1912, the composition often moves upward, like a fan, creating an overall effect of vertical arabesques that call up gothic glass windows.

A turning point was reached in 1913 with *Oval Composition with Trees* at the Stedelijk Museum of Amsterdam, corresponding to the moment when the cubism of Picasso and Braque influenced Mondrian the most. Yet he managed to combine several tree sketches into a composite image. He even indulged in a *trompe l'oeil* pun by giving his painting the textured appearance of tree bark. This was the first time that Mondrian used an oval format. The painting was exhibited in the fall of 1913, and when Dr. Bremmer bought it Mondrian told him that it represented one single tree in the Luxembourg Garden! Soon, he would not need any source in nature, and would just work from previous drawings or paintings, such as the series of Paris scaffoldings, so as to generate a grid of vertical and horizontal lines. After 1913, Mondrian completely abandoned naturalistic subjects, as for example in *Composition in Blue, Grey and Rose* from 1913, which can be seen at the Rijksmuseum Kröller-Müller in Otterloo. Here, the composition has a center, a sort of cross which provides a median axis, and the contrast between soft tonalities of pink and blue creates a delicate mosaic. In *Composition no. 7* (1913) at the Guggenheim Museum in New York, no theme or pretext is necessary. Objects and light are unified by a common atmospheric luminosity, and there is no need for a violent disintegration of the object, since a coloristic fragmentation equalizes everything in a pure light in which objects get smaller and fade away. *Oval Composition with Clear Colors* (1913) in the Museum of Modern Art in New York, plays with the theme of façades and scaffoldings, and asserts the drift toward the horizontal, while *Oval Composition* (1913–14), in The Hague, just allows one to distinguish the letters KUB on the right-hand side; this refers to an advertisement for French soup, but the letters function very differently from the newspaper cuttings that Braque and Picasso had inserted into their cubist compositions of 1911–12: they are almost identical with the other straight lines, and the lower curve of the B frames the oval limit of the motif.

A critic who immediately perceived Mondrian's originality was Apollinaire. He praised Mondrian's "highly abstract cubism" whose trees and one portrait "displayed a sensitive cerebral quality," and went on: "This kind of cubism follows a different path from that apparently taken by Braque and Picasso now, as their quest for materiality currently excites such interest."[36] The stress on *recherche de matière* is perceptive: Mondrian does not want to layer his surfaces with "collages" that leave material texture perceptible; on the contrary, his effort goes in the opposite direction, the "ascension away from matter" as he had written in a letter to a friend in 1909.[37] The accentuation of vertical lines, the reduction of the number of planes, and the avoidance of chiaroscuro transitions were meant to lead to a purely spiritual contemplation. This "art of destruction"[38] was too radical to be appreciated in 1913. Apollinaire's sympathetic mention was the only sign of recognition, and Mondrian returned to the Netherlands in 1914, where he refined his abstract art.

Apollinaire also had a kind word for Giorgio de Chirico in 1913, although the praise was qualified. In his review of the Salon d'Automne exhibit of November 1913, he mentioned "M. de Chirico, a painter at once unskillful and highly gifted," who exhibits "curious landscapes full of novel intentions, of solid architecture and great sensibility."[39] The remark on the lack of technique is not disparaging, as Apollinaire had already praised Douanier Rousseau for his ungainly touch and painstaking adherence to details. As the example of Mondrian, whose technique was impeccable, has shown, the production of an original painting has little to do with the mastery of brush strokes. Some of de Chirico's sketches and even canvases are indeed technically ungainly, clumsy, or badly finished; it was more important to let an idea pass through rough forms, crude colors, and naive contours than rely on the mimetic fallacy.

In the fall of 1913 Apollinaire had already met de Chirico and was on excellent terms with him, reading from *Alcools* to him, and launching a fruitful friendship that culminated in the artist's famous portrait of Apollinaire in 1914. De Chirico had evolved from an early symbolist fascination for Greek and Roman antiquity in the spirit of Böcklin to a more modern idiom that freely incorporated emblems of the industrial age, such as smokestacks, industrial chimneys, trains, stations, and clocks, or his classical piazzas, towers, columns, *palazzi*, and statues of Ariadne. Picasso had dubbed him the "train-station painter" (perhaps knowing that de Chirico's father had built railroads in Greece). By 1913, de Chirico began combining these symbolic elements in unlikely juxtapositions that went beyond the realistic setting one might expect, say, an old Italian town in which the smoke of a locomotive, oblique columns, and the statue of a goddess are found together; one could see two iron artichokes on a city background with a speeding train, as he painted in *The Melancholy of the Afternoon* (1913), or bananas, pineapples, and a classical marble head which we find in *The Transformed Dream* of the same year. Each element was taken as a "sign,"[40] and these signs could be combined at will, in curiously static allegories whose per-spective was always a little skewed. These haunted allegories became the distinctive feature of de Chirico's "metaphysical painting." The allegorical semiology gave the impression of an anguished wait for something other-worldly about to happen in a frozen future. The theatricality of those signs is foregrounded, everything turns spectral, no less the markers of modernity than the markers of antiquity.

We might conclude from this overview to the relativity or to the lability of the notion of "being modern". Nevertheless, what stands out as a com-mon feature is a decision made by all these artists to reject an older mode of expression deemed to be worn out and irrelevant. This bold decision was accompanied, however, by a retrospective look that took the entire tradition in which their works are inscribed into account. Thus, in the name of similar notions like the "spiritual" or the "metaphysical," Mondrian and de Chirico seemingly move in opposite directions, Mondrian going toward pure abstraction, a grid of non-representational vertical and horizontal lines, while de Chirico multiplies opaque allegories that announce the surrealist school of painters. Yet Clement Greenberg pointed out that it was Mondrian who drew the logical consequences of the exaggerated perspectives of de Chirico's "metaphysical" paintings. In 1912 and 1913, de Chirico had skewed depths, juxtaposed jarring perspectives, interpolated contradictory shadows, and thus generated a universe of impossible piazzas, ramps, and stations. This "interplay of subtle dehiscences" was meant to negate illusionism, while highlighting the flat aspect of planes and volumes.[41] Thus, de Chirico's true heir was not Dalí, who used the formulas of academism to incorporate surrealist themes, but Mondrian, whose abstraction completes the evolu-tionary line that runs from Giotto to Manet and Cézanne. Mondrian became "modern" out of neo-expressionism and cubism, while de Chirico became "modern" out of neo-classicism.

In a similar manner, one can say that Stein became "modern" as soon as she was able to graft the technique of cubism on to an exploratory and playful language that followed the ultimate suggestions of American prag-matism, in which the value of experience is asserted above everything else. Meanwhile, Williams became "modern" by combining an initial Romanti-cism in a broad sense, going from Blake to Whitman, to the quasi-painterly experiments of imagism. Frost became "modern" when he was able to com-bine the naturalness of local diction with the dramatic perspective inherited from Browning's histrionic monologues. Cather became "modern" when she used the same American provincialism and universalized it by the depth of her mythological associations with elemental forces, subtly subverting the social coding of sex and gender. The same might be said of Lawrence, with the added dimension of a personal experiment with his own Oedipal attachments, and a more decisive confrontation with primitivism. Finally, Joyce became "modern" in several stages, each very precisely documented in the psychological evolution of the hero of *A Portrait of the Artist as a Young Man*. The progression from deliquescent symbolism to a more tonic naturalism would not have sufficed to qualify him as a "modern" had he not gone beyond the concept of style as a progression in technical mastery and of moral heroism to develop a concept of style as a way of probing subjective, sexual, and social issues. To achieve this, he had to overcome his youthful narcissism through self-parody, and *Giacomo Joyce* (composed in 1913 and 1914)[42] was a perfect stylistic exercise in poetic debunking, while announcing the emergence of a deft, musical, and precise prose that found a perfect place in *Ulysses*. Joyce also needed to construct a hermeneutic pattern in which opposites, male and female, passively introspective and active, poet and politician, sadist and masochist, would find a satisfactory resolution, which he achieved in *Exiles*. His work on his play in 1913 taught him to use private fantasies and dream narratives and incorporate them in a scheme that combined universal history, the history of Ireland and of himself, as he would do with *Ulysses* and after, in his *Work in Progress*. Then, late modernism had expanded, trying to overcome boundaries and bypass borders, not even stopping at the limit of national languages: the whole world had become its "chaosmos."

Chapter 5

Global Culture and the Invention of the Other

Pre-War Exoticism

A taste for the exotic was prevalent in the fashion of 1913, which, rewriting belle époque formality in the direction of freedom, was starting to let the body breathe and move, become muscular, nervous, and lithe. In that connection, Debussy's *Jeux*, which used tennis as a ballet's argument, was more revealing of current trends than the archaic Russian pastoralism and the stunted gestures of the *Rite of Spring*. The new dynamism was shared by men and women, who were striving to be as "singular" as possible by avoiding the old "uniforms" that tended to distinguish working men's trades, classes, and ethnic provenance. At a time when each craft had a recognizable work uniform, women's magazines were deploying an imaginary of the rich foreigner visiting abroad, and deploying a grammar of immediately recognizable types – the snobbish British man in tweeds, the practical American with his gadgets, the impoverished Polish or Russian noble, the monocled and scarred Prussian officer, the Turks and Hindus with their turbans and colored flare trousers.[1] The sartorial inventions in 1913 were purposefully imitative, going back to medieval models or exotic clichés. The most representative designers of this trend were Fortuny and Bakst, who were connected by Proust when he described the "Fortuny gowns" worn by Madame de Guermantes, garments imitating the costumes worn by Venetians in Carpaccio's paintings. These lush velvets and embroidered brocades evoked a dream Venice, and beyond that, the sumptuous pageants of the Byzantine period:

Like the theatrical designs of Sert, Bakst and Benoist, who at that moment were recreating in the Russian ballet the most cherished periods of art with the aid of works of art impregnated with their spirit and yet original, brought before the eye like a stage décor, and with an even greater evocative power since the décor was left to the imagination, that Venice saturated with oriental splendour . . .[2]

The French Russophilia of the years 1909–14 had had political and economic origins (as Russian loans were in great demand), while being typical of a global craving for the oriental under all guises, whether it came via Venice, Vienna, St. Petersburg, or Tonkin.

Following Proust's lead, I want to insist on the relative artificiality of this creation, an artificiality that belongs to the genre; Proust was not foreign to the pleasures of pure imagination, and knew how to transform a Breton port like Balbec into a Persian temple. Like Proust, I want here to insist upon the idea of "inventing" a tradition,[3] in order to describe more than the fashion for *japonisme* of the last decade of the nineteenth century, or the newly discovered Negro art that made such a strong impression on Picasso, Derain, and their friends. I am alluding here to a concerted effort by a number of intellectuals and artists to broaden the sphere of European consciousness by going back to other and more ancient traditions, in such a way that they were both discovering unknown horizons, setting new boundaries, and "inventing" in the etymological sense (that is, *invenire*, finding what is there to encounter) the dimension of the missing Other. The process was connected with a critique of the European starting point, be it scathing, as with Du Bois, or tolerant, as with Tagore.

Christ and Airplanes

Apollinaire's "Zone" can be taken as the quintessential modernist text of 1913 and is therefore a good place to start from if we want to understand the tensions bequeathed by the nineteenth century's "discovery," conquest, and subsequent ruthless exploitation of Africa. Here is the famous finale of "Zone":

> You walk towards Auteuil you want to walk home and sleep
> Among your fetishes from Guinea and the South Seas
> Christs of another creed another guise
> The lowly Christs of dim expectancies
>
> Adieu Adieu
>
> Sun corseless head[4]

As if to contradict the ambiguous appeal to other "fetishes" and religions, a passage from the 1917 lecture on "The New Spirit and the Poets" that I discussed briefly in chapter 1 increases the distance between his newly found nationalism and former cosmopolitan ideals:

> A cosmopolitan lyric expression would only yield shapeless works without character or individual structure, which would have the value of the commonplace of international parliamentary rhetoric. And notice that the cinema, which is the perfect cosmopolitan art, already shows ethnic differences immediately apparent to everyone, and film enthusiasts immediately distinguish between an American and an Italian film. Likewise the new spirit, which has the ambition of manifesting a universal spirit and which does not intend to limit its activity, is none the less [. . .] a particular and lyric expression of the French nation, just as the classic spirit is, *par excellence*, a sublime expression of the same nation. (*Selected Writings*, 30)[5]

Because of this irrepressible surge of nationalism, Apollinaire is busy preparing the regeneration of the French race, a race that he felt was being bled to death in 1917 by the war's mass attrition. This is the theme of *Les Mammelles de Tiresias*, a "surrealist" play later claimed by André Breton as providing the impetus for surrealism:

> I imagine that, if women could bear no more children, men could make them, and why in showing it to be so I express a literary truth which could only be termed a fable outside literature, and I thus cause surprise. But my supposed truth is no more extraordinary or unbelievable than those of the Greeks, which show Minerva coming armed out of the head of Jupiter. (*Selected Writings*, 233)

Just as airplanes give new validity to the fable of Icarus (*Selected Writings*, 233), Christ stands out as the very first airplane pilot in a poem that has "religion" rhyme with "les hangars de Port-Aviation":

> It is Christ who better than airmen wings his flight
> Holding the record for height
>
> Pupil Christ of the eye
> Twentieth pupil of the centuries it is no novice
> And changed into a bird this century soars like Jesus[6]

Are African or Oceanian Christs deemed "lowly" ("Christ inférieurs des obscures espérances") just because they haven't yet mastered the art of flying airplanes? These darker peoples obscurely clinging to their "fetishes" do tend to walk on foot more than they cross continents by sea or air, and thus are not unlike the poet, who has had "enough of living in Greek and Roman antiquity." He craves the liberation brought about by scientific progress, its immediate uplift and surprising innovations – all of which create a new technological sublime. As we have seen, Apollinaire's modernism shares fundamental features with Italian futurism, such as the cult of the machine. It is a true "modernism" insofar as it is underpinned by a belief in progress, unlike Dadaism, born in 1917 from a rejection of the war, and marked by the slogan "Dada is not modern." In Apollinaire's terms, an international modernism should strive to distinguish itself from a vague cosmopolitan spirit, and will not try to abolish the nationalisms that had flared in open conflict. The solution lies in attempting to harness them and bring them closer to a vision of progress and modernization. This is also why a pioneer of the dissemination of Japanese and Chinese culture like Fenollosa had first acted as a museum curator for the Emperor, saving from destruction or oblivion the shrines and ancient art pieces that were considered rubbish by the eager Meiji modernizers. We need to explore once more the paradox of cosmopolitanism buttressed by nationalism; the international recognition of writers and artists coming from beyond the pale of Western culture was emerging while those developing countries were caught up in the universal race to industrialization, imperialism, and the development of cutting-edge military technologies, all this underwritten by growing nationalist ideologies.

Fenollosa and Pound

Fenollosa is an exceptional example of this process. He came from an old Spanish family, was born in Salem, and was educated at Harvard, where he studied philosophy.[7] It was as a Hegelian philosopher that he was invited to teach in Japan in 1878. He taught logic, philosophy, and political economy at Tokyo Imperial University, which left him time to discover the artistic treasures of the imperial past, then treated as little more than junk. Ten years later, he had helped found the Tokyo Fine Arts Academy and the Imperial Museum, where he became the director. He converted to Buddhism and was later made a high priest. He was decorated by the Emperor for his important services to Japan, which included an inventory of national treasures. He returned to the United States in 1890, and founded the department of oriental art in the Boston Museum of Fine Arts. While in Tokyo he met Mary, who had been widowed very young, and who had gone there with her second husband. Mary was known as a talented writer: she had published poetry, short stories, and novels between 1899 and 1906. She was awarded a literary prize in 1906, and later her two novels were made into silent films.

Mary returned to Boston to be reunited with Fenollosa, as they were working in the Boston Museum together. In 1895 Fenollosa divorced, and married Mary soon after, which created a scandal. Fenollosa was dismissed from the museum in 1896, and went back to Japan the next year with Mary. He started teaching again in Tokyo, deepening his knowledge of Noh and Buddhism, and returned a few times to America and Europe to lecture on Asian art and on educational problems. He died suddenly in London in 1908, leaving a mass of unpublished notes and book manuscripts for Mary to edit. This is what she did with *Epochs of Chinese and Japanese Art*, spending three years and almost all her money on the project (she had to return to Japan to check the dates and facts). The first edition was published in 1912, and by the time of the second edition a year later she was exhausted, and wanted to retire and be with her children in America. She contacted Ezra Pound, who was then the emerging young star of modernism, and offered to have him edit the remaining manuscripts left by her husband. She made the offer in September 1913 during a dinner in London, after which she gave Pound all the notebooks and manuscripts on which her husband had been working at the time of his death. These were mostly notes on the Japanese language, and translations from various poems and Noh plays. Pound had expressed a certain interest in Chinese poetry earlier, but the gift propelled modernism into uncharted seas, exactly as Japanese prints had taught the impressionists to look at nature differently 40 years earlier.

The gift of the notebooks and manuscripts pushed imagism beyond itself, toward an Eastern literature that became suddenly accessible to enthusiastic non-specialists, and added to the cult of fleeting instants perceived in a flash by privileged observers the weight of another culture that was to unfold slowly in all its complexity. Mary Fenollosa made Pound her husband's sole literary executor because she had recognized a fellow poet in the young American, and also a vibrant agitator who cared for precise language and rare documents (as with the manuscripts of the troubadours' songs) yet eschewed official scholarship as much as her late husband had done. Pound was of course not a specialist, and while this relative incompetence was the cause of many blunders (for instance, he never realized that Li Po and Rihaku were the same famous poet, one name being in Chinese, the other in its Japanese transliteration), those very limitations prevented him from falling into the rampant orientalism of British Museum sinologists. Thus Pound wrote excitedly to William Carlos Williams in December 1913: "Dorothy is learning Chinese. I've an old Fenollosa treasure in mss."[8] Already by October 1913 Pound had been helped by his friend Allen Upward, who had read him translations of Confucius and Mencius in the precise French of Pauthier's 1841 version. Upward had published his own *The Sayings of Confucius* in 1904, which led Pound to ask him to go back to these and use them for an article in *The New Freewoman*. Upward obliged with a selection from Confucius' *Analects*. Interestingly, in the editorial context evoked earlier, one of the teachings of "K'ung the Master" was to forbid egoism: "There were four things from which the Master was entirely free. He had no foregone conclusions, no arbitrary decisions, no obstinacy, and no egoism."[9] This is perhaps what triggered a different series of essays on Chinese philosophy in *The Egoist*. Starting with the first issue of *The Egoist* in December 1914, the sinologist William Loftus Hare published a series of learned discussions of "Chinese Egoism."

The consequences of the unexpected gift of the Asian "treasure" were momentous. As we have seen, Pound spent the winter of 1913/14, from November to January, with Yeats in a cottage near Coleman's Hatch, on the outskirts of Ashdown forest. Pound acted as a secretary, taking dictation, classifying correspondence, reading aloud to the Irish poet at night. They shared stories, discussed translations, examined drafts of poems, and also started sorting out Fenollosa's notes. Pound sent his version of *Nishikigi* to *Poetry* at the end of January 1914, using Fenollosa's rough crib. He later published *"Noh" or Accomplishment*, which contains Fenollosa's essays on Noh, along with a selection of canonical Noh plays translated from his papers. Yeats wrote the introduction to the book. Pound also worked on Fenollosa's translations of Chinese poems accompanied by Japanese glosses. The result was *Cathay* in 1915, a collection of poems that, as Eliot said, reinvented Chinese poetry.[10] Among them, "The River-Merchant's Wife," "The Jewel Stairs' Grievance," and "Exile's Letters" are masterpieces of creative translation. Even his earlier "In a Station of the Metro" was construed in his article on Vorticism as being a Japanese haiku or hokku.[11] Finally Pound tackled Fenollosa's notes on the Chinese ideogram ("The Chinese Written Character as a Medium for Poetry"), which provided the foundation for a wholly new system of poetics. Here is how the argument of a Noh play like *Nishikigi* was presented by Fenollosa: "Among the most weird and delicately poetic pieces is Nishikigi, in which the hero and heroine are the ghosts of two lovers who died unmarried a hundred years before."[12] Obviously, the magical world of Noh could be easily assimilated to the Irish folklore then explored by Yeats. While Noh is an elite art devised for the aristocracy, its themes are mostly pastoral and its characters priests, fairies, ghosts, and peasants. Fenollosa had compared its sophisticated art with the masterpieces of Greek tragedy. Pound went even further, following Fenollosa's example, when he turned into a disciple of Confucius. For him, China would replace Greece in his new "paideuma."

Tagore's Prize

If Pound took the initiative with China and Japan, it was Yeats who was responsible for the discovery of Tagore. When the Nobel prize in literature was given to Rabindranath Tagore in 1913, he appeared as a poet, playwright, educator, and religious leader whose work had had a strong impact on Yeats. Tagore received the prize mainly because of the success of the English translation of his *Gitanjali: Song Offerings* (1912). *Gitanjali* then went through a dozen printings in London just after its publication. In his telegram of acceptance, Tagore thanked the Nobel committee for having "brought the distant near, and made a stranger a brother." Such optimism may seem unfounded just one year before the outbreak of a world war, but it is consistent with Tagore's friendship with Gandhi. Both of them looked beyond the ugly European military confrontation to a post-colonial stage. Tagore had been visiting London in the spring of 1912, and had been launched and feted by Yeats. Yeats said at a banquet in July: "To take part in honouring Mr. Rabindranath Tagore is one of the great events of my artistic life. I have been carrying about me a book of translation into English prose of a hundred of his Bengali lyrics written within the last ten years. I know of no one in my time who has done anything in the English language to equal these lyrics."[13]

The translations were prose translations, and Pound, who had heard Tagore sing the poems to a musical accompaniment, knew how different they were in the original. The prose paraphrase kept little of their melodic charm. A typical section from *Gitanjali* illustrates well the neo-Whitmanian unanimism of Tagore's songs: "The same stream of life that runs through my veins night and day runs through the world and dances in rhythmic measures. // It is the same life that shoots in joy through the dust of the earth in numberless blades of grass and breaks into tumultuous waves of leaves and flowers. // It is the same life that is rocked in the ocean-cradle of birth and of death, in ebb and flow. // I feel my limbs made glorious by the touch of this world of life. And my pride is from the life-throb of

124

ages dancing in my blood this moment."[14] Pound initially shared Yeats' infatuation with the Bengali poet, and wrote two pages of introduction to the six poems by Tagore published in the December 1912 issue of *Poetry*. There, he asserted that he felt that "world-fellowship" had come "nearer" because of this visit, and he stressed the refinement of the poet, who, he said, made him feel "like a painted Pict with a stone war club" by comparison.[15]

Meanwhile, Tagore took a trip to the United States in November 1912. He first stayed in Urbana, Champaign, where his son was doing agronomical research. He wrote to Pound from there, complaining of his solitude. Pound narrates an anecdote about Tagore in January 1913: someone has asked how Tagore could be taken as a Bengali patriot, when he had written an ode to the king. A student of Tagore explained that his master had tried to write a nationalist poem, that he had failed, and then offered a poem written previously and said: "It's addressed to the deity. But you may give it to the national committee. Perhaps it will content them."[16] Witty as this is, it is the aspect of Tagore with which Pound grew disenchanted, and he would often make fun of his hazy syncretism, which, as Foster notes, anticipated the later craze for Khalil Gibran's vague spiritualism.[17] "As a religious preacher [Tagore] is superfluous," Pound wrote to Harriet Monroe.[18] He added: "We've got Lao Tse. And his [Tagore's] philosophy hasn't much in it for a man who has 'felt the pangs' or been pestered with Western civilization. I don't mean quite that, but he isn't either Villon or Leopardi, and the modern demands just a dash of their insight."[19] This would be Pound's view afterwards: Tagore was good if considered as a foreign lyrical voice, a contemporary Kabir, but should not be taken seriously as a thinker, especially when he pretends to be a sage with a mission, disseminating a universal message of peace. In fact, this aspect of Tagore sounded very much like theosophy, which was a reason why Yeats had been drawn to him in the first place. There was also the nationalist aspiration of Bengalis and Hindus striving to achieve if not immediate independence from Britain at least some form of home rule. Even if Tagore, because of his religiosity and universalism, was not a staunch nationalist, Yeats projected on to him his own resistance to English imperialism.

In January 1913 Tagore traveled to Chicago, where he met Harriet Monroe and lectured on India and the problem of evil. He then went to Rochester, where he gave a lecture on "Race Conflict," a symptomatic theme that he thought relevant for an American audience. During this trip to America and when he was returning to London, his prose translation of *Gitanjali* (slightly retouched by Yeats) along with two plays, *King of Dark Chamber* and *The Post*

Office, were published. Their success in England and beyond was such that Tagore was short-listed for the Nobel prize, a success that was credited to Yeats' vigorous campaign of promotion. Tagore returned to India in September 1913 and was in Calcutta when he heard that he had been awarded the prize. He was celebrated by his friends, and took the opportunity to settle old accounts in a speech he gave there, which infuriated many. Tagore had also started distancing himself from Yeats, whose patronizing attitude he politely bore but resented. It was also in 1913 that Tagore sent a first message of welcome greeting Gandhi, who had begun preaching non-violent resistance to the Indian minority in South Africa.

For Pound, the distinction granted to Tagore was just a proof that he had lost any relevance. He judged everyone quite severely in 1917: "Tagore got the Nobel Prize because, after the cleverest boom of our day, after the fiat of the omnipotent literati of distinction, he lapsed into religion and optimism and was boomed by the pious non-conformists. Also because it got the Swedish academy out of the difficulty of deciding between European writers whose claims appeared to conflict. Sic. Hardy or Henry James?"[20] He notes, however, with evident glee that this had been a "damn good smack" for the British Academic Committee led by Gosse, who had turned down Tagore "on account of his biscuit complexion" and elected two nonentities instead. Like Yeats, Pound had read Tagore's religious rhapsodies as another variation on theosophic rhetoric, whereas the Upanishads were a serious and essential part of his culture. Tagore belonged to the reformist Hindu sect founded by Rammohun Roy, Brahmo Samaj. It rejected ordinary Hinduism and embraced a "deity" that was purposely left vague and formless. It was a religion which was an esthetic at the same time, and their fusion prevented Tagore from being a modernist, at least in the sense that modernism implies a questioning of these values, and he steadily refused the accolade of modernist masters that he felt too condescending. In his essays of the twenties and thirties Tagore criticized Eliot, Pound, and their followers for being too alienated, despairing, and nihilistic. In his vision, the poet was to become the god of his universe, thus feeling ethically responsible for all other creatures. Indeed, he embodied the Romantic ideal of the poet as priest and prophet with a vengeance.

Ethiopia

It was not only to the East that European and American modernists were looking. A key term in 1913 was "Ethiopia," as it signified a new African utopia. W. E. B. Du Bois' pageant, *The Star of Ethiopia*, was presented in New York in 1913 to commemorate the Emancipation Proclamation. It was such a success that it was shown again in DC in 1915 and in Philadelphia in 1916. At the same time, the German ethnographer and anthropologist Leo Frobenius published the third volume of his trilogy based on his African expeditions, *Und Afrika sprach*. The third volume, published in 1913, was entitled *Unter den unsträflichen Aethiopen* (literally, "Among the Unpunishable Ethiopians"). That same year saw the American version of the first two volumes, an important source of inspiration for Du Bois, in spite of Frobenius' ambivalence. The American philosopher of a divided black consciousness and the German ethnographer who was producing a scientific study of ancient African kingdoms were both striving to understand Ethiopia. They both unearthed its rich cultures, deepening the turn to African art that had already caught on with Picasso and Apollinaire in Paris. Just as China was being "invented" by the London imagists in 1913, so too was a new vision of Africa being taken as a critical measure and model, paving the way to the recognition of the power of *négritude* which Léopold Senghor brandished one decade later. And a little later, after his London and Paris years, Pound would provide another bridge from Rapallo when he started connecting Frobenius' *Sagetrieb* with a Confucian tradition deployed in the historical chronicle of the China *Cantos*.

I will limit myself to Frobenius' and Du Bois' parallel but diverging trajectories as they offer modernist variations on the nineteenth-century genre of "Ethiopianism." The genre went back to the African American experience in the late eighteenth century, to sermons and political tracts which all quoted the same lines from Psalm 68: 31: "Princes shall come out of Egypt; Ethiopia shall soon stretch out her hands unto God." This was variously interpreted as a prophecy announcing Africa's impending liberation and political renascence or its complete conversion to Christianity.[21] Let us note that Ethiopia figures prominently in the Bible, from Genesis 2: 13 to the wonderful story of the conversion of the Ethiopian eunuch who reads the prophet Esias without understanding the meaning and is helped by Philip in Acts 8: 27. Paul Laurence Dunbar's "Ode to Ethiopia" hailed the country not just as a nation in Africa but as a "Mother Race" whose glory should inspire all African Americans. Customarily, the rise of Africa was presented as heralding the decline of the West, tainted because of the sin of slavery. In this context, one needs to remember two dates: 1884, when the Berlin conference office ratified and justified the "scramble for Africa" among Western nations, and 1896, when the battle of Adwa saw the ignominious defeat of the Italian army by Emperor Menelik's troops.

In 1896, Abyssinia (the name of the old Ethiopia) remained, with Liberia, one of the only two independent countries in Africa, and was thus for a while not considered fair game by European colonial powers – at least until Mussolini. In 1931, just before the renewed colonial or imperialist aggression, Abyssinia changed its name back to Ethiopia, proudly reclaiming the old Greek term meaning the "land of the burnt faces." When in 1890, before Adwa, Du Bois was asked to give the commencement speech at Harvard, he chose to give a short lecture on Jefferson Davis, the only president of the Southern Confederacy. Davis was surprisingly presented as "a representative of Civilization," but the blond hero was in dire need of the counterweight brought by a rather submissive Negro. Adapting freely Hegel's dialectic of master and slave, Du Bois predicted that civilization would be enhanced by the cooperation between aggressively individualist landowners and recently enfranchised ex-slaves – then and only then would the Strong Man and the Submissive Man be able to acknowledge one another. Indeed, it was not too far-fetched to say that Davis embodied the manly virtues of Germanic culture: "A soldier and a lover, a statesman and a ruler; passionate, ambitious, and indomitable; bold reckless guardian of a people's All – judged by the whole standard of Teutonic civilization, there's something noble in the figure of Jefferson Davis." He was nevertheless a symbol of the ideology of white supremacy, an ideology based on "the idea of the Strong Man – Individualism coupled with the rule of Might."[22] The white owner needed the counterweight supplied by a more artistic, freer, and less driven race. Thus Du Bois concluded with a flourish: "You owe a debt to humanity for this Ethiopia of the Outstretched Arm," and was greeted by astonished and wild applause.[23] The haunting question remains: what was the outstretched arm saying? Was it to suggest submission, devotion, or the closed fist of defiance?

Ethiopia surfaces again in Du Bois' daring modernist novel, *The Quest of the Silver Fleece*, published in 1911. At one point, Zora, the heroine of the story, has come from the Southern swamps to become a maid in Washington; then she travels with the rich and cynical Mrs. Vanderpool, and starts reading not only the newspapers but also history and literature:

> Zora was curled in a chair with a book. She was in dreamland . . . Hour after hour, day after day, she lay buried, deaf and dumb to all else. Her heart cried, up on the World's four corners of the Way, and to it came the Vision Splendid. She gossiped with old Herodotus across the earth to the black and blameless Ethiopians; she saw the sculptured glories of Phidias amid the splendor of the swamp; she listened to Demosthenes and walked the Appian Way with Cornelia – while all New York streamed beneath her window.[24]

Figure 8 *The Star of Ethiopia.* W. E. B. du Bois Library

Thereafter, the spirit of Ethiopia is embodied by Zora, the willful and free heroine of *The Quest of the Silver Fleece*, a modernist text that plays self-consciously on mythological parallels. In his novel, Du Bois reconciles progressive socialism with black nationalism under the general heading of a critical rewriting of Greek myths and legends. Zora emerges triumphant as an Ethiopian queen who unites the most ancient wisdom and the new knowledge brought to the uneducated masses by multi-racial schools. In the end she manages to marry Bles', the young man whom she had seduced at the start.

Two years later, the Ethiopian rhetoric reaches its most perfect expression in the 1913 pageant:

> Hear ye, hear ye! And learn the ancient glory of Ethiopia, All-mother of men; whose wonders men forgot. See how beneath the Mountains of the Moon, alike in the Valley of Father Nile and in ancient Negro-land and Atlantis the Black Race ruled and strove and fought and sought the Star of Faith and Freedom even as other races did and do. Fathers of Men and Sires of Children golden, black and brown, keep silence and hear this mighty word.[25]

The Mountains of the Moon were taken as theme in Du Bois' poem "Children of the Moon," and refer to Ptolemy's geography – the semi-fictitious mountain range could be identical with the Ruwenzori Mountains in Africa. Hence the children of the moon are ancient Negroes from Central Africa. Du Bois is alluding to the Nile–Congo watershed, or rather to a time before the division of African peoples between Congolese and Egyptians or Nilotics. The aim of the united Negroes will be to build a "Tower of Eternal light" or the Obelisk of the Egyptians, a stone monument thought to represent a sunray. In 1911, Du Bois chose to illustrate *The Crisis* with a winged disk for the sun and a black face on it. Those wings were the wings of Ethiopia, as in the famous quote from Isaiah 18: 1: "Woe to the land shadowing with wings, which *is* beyond the rivers of Ethiopia." Like Isaiah, Du Bois never abandoned the idea of uniting all these "scattered" nations of black Africa until they would become a new Zion.

When *The Star of Ethiopia* was performed in New York, it staged over a thousand actors and had an audience that numbered 30,000 people. Although attendance was always high then and at the later stagings, the pageant was so huge and costly that it could not be financially successful. It consisted of a prologue and, in five scenes – the Gift of Iron, the Dream of Egypt, the Glory of Ethiopia, the Valley of Humiliation, and the Vision Everlasting – covered 10,000 years, beginning with prehistoric black men and the invention of iron artifacts, passing to the rise and fall of the Ethiopian kingdom near Egypt, moving on to describe the sad plight of black nations later subjected to the humiliation of slavery. It was in fact a history of Pan-African nationalism, since Du Bois believed that it was crucial to give a sense of dignity to the American Negroes who should consider that they came from a more ancient and moral culture than the one in which they found themselves at present. A pageant that called upon famous characters like the Queen of Sheba, Solomon, Toussaint L'Ouverture, Nat Turner, John Brown, and Harriet Beecher Stowe was supposed to be the best tool to monumentalize Negro history and celebrate a recent emancipation. It incorporated music from *Aida* and Negro spirituals, including music by the black musical theater team of Cole and Johnson. This huge effort can be best understood in the context of the popularity of pageants in the first decade of the twentieth century.[26] They were used to promote patriotism and civic pride, and in this case, the aim was to reawaken a national pride in the African American people at a time of heightened segregation and racial tensions. The pageant achieved its main goal, the creation of national pride among a younger black generation, and is a determining factor in the triggering of the Harlem Renaissance – yet, as Du Bois was to complain later, almost no white person was to be seen in the audience.

Du Bois soon felt the need of a more scientific approach. When he published his compendium of African lore as *The Negro* in 1915, the book was in great part based upon the American translation of Frobenius' *The Voice of Africa* (1913). Here is what he writes about Ethiopia: "The history of the Sudan thus leads us back again to Ethiopia, that strange and ancient center of world civilization whose inhabitants in the ancient world were considered to be the most pious and the oldest of men."[27] In that historical survey, slavery is called "the Rape of Ethiopia" – "a sordid, pitiful, cruel tale."[28] Nevertheless, the epic survey of *The Negro* ends on a positive note – there is always something new coming from Africa: "Semper novi quid ex Africa!"[29] The same Latin tag is used at the beginning of Du Bois' remarkable essay "The African Roots of the War" published in May 1915 in the *Atlantic Monthly*.

War and Slavery

Pointing to the series of incidents surveyed in the introduction to this volume – Fashoda pitting France against England, Tripoli opposing Italy and Turkey, Delago Bay opposing England and Portugal, Germany and France at Agadir, Germany and the Dutch versus England in South Africa – Du Bois shows that the world war could have been triggered earlier in Africa. It is no coincidence that the culmination of atrocities accompanying the "rape of Africa" should have been in the Belgian Congo, just as Belgium was the first theater of war on the Western front. As Du Bois argues, the 1884 Berlin conference could never establish a perpetual colonial peace because it did not attempt to regulate a state of peace but merely organized international war and plunder: "The methods by which this continent has been stolen have been contemptible and dishonest beyond expression. Lying treatises, rivers of rum, murder, assassination, mutilation, rape, and torture have marked the progress of Englishman, German, Frenchman and Belgian on the dark continent."[30] The core of the essay is the original idea that the plunder of Africa by European powers was more than an offshoot of international capitalism, because it underpinned the very concept of capitalism. The rivalries of international capitalism not only created a deep fault in European consciousness, pointing to a weakness shared by white laborers and socialists, but also inscribed the idea of plunder in the psyche of Western man. It was because of this internal division that the socialists were unable to oppose the war when it was brewing.

> With the waning of the possibility of the Big Fortune, gathered by starvation wages and boundless exploitation of one's weaker and poorer fellows at home, arose more magnificently the dream of exploitation abroad. Always, of course, the individual merchant had at his own risk and in his own way tapped the riches of foreign lands. Later, special trading monopolies had entered the field and founded empires over-seas. Soon, however, the mass of merchants at home demanded a share in this golden stream; and finally, in the twentieth century, the laborer at home is demanding and beginning to receive a part of this share.[31]

This is what Du Bois calls a "new democratic despotism," a term that had not been understood until then. This gave rise to a momentous paradox lying at the core of the Western concept of democracy:

> It is this paradox which has confounded philanthropists, curiously betrayed the Socialists, and reconciled the Imperialists and captains of industry to any amount of "Democracy." It is this paradox which allows in America the most rapid advance of democracy to go hand in hand in its very centers with increased aristocracy and hatred toward darker races, and which excuses and defends an inhumanity that does not shrink from the public burning of human beings.
> Yet the paradox is easily explained: the white workingman has been asked to share the spoil of exploiting "chinks and niggers." It is no longer simply

the merchant prince, or the aristocratic monopoly, or even the employing class, that is exploiting the world: it is the nation; a new democratic nation composed of united capital and labor. The laborers are not yet getting, to be sure, as large a share as they want or will get, and there are still at bottom large and restless excluded masses. But the laborer's equity is recognized, and his just share is just a matter of time, intelligence and skillful negotiation."[32]

The European nations and America rule the modern world and their success derives from having created a new sense of community not founded on values established by patriotism, nationalism, or traditional religion but on "wealth, power, and luxury for all classes on a scale the world never saw before." This accumulation is created at the expense of the "darker nations of the world" that are concentrated in Asia and Africa, and also South and Central America, the West Indies, and the islands of the South Seas.

Du Bois' rigorous demonstration then gives way to an impassioned plea for justice. He expresses the hope that feminine figures like Queen Nefertiti of Egypt, a black woman, will yet again have access to power. Here is how he concludes his essay:

> Twenty centuries after Christ, black Africa, prostrate, raped, and shamed, lies at the feet of the conquering Philistines of Europe. Beyond the awful sea a black woman is weeping and waiting with her sons on her breast. What shall the end be? The world-old and fearful things, War and Wealth, Murder and Luxury? Or shall it be a new thing – a new peace and new democracy of all races: a great humanity of equal men? "Semper novi quid ex Africa!"[33]

An Africanist like Leo Frobenius could not have disagreed with this Latin motto. Born in 1873, five years after Du Bois, the son of a Prussian officer, Frobenius made good the promise provided by his first name, Leo, and took Leo Africanus as his godfather. Although he never had any formal academic training, although his PhD was refused, he nevertheless founded several research institutes devoted to African cultures in Germany, the first one in 1898 being the African Research Institute. He finished his career as director of the Municipal Museum of Ethnology in Frankfurt from 1934 to his death in 1938, which led to speculation that he was a crypto-Nazi and that he was allowed to remain in that position by Hitler because he justified the doctrine of inferior darker races. He had an unlikely defender in Ezra Pound, who asserted that "The modern university was founded at Frankfurt by Leo Frobenius."[34] Frobenius is a complex figure, who had indeed been influenced by Spengler in his theories of "cultural circles" or "cultural morphology." As early as 1898, when he published the *Origin of African Cultures*, Frobenius rejected the *doxa* then prevalent that Africa was a dark continent devoid of history, as Hegel had assumed. He demonstrated that on the contrary it had been the theater of the rise and fall of ancient empires and warring kingdoms. Just as Fenollosa had reclaimed a Japanese past for the Japanese, Frobenius was rediscovering African culture in nations that had forgotten the richness of their cultural past while demonstrating the enmeshed historicity of African civilizations.

This he did with a battery of concepts that correspond to diffusionism, the ethnological movement that Boas had encouraged in the US. Frobenius' main concept was that of *paideuma*, a term later borrowed and used systematically by Pound. It is a living culture which functions as a form-producing *Gestalt* since it is endowed with a specific manner of creating meaning and a whole style of being. This led him to study side by side artifacts of material culture (arrows, pots, burial sites, the architecture of buildings and villages, decoration marks on the body, dance types, dresses, masks, etc.) and local myths, legends, and folklore. This is why all his books read like novels and are full of vivid legends when they document his 12 expeditions that started in 1904. Frobenius then developed the concept of *Kulturphysiognomik* in 1923, which led him to talk systematically of "cultural symptoms." A note to his 1913 *Unter den unsträflichen Aethiopen*,[35] the third and last volume of his trilogy documenting his African expeditions, *Und Afrika sprach*, explains that he uses indifferently "systems" and "organizations" "by which I mean ripened and completely formed universes of cultural manifestations" ("ausgereifte aus- und durchgebildete Erscheinungswelten"), a notion that allows him to regroup isolated "individual features" or "symptoms."[36] These symptoms are categorized in cultural complexes that follow an organic logic, while being nevertheless radically historicized at the same time. For "cultural morphology" sends us back to the idea of human cultures as living organisms underpinned by an unconscious "will" to express itself, a *Sagetrieb* – or "a drive to express" – a coining that would strike Pound so forcibly in the late thirties that he made it into one of his key concepts. As we have seen, Frobenius' sense of agency greatly influenced Leopold Senghor in his militant reclaiming of *négritude* in the interwar years.

Inventing the African *Paideuma*

The first two volumes of *Und Afrika sprach* were translated into English as *The Voice of Africa* (*VA*) in 1913.[37] The tone is surprisingly racist at times; for instance, in a moment of recrimination against the Yorubas in Lagos who multiplied problems and even murdered one black helper during the 1910–12 expedition, Frobenius vents his rage with damaging generalizations: "At one fell swoop, I gained a view of the dreary moral waste of the black man's soul. I never believed that human beings could exist who lied so vilely and so much as a matter of course" (*VA*, 107). The lesson that this teaches is pointedly Eurocentric: "Woe betide the Europeans who forget their unity of race and culture in the bush of Africa! Woe! For the beast slumbers in the heart of us all and should the blacks no longer feel constraint and white men goad them on, unthinking, against their fellow-whites, then in the day to come, when, conscious of their masters' failings, then – brutes as they really are – they will learn at last to tear them down, rend them in pieces and lap their blood" (*VA*, 107). At times, Frobenius sounds ominously like Kurtz in *Heart of Darkness* just before his final breakdown . . .

Frobenius was a highly idiosyncratic writer and self-taught explorer whose strong personality could be shamelessly on display, which led to his rejection as a fraud and quack by British ethnographers. Moreover, he never questioned European supremacy and the existence of colonialism, and he seemed to assume that the best way for Africa to renew its old culture and emerge from centuries of backwardness and oppression was to seek the help of enlightened Western nations like Germany or England. Indeed, this was the motto of the 1913 book: "Fiat Lux!" (*VA*, xiii). African enlightenment should be based upon a deeper knowledge of the complexities of ancient cultures and kingdoms. However, there was a pragmatic edge to these scholarly activities. In a curious passage entitled "An Explanatory Note" Frobenius managed both to condone Western colonialism and criticize the American system that abusively refused to grant full dignity to black people:

> The introduction to the great problems involved in the previous history of Africa, which are set up in the recital of our experience among the "Savages of Africa," ought to interest all specialists in general, and in particular to be of unusual value to the colonial politician who would conduct the affairs of the countries through which we traveled either from his arm-chair at home in Europe or in the district itself. For the "German Inner African Exploration," which God grant, may still have a prolonged existence under whatever flag, and whose archives will continue to be uninterruptedly increased, has for its ideal task not only the establishment and exposition of the recorded and the prehistoric conditions of Africa, but the creation of practical values and, above all, of a utilitarian standard. [. . .]
>
> That the working capacity of the so-called "negro" population of Tropical Africa represents the highest asset possessed by these lands is a fact fully recognized to-day, and which cannot well be emphasized too strongly. Now,

an eminent English colonial politician of great practical experience recently expressed himself to me as follows: "As far as my experience goes, the European colonizing powers bring about the same conditions on all the tropical coast-lands of Western Africa as in America. But it is a thoroughly unsound state of affairs. If, now, the state of things has already assumed a horrible complex-ion in America, it may in the course of time even end in a racial conflict for us Europeans in Africa, where the struggle for existence amongst the aboriginal nations is on such a very extensive scale." I can subscribe to every syllable of this pronouncement. (*VA*, vi–vii)

As we have seen, given his shrewd skills of observation, his wish to be pragmatic and not deluded by ideals, his philosophical organicism, and his insistence on how ideas have to be evaluated "in action," Frobenius' vocabulary often turns medical: the health of a culture is systematically opposed to disease. He suggests in many places that the Europeans have in fact corrupted the Africans. And if we ask "What is the ultimate cause of the disease?", like Du Bois, Frobenius never wavers in his answer: the answer is slavery. Observe the mixture of condescension, prejudice, and anti-colonialist critique in this passage:

I have frequently explained that servility is not the greatest fault possessed by the negro. [. . .] He begs for what can be of no earthly use for him and tries his hand at begging for one thing after another. The horrible peculiarity may have its source in the evil habits engendered by the slave-trade and the commerce with Europeans, which it brought in its train. (*VA*, 147)

Frobenius sharply observes that the general moral corruption that slavery has brought about has destroyed the ancient reverence for the "native holders of power" like the traditional chiefs and priests. "These natives have been accustomed and trained to a government of bloody repression, and attained to both power and honour by its exercise" (*VA*, 48). This has created a sort of vacuum, which has in its turn destroyed the usual relationships between people; they have even forgotten their own mythologies, which is why Frobenius deems it essential to collect traditional tales.

Although the inland tribes may have forgotten the greater part of their mythology, the reason of it is, partly, that unhappy slave traffic to which they were subject, which absorbed all their activities to such an extent and so lowered their estimation in which life should be held, that human offerings occupied an unusually large space in the ritual observance of West Africans, whose cruel disposition is innate. Exactly as happened in Benin, the wealth and piety of a Yoruban was reckoned by the number of human sacrificial victims he could afford. And this too, I consider a result of the trade in human flesh, fostered in is time by Europeans, although doubtless the germs of such abuses already existed. (*VA*, 148)

In conformity with nineteenth-century models, the account of Frobenius' travels often takes the form of a travelogue documenting a descent into darkness. He pays attention to the progression of Islam in countries like Senegal and Sudan, adding that Islam is fundamentally foreign to the African *paideuma*. He describes at some length the destruction of Timbuktu by the Mossi in 1329 and documents the rise and fall of many empires in central Niger. His somewhat disordered chronicle turns into a compendium of all the legends, myths, and rituals he has observed, a rag-bag of myth and history as well as an explorer's logbook (a "descriptive catalogue" as he writes on page 612). The tone changes when he reaches Ethiopia – a culture whose "Asian" origins he tries to demonstrate. His trips took him from Senegal to the sources of the Nile. There he reaches "Nubia" or the "ancient classical land of Ethiopia," a country whose inhabitants were considered the "most pious" and the "oldest of all mankind" (*VA*, 620). He sets out to show that this culture was not a tributary of Egypt but pre-dated the culture of Egypt, and that Egyptian lore borrowed its main elements from it. The key factor of the old Nubian religion was the ritual slaying of the king at the hands of the sacred priests, a tradition analyzed in the third volume on the "unpunishable" Ethiopians. Nubia was conquered by Egypt, which adopted its respect for the caste of the priests. Later on, Nubia chose to become Christian against Egyptian polytheism and started a long connection with Byzantium, as early as AD 547 and until at least 1486.

By comparing a number of semantic radicals, objects such as swords with a cross-shaped handle and certain African legends, Frobenius accepts the claim that the Nubian people might be descended from Jewish tribes. Although he does not fully substantiate this claim, it brings grist to his mill since he wants to prove that the most ancient people of Africa is a branch of an Eastern or Asian group which might be Perso-Byzantine in origin. Frobenius rhapsodizes lyrically about the ancient Perso-Nubian culture that has invented the domination of priests over the people, controlling all the aspects of everyday life. His expedition eastward allows him to leave behind the "venomous," "diseased," "rife with germs," "poisonous" atmosphere of the coastal west, which is "neither white not black in colour, neither European nor African in temperament, but a bastard and a mongrel, in whom the vices of two races and two continents are intermingled"

(*VA*, 652). Against this miasmic mixture, the true spirit of the inland plains rises purely:

> The Inland Spirit is one of power, of action and of will. The Inland Spirit is full of vigour and of might, not cunning like the Spirit of the Coast, not intent upon acquiring lucre and well-being, not for ever thinking of an end in view. For what it delights in is activity for action's sake; the struggle for life in sheer joy of battle; the joy of movements; these inspire it with happiness and vital energy. (*VA*, 652)

Finally, Frobenius boldly generalizes this dialectical clash to most African countries, which he sees as split between the coasts, tainted by mercantile exchange, and inland territories still imbued with the idealistic spirit of death-defying heroism.

In fact, Frobenius is more attentive to African *realia* than these broadly epic traits and these mythical dichotomeis suggest. His account of the clashes between the Komaï, those allegedly "disruptive tribes" of North Cameroon, and their Fulbe masters, who enslave them and make them till the land, and the partly blind colonizers of the German administration, is a model in the sociology of colonial mores showing how European power thrives on local oppression (*VA*, 665–9). Like Du Bois, he is aware that quite often the rule of the white man that marked the colonial expedition of the late nineteenth century was disguised as an attempt to stop an indigenous slave-trade. Frobenius concludes his book with a paean to the old African civilization, a culture that should not need the Europeans to find its own roots. This time, the term "symptom" is used in a negative sense: "Does this not supply the evidence of the greatness of the mistake committed in the policy of inciting the people to exercise their own intellectual activity with our modern factors in civilization productively on the Coast, where its results are only grotesque and most undesirable symptoms?" (*VA*, 682). It becomes clear that what was described as an efflorescence of the "Spirit of Africa" is in fact a historical phenomenon; this has been created by men – and Frobenius does not simply accuse the white colonizers, but shows perceptively how the warring factions and tribes contributed to the destabilization of their societies, paving the way to another and wider plunder.

It would be reductive to accuse either Du Bois or Frobenius of being "racist," of believing uncritically in an essence of race that would define specific human groups. If one reads their texts closely, the lingering essentialism is soon replaced by the wish to create "more light" and such an endeavor led them to historicize their discoveries and thus to politicize their analyses.

True, Du Bois aims at being a poet and a prophet of the black race, using what he finds in ethnographic literature as an inspiration to seek equality and freedom. True, Frobenius is a symptomatologist of the continents seen as living cultural organisms, more or less healthy *Erlebte Erdteile*. In 1913, Frobenius would not question German colonialism but aimed at making it more effective and helpful. But he saw the role of the German administration as that of undoing centuries of oppression and slavery, often perpetrated by Muslim conquerors who gave a model to the Europeans: "If we Europeans want to take these people under our protection, we have to behave facing them entirely differently from the islamic half-barbarians who just see them for their financial value."[38] Thus he ended his "Ethiopian" book with a similar admonition: "The poor people who live in Ethiopia know the invaders from the steppes and the more recent conquerors only as a steady and always renewed stream of bloodthirsty slave-hunters, raping women and stealing crops. And when Europeans want to appear as leaders intent upon re-building a strong nation, their efforts do not elicit any confidence."[39] At least he could rejoice that some of them managed to remain independent, or "unpunishable."

Ethiopia was the only name that could be invoked in 1913 to depict both a nation-state and a whole continent. As a synecdoche, Ethiopia described for Frobenius almost all of the northern half of the African continent from the Atlantic coast to the Red Sea. For Du Bois, it allegorized his entire African dream, a nationalist utopia that he tried to make real by exiling himself at the end of his life when he deserted a decidedly racist America and chose to live in exile in Ghana. In 1913, however, Ethiopia called up epic legends, the rich lore of the most ancient races of Africa, ranging from Egypt and its confines to the heart of a dark continent, sending a message of defiance and even hope for a brighter future. If Du Bois remains a Hegelian at heart, Frobenius betrays Nietzschean leanings. The very title of his trilogy confirms this echo: *Und Afrika sprach* calls up *Also sprach Zarathustra*. They both had to "invent" a workable Ethiopia, and they did this without relinquishing a sense of political urgency or agency. Thus Du Bois' "A Philosophy for 1913": a racial manifesto doubling as an anti-racist credo, provided a new year's resolution to which Frobenius, or for that matter Tagore and Apollinaire as well, would have subscribed:

Boldly and without flinching, I will face the hard fact that in this, my fatherland, I must expect insult and discrimination from persons who call themselves philanthropists and Christians and gentlemen. I do not wish to meet this despicable attitude by blows; sometimes I cannot even protest by words; but may God forget me and mine if in time or eternity I ever weakly admit to myself or the world that wrong is not wrong, that insult is not insult, or that color discrimination is anything but an inhuman and damnable shame. . . . In fine, I will be a man and know myself to be one, even among those who secretly and openly deny my manhood, and I shall persistently and unwaveringly seek by every possible method to compel all men to treat me as I treat them.[40]

Chapter 6

The Splintered Subject of Modernism

Du Bois is perhaps most famous for his concept of a divided self: a "double consciousness" defined for him the specificity of an African American identity, yet this "twoness" ("an American, a Negro; two souls, two thoughts, two unreconciled strivings; two warring ideals in one dark body, whose dogged strength alone keeps it from being torn asunder"[1]) can be generalized to most modernist subjectivities. It will be necessary to visit locales like Russia, Germany, Portugal, and France to understand how the birth of modernism was also the birth of a fissile subject. Its roots can be found in deep underlying trends like the aftermath of slavery, Western imperialism, nascent industrialization, a general increase in communication, the speed of travel, and population density, and they surface in the artistic or literary documents of movements like post-symbolism, expressionism, simultaneism, and futurism. However, a constant remains: the newly globalized world entailed either a sharp division or a slower splintering of the old self. A new subjectivity was born at the same time as modernist literature was produced. It was a noticeable groundswell in which the arts, literature and politics gathered speed together so as to undo the old bourgeois sense of self as ownership and "propriety." As Simmel and later Walter Benjamin analyzed the process, modern living habits in big cities hollowed out subjective interiority, reducing the inner life of the mind to the blank recording of sudden juxtapositions and the warding off of countless jolts and shocks. I will survey the patterns of this emerging subjectivity by highlighting several symptoms of its deployment: first, a modern scientific view saw dissection as a new way of probing the innards of man and woman. By applying a mental scalpel to the lyrical self, as we will see in Gottfried Benn's early works, the modern spirit appears as vivisective. The self then explodes in lyrical rhapsodies opening onto echolalic others, as is evinced by Trakl's short career, until the subjective agency disappears as such, layered over with symbols, allegories, and intertextual polyphonies as with Biely, Blok, and Mandelstam. One observes the final dissociation of the self when it generates fully fledged personalities as different selves, as with the "heteronyms" invented by Pessoa and Valery Larbaud.

Benn and Trakl: From Expressionism to Nihilistic Lyricism

Gottfried Benn was perhaps the most radical author of 1913 in that he consciously declared war on the old subjectivity, and systematically sapped its idealistic trappings. He was 26 when he published his first collection, *Morgue and Other Poems*, in 1912. Benn was, like Williams and Céline, a medical doctor, and like Céline became a sympathizer of the National Socialist movement after the war. He had studied at the military hospital in Berlin and left the army in 1912 to perform odd medical jobs in laboratories, sanatoriums, and even cruise ships, which left him free to write at night, after shattering encounters with disease and death. A regular at Café Megalomania where most avant-garde Berlin artists would flock, he had a brief affair with the high priestess of the poetic avant-garde, Else Lasker-Schüler, whose *Hebrew Ballads* had just been published to great acclaim. Lasker-Schüler published Benn's poems in the expressionist magazine *Der Sturm* and warmly praised his verses. When the war broke out, Benn served as a military doctor in Brussels and Antwerpen, where he was in charge of both the army prostitutes and the jail. After the war, he returned to Berlin and specialized in venereal diseases. His play *Home Front*, forcibly reflecting the horror of the war, was couched in a quasi-surrealist language that aggressively expressed revulsion at humanity. This play and the poems were taken as beacons of leftist literature in the post-war years, although Benn had chosen a different camp, turning into a neo-Nazi sympathizer. Later, the Nazis censored him because of his nihilism and his experimental language, and he distanced himself from them, although, like Heidegger in the thirties, he believed that a national revolution would save the German spirit from the morass. It would be an expressionist revolution, similar to the aspirations of the futurists who, for a time, expected the fascist regime to institutionalize avant-garde art.

The 1912 collection *Morgue* was shockingly obsessed with physical decay and the ills of the flesh. Benn's medical expertise conveys a morbid view of humanity as a disease-ridden species bound for the dissecting table. "Little

Aster" presents a "drowned truck-driver propped on the slab" with a lavender aster stuck between his teeth. The doctor "cuts out the tongue and the palate" with a long knife, by accident making the flower slide into the open body. Undisturbed, he sews up the whole, and exclaims: "Rest softly, / little aster!"[2] The utter refusal of sentimentality is enhanced by the poet's bidding adieu to the flower and not to the man – the dead driver is a bag of flesh that one cuts open and sews shut. The only saving grace is a flower even if it, too, is doomed to be forgotten, sewn in the dungeon of a rotting corpse. Another poem evokes a "Night Café" with startling images of walking diseases and bodily defects. After a view of the orchestra, Benn pans on the customers: "Green teeth, pimples in his face, / waves to conjunctivitis. / Grease in his hair / talks to open mouth [. . .] Young goiter is sweet on saddle-nose. / He treats her to three beers." Suddenly, "The door dissolves: a woman. / Desert dried out. Canaanite brown. / Chaste. Full of calves. A scent comes with her. Hardly scent. / It's only a sweet leaning forward of the air / against my brain." The sensual images are brutally deflated: "A paunched obesity waddles after her."[3] The desirably exotic woman is a vision expressed in the poetic equivalent of the speaker's interior monologue, a technique that Benn had mastered early in his prose pieces.[4] Feverish sexual visions tantamount to hallucinatory day-dreaming clash with the sordid reality of degraded flesh.

The collections *Alaska* and *Sons*,[5] both from 1913, appear more properly modernist as the urban setting takes precedence over the dissecting table. These Berlin poems describe subway trains or speed-line trams as claustrophobic hells on rails in which desire and disgust vie with one another. The philosophy becomes more Darwinian, reminding us of our proximity with primal ancestors slithering in a slimy bog. Men are "sickly, corrupted gods"[6] who need to be humiliated by being plunged back into their original element. The lyrical factor recurs under the form of seascapes or Southern vistas. Then, a Romantic or Schopenhauerian wish to become one with nature is presented as a suicidal release slipping back into the maternal element of the sea. For Benn, there is "no consolation here," as he says in a poem with that title. Even a beautiful landscape just calls up "an Illysus with meadowy banks / Eden and Adam and an earth / of nihilism and music.[7] Thus Benn's early poems stage a redoubled nihilism – a reduction of humanity to almost nothing is accompanied by the remedy, which consists in artistic expression, the only purposeful activity remaining in the face of absurdity. Benn anticipates trends and terms of fifties existentialism, while pushing German expressionism toward the standards and criteria of international modernism.

Georg Trakl, too, often enlisted in the expressionist camp, partakes of a similar debunking of the traditional bourgeois ego. While in Vienna, he befriended the controversial architect Alfred Loos and the satirist Karl Kraus, and he was helped financially by Ludwig Wittgenstein. A close companion of Oscar Kokoshka, whose *Franziska*, an expressionist portrait, decorated his bedroom, Trakl would visit the painter's studio near the Prater; both thought his verses to be the linguistic equivalent of expressionist painting. Trakl was defended, in spite of all his shortcomings (drunkenness, addiction to various drugs, and anti-social behavior), by Ludwig von Ficker, who edited the influential magazine *Der Brenner* in which most modernist writers were published. It was thanks to *Der Brenner* that Trakl had a regular outlet for his tortured poems.

1913 was a good year for Trakl since it saw the publication of his first collection, simply called *Poems*, beautifully printed by Kurt Wolff. This slender collection made him well known in the intellectual circles of Vienna. Its poems do not attain the intensity and maturity of the poems published posthumously a year later: Trakl died on November 3, 1914, of an overdose, shortly after a suicide attempt following the battle of Grodek (October 6–11) led to his being committed to the mental health unit of the hospital of the Austrian army. The handsome volume can be described as imagistic in technique, with a stress on melancholia (two poems have that title). Most images are generated by the initial evocation of an autumnal landscape full of pastoral grace, and then a gust of wind, a coming storm, the approach of night make all participants shudder, and evocations of rotting fruit, dead leaves, and suddenly aging characters transform the serene setting into an allegory of irreversible decline, a memento mori and a funereal chant.

A lighter mode is illustrated by "Trumpets," which gives a visual and aural equivalent of wild fanfare music:

> Under trimmed willows, where tanned children play
> And leaves blow, tone trumpets. A churchyard shudder.
> Banners of scarlet crash through the maples' grief,
> Riders along ryefields, empty mills.
>
> Or shepherds sing at night and stags step
> Into the circle of their fire, the grove's ancient sorrow,
> Dancers fling themselves up from a wall;
> Banners of scarlet, laugher, insanity, trumpets.[8]

"Helian," written in January 1913, a more ambitious poem, was presented by Trakl as "the most painful poem I have ever written."[9] Its mood is dark, with disjointed images of madness, leprosy, skulls intermingling. It ends on an intimation of blissful death: "O you crushed eyes in black mouths, / When the grandson in his mind's gentle night, / Lonely, ponders the darker ending, / The quiet god closes his blue eyelids over him."[10] Helian was one of the many masks donned by Trakl, otherwise known as Christ, Elis, Sebastian, Prince Myschkin from *The Idiot*, or Caspar Hauser, the eighteenth-century "innocent" murdered by a mysterious killer. Trakl's "Caspar Hauser Song" rewrites a poem by Verlaine, whose similarity to Trakl is notable, and includes the consumption of alcohol as well as bohemian acting outs. Published in November 1913, "Helian" was inspired by Wassermann's 1908 novel *Caspar Hauser: The Enigma of a Century*.[11] It confirms Trakl's identification with one who is "not-yet born," soon to be murdered. Trakl is categorized as either a "decadent," an "expressionist," or an Austrian "imagist," whose trajectory was too short not to baffle. He kept announcing his doom, reinforced by his incestuous relationship with his sister, whom he had complimented by writing: "Where you walk, there is autumn and evening."[12] Here is the self-dramatization of an Austrian Rimbaud, whose complex relation to Catholicism makes him a precursor of Thomas Bernhard.

The Russian Metamorphosis

In a similar dialectical articulation of literary trends and modified subjectivities, the triumph of symbolism in the first years of the twentieth century marked the Russian "silver age" (from 1895 to 1914). Like Virginia Woolf, Alexander Blok, the most visible poet of Russian symbolism, dated the waning of symbolism and the crisis of the old subjectivity to 1910. He notes that this was the year of Tolstoy's death and adds: "Also in 1910 came the crisis of symbolism . . . In this year, trends emerged which eventually adopted a position hostile both to symbolism and to one another: Acmeism, Egofuturism and the first shoots of Futurism."[13] In the aftermath of the failed 1905 revolution "the hangover of false mysticism" that followed it led to new experiments. No one played a more important role than Andrei Biely in the metamorphosis of late symbolism. Blok's early poems testify to the dynamism of the second wave of Russian symbolism, but after 1911 he was searching for new forms, finally achieving poetic renewal in imagistic vignettes like this one, dated October 10, 1913:

> Night, a street-lamp, a pharmacy.
> A meaningless and murky light.

A quarter of a century
Can pass – no change. No hope of flight.

Die, and go back to the beginning.
Just as before, fate will repeat
Night, the canal's cold waters rippling,
The pharmacy, the lamp, the street.

(Selected Poems, 175)

The lament for an impossible renewal is rendered in a neat chiasmus repeating and inverting the initial series, making us experience a Nietzschean eternal return of the same in a street of St. Petersburg. Blok needed other voices to progress; he found one in a poet whom he saluted early, Anna Akhmatova:

TO ANNA AKHMATOVA

Beauty's terrible, they'll tell you –
Round your shoulders languidly
You will draw a Spanish shawl,
Put a red rose in your hair.

Beauty's simple they will tell you –
Awkward, with your flowered shawl
You will cover up the baby,
Let the rose lie on the floor.

But, as you are listening vaguely
To the words you hear around you,
You will suddenly turn pensive
And will murmur to yourself:

"I'm not terrible or simple,
Not so terrible that I would
Simply murder, or so simple
Not to know life's full of terror."

(Selected Poems, 215; December 16, 1913)

This spin on what Rilke saw just then as the essence of beauty (in the first Duino elegy, "Beauty is only / the first touch of terror / we can still bear"[14]) leads to the feminine by acknowledging that only a woman poet has the right to be terribly simple and innocently dramatic at once. In December 1913, Blok's fantasy of "New America" opposed the barren landscape of

Russia's steppes with images of an Americanized and industrialized country. The heroic past of Russian history with its roll-call of battles, heroes, and fallen soldiers starkly contrasts with the emergence of a modernity defined by industrial progress. The "fierce Cossacks" whose "pigtails are flying" in battle are replaced by "tall factory chimneys," and "factory sirens that scream." The modernity of "A many-floored factory building, / And townships of working-class slums" nevertheless grants a measure of hope for the future: "Yes, above the bleak steppe-lands, the rising / New America shines like a star!" (*Selected Poems*, 245)

The theme of eternal Russia facing the dilemmas of pre-revolutionary times received a different treatment at the hands of the master of the Acmeist school, Osip Mandelstam. The Acmeists accepted the formal heritage of symbolism while rejecting the vague subjectivism and the heady mysticism of its practitioners. Against lyrical wobbliness, they extolled the craft of verse, the discipline of the well-shaped line. Mandelstam's first book of poetry, *Stone*, published in 1913, is thoroughly Acmeist. Most of the poems were given to *Apollo*, where no fewer than three Acmeist manifestos were published in 1913. Acmeism was in advance of its times, announcing the neo-classical experiments of T. S. Eliot and Ezra Pound in the twenties when they returned to the stricter forms, rhymed quatrains. A similar mixture of tones allied with formal virtuosity marks Mandelstam's "Petersburg Stanzas" written in January 1913. They were so powerful that Mayakovsky, then a futurist, immediately memorized them.

> Above the yellow loom of government buildings
> The swirling snow fell thick all through the day;
> Pulling his overcoat close, a law student swings
> His arm out wide, and settles back in his sleigh.
>
> Steamers are moored until spring. Where the sun is hot
> The thick glass of cabin window glows.
> Russia, like some enormous dreadnought,
> Lies at her dock in ponderous repose.
>
> The Neva has embassies from half the globe,
> The sun, the Admiralty, and silence.
> And the state is wearing a stiff purple robe
> As poor as a hair shirt worn, for penitence.
>
> The heavy weight a northern snob must bear
> The ancient burden of Onegin's anguish;
> The wave of a snowdrift on the Senate Square,
> Smoke from a fire, a bayonet's cold flash . . .

147

Skiffs scoop the water, and the gulls
Swoop down to gather on the rigging warehouse
Where *muzhiks* wander, selling spiced drinks and rolls,
As if they were an operetta chorus.

A line of motors rushes through the haze;
Ashamed of his poverty, his walk sedate,
Queer proud Evgeni, with his absurd ways,
Breathes gasoline and curses at his fate.[15]

The stately equipoise of the rhymed lines should not make us forget that Mandelstam grafts onto the "northern metropolis" the modern spirit defined by London, Paris, Berlin, and New York. At the same time, he suggests the permanence of an "acropolis" that connects it to classical Athens and Rome. Elsewhere, he takes as topics "An American Girl" doomed to go down on the *Titanic*, the screening of a "Silent Movie," or a couple playing tennis, then a new Western craze. The main topic of *Stone* is the city, St. Petersburg: the title, *Kamen* (*Stone*) calls up the fact that the name of its founder, Peter I, means "stone." Many poems offer meditations on buildings, such as St. Peter's in Rome, Hagia Sophia, or Notre Dame: the craft of architecture becomes the equivalent for the craft of verse. Behind what look like purely descriptive exercises, one detects the lineaments of an arch social critique.

Mandelstam zooms in on the sites of Russian power: the privileged student leaves a select law school to jump into a sleigh,[16] we see the centers of administrative power, embassies and the Admiralty, an imposing 1809 building to which another poem is devoted (*Stone*, 139). Mandelstam multiplies intertextual layers, refers to Gogol's "The Overcoat," Pushkin's *Eugene Onegin* (Onegin is the "northern snob" alluded to in line 13) and to the latter's *Bronze Horseman*, whose protagonist, Evgeni, is mentioned in the last stanza. Evgeni, "queer" because half-mad, has lost everything after a flood of the Neva; distraught, he curses the bronze horseman, Tsar Peter's equestrian statue. But the horseman pursues him, makes him promise not to curse any more, leaves him raving, demented. Pushkin did not want to choose between imperial absolutism and popular resentment at his oppression. These quoted texts take St. Petersburg as locale, but other topical allusions are more ominous: the dreadnought recalls Russia's ignominious defeat at Port Arthur in January 1905, when the Japanese warships destroyed the Russian fleet. The British navy launched the *Dreadnought* in 1906, in its race against Germany, while remaining suspicious of the Russians, who had sunk a British steam trawler in the North Sea in October 1904. And the glinting bayonets on

Senate Square evoke the brutal suppression of the Decembrist revolt that took place there in 1825, and as recognizably the recent slaughter by the army of hundreds of unarmed strikers who were demonstrating near the Winter Palace on January 22, 1905. Finally, the arresting image of ice-bound ships, a common occurrence, also alludes to Ovid's *Tristia*, a poem that Mandelstam loved and was to use later. Evgeni's helpless curses evoke the general distrust felt by the population for the tsarist regime after 1905, when the Petersburg intelligentsia expected a revolution that was brewing. When it erupted in October 1917, writers like Blok and Biely embraced it but Mandelstam remained cautious.

Such a political reading of the "Petersburg Stanzas" is confirmed by "1913," published in 1914 and included in the second edition of *Stone*:

1913

No triumphs and no war!
O iron ones, how long must we serve,
We who are condemned to preserve
The Capitol secure?

Have the thunderbolts of Rome –
The people's wrath – been tricked?
Do those sharp beaks rest that are fixed
On the orator's tribune?

Or does the sun's battered wagon
Carry bricks of dried clay
And are Rome's rusty keys
Held by one prematurely born?

(*Stone*, 159)

First published in *Apollon* in September 1914 under the title of "Before the War," the poem develops an analogy with classical Rome. The turbulent transition between a dying republic, in which orators like Cicero tried to preserve a balance of powers by using the resources of eloquence, and a "prematurely born" Caesar who came to power by military force, offers an analogy with the ideological tensions rife in 1913. The thunder of war (*peruny*) alludes to the Slavic god of thunder Perun, while calling up the troubled times of international war and the looming civil war. Again, formalist control barely hides a brewing world of social and political unrest, while typically Russian allusions to myth and literature merge with classical lyricism.

Biely's Breakthrough

If the culmination of "high modernism" in the English-speaking world occurred in 1922, it took place in 1913 for Russian literature, first in poetry with Mandelstam's *Stone*, then with Andrei Biely's *Petersburg*. The "Petersburg Stanzas" could serve as an epigraph for the novel in which each chapter is preceded by a quote from Pushkin, mostly from *The Bronze Horseman*. One often hears that *Petersburg* is a Russian *Ulysses*, a comparison which is somewhat overwhelming. True, it is a city-novel, an urban fantasmagoria in which St. Petersburg assumes control over the characters' lives and fantasies; it is also a father-and-son story, and it is linguistically playful and innovative, with sparkling dialogues that instantly dramatize moods. It might be more prudent to say that *Petersburg* stands as the equal of Wyndham Lewis's great novel, *Tarr*. In fact, it looks very much like the *beginning* of *Ulysses*, calling up what Michael Groden has defined as its "initial style,"[17] a style reserved mostly for the sections concerning Stephen Dedalus: a free-floating poetic prose moving from interior monologues to dialogues and third-person vignettes evoking everyday life in the city. If one studies the evolution of Biely's text, one sees that, unlike Joyce who kept on adding for a decade to what was originally a simple story meant for *Dubliners*, Biely worked by concentration and suppression. Biely began writing *Petersburg* in October 1911, and finished his manuscript in November 1913; the novel was published in three issues of *Sirin* (nos 1 and 2 in 1913, no. 3 in 1914), and was published as a book in 1916. Biely rewrote it, abridging it substantially in the Berlin edition of 1922. Symptomatically, he did not avail himself of the war years to expand a text that would include almost everything, as Mann, Proust, and Joyce did, but reduced it to a symbolist novel, making it more tense and also more enigmatic.

Biely began his literary career with a *succès de scandale* in 1902 while he was still a student: the publication of *Dramatic Symphony* opened the artistic salons to him when it turned out that the pseudonym Biely hid a very young man, the son of a gifted mathematician.[18] The success was repeated when he published *The Silver Dove* in a serialized version in 1909, which was one of the first novels to deal with the aborted revolution of 1905. Like *The Silver Dove*, the action of *Petersburg* is situated in 1905, but whereas the second novel is a city novel, *The Silver Dove* takes place in the countryside, and pits a young aristocrat against a sect of mystics. He has left his aristocratic fiancée and been accepted as the progenitor of a future savior of humanity. He is brutally murdered at the end, when the carpenter who is the head of the sect starts becoming jealous of him. Biely believed that

Russian culture was in a state of crisis in 1909–11 (a few of his essays bear the title "The Crisis of Culture"), hoping for a rebirth bound to follow either from the revolution or from a conversion to new values. He finished the first version of *Petersburg* while in Basel, where he and his wife had become disciples of Rudolf Steiner, the inventor of anthroposophism. He came back to Russia on the eve of the revolution. The plot of the novel is in great part shaped by the dealings of a group of mystical anarchists who hope that the son of a prominent politician will blow up his own father with a bomb provided by them. This plot evokes Dostoevsky, half-way between *The Possessed*, with its nihilist conjurations, and *Brothers Karamazov*, with its treatment of the Oedipal murder. It is couched in the style of Gogol, with a distinctively hallucinatory flavor.

Is the novel one single hallucination? At times, Biely seems to say so, as in a letter he wrote just after he had finished *Petersburg*: "The real place where the action of the novel is taking place is the soul of some character not given in the novel, a character overstrained by the working of his brain. [. . .] The whole novel might have been called 'Cerebral Play'."[19] These terms recur throughout the novel; thus, at the end of chapter 1, a brief recapitulation tells us that the two main characters that we have glimpsed, Senator Ableukhov and his son Nikolai, are ephemeral shadows, mere "cerebral play" because produced by the imagination of an internal narrator.[20] This captures well the blurred or cropped contours of most dialogues and reflections that seem to hover between consciousness and daydreams, yet the novel cannot be just the author's dream. Indeed, in a restatement of the same idea close to the end, Biely points to narrative excess, hinting that the contents of the text cannot be subsumed by a single narrator's dream. He explains that although the Senator's wife, Nikolai's mother, has returned home after two years in Spain with her Italian lover, this has not been registered by the main protagonists. The text is laid out like a prose poem:

> These twenty-four hours! –
> – these twenty-four hours of our narrative have expanded and
>   scattered in the spaces of the soul: the authorial gaze has
>   gotten all tangled up in the space of the soul.
> Cerebral, leaden games have plodded along within a closed-in
>   horizon, a circle that has been traced by us –
> – in those twenty-four hours!
> [. . .] And as usual; the heroes of the novel – following our
>   example – had forgotten about Anna Petrovna.
>
> (*Petersburg*, 265)

Biely constructs his narrative like a mirror of the universe in which he participates as a privileged narrator, but this is a post-Einsteinian universe, in which point of view and duration shift constantly. There is no reason to grant the author omniscience – he merely points to ever-expanding spirals of meaning. The author's mind does not contain all the linguistic, narratological, and stylistic games deployed by his textual mechanism.

The novel is built quasi-scientifically by the intersection of three triangles that overlap and dovetail repeatedly: the family triangle, made up of the aging father, suspicious of his rebellious son, unable to bridge the gap between them, and the unexpected return of the mother; the lover's triangle, in which we witness Nikolai's infatuation with Sofya, the flirtatious wife of a friend of Nikolai's; and the triangular political plot, in which the naive revolutionary Doodkin, a student friend of Nikolai, is manipulated by an agent provocateur, Lippanchenko. This is the part of the plot that gives the novel its dynamism, its coherence, and its tension – for Nikolai has mistakenly started the mechanism of the bomb and we hear it ticking most of the time, until it explodes – without killing anyone. The layered plots do not stop there; they encompass the whole city of St. Petersburg, which functions as a key character in a prose-poem devoted to its streets, canals, and monuments. Biely does not gloss over its ruptures and divisions, evoking its two sides, the fashionable area where power resides on the Nevsky Prospect, Russia's "window on Europe," and Vasilyevsky Island, full of working-class slums seething with revolutionary unrest. The class division is connected with a further racial divide: Nikolai and his father Ableukhov come from Khirghiz stock and both identify with the Asian side of Russia. Depressed after the departure of his mother, Nikolai spends his time reading Kant, whose bust is enthroned in his room, meeting suspicious students, pacing up and down in a Bokhara dressing gown wearing a Tartar skullcap. As for the Senator, he has had to go to Tokyo to negotiate a peace treaty following the fall of Port Arthur, and now he sees his son as a young Mongol, which suggests a link between communism and the invasion of Asian tribes bringing "creative destruction."

At the end, while father and mother reunite, Nikolai, who has almost brought about his father's death, flees abroad. He lives in Palestine, where he learns the news of his father's death, and spends some time in Egypt. He has become religious and instead of Kant now reads the Platonist Grigory Skovoroda, the "Russian Socrates" of the eighteenth century. Has he found his center? Is there any center of consciousness? This is doubtful, as the celebrated prologue to the novel states that St. Petersburg cannot function as a center (it is too close to the western border of Russia) and has been displaced by the modern metropolis of Moscow, which became the official capital in 1914. If St. Petersburg is not the capital, the narrator says, there is no Petersburg, its very existence is imaginary: "But if Petersburg is not the capital, then there is no Petersburg. It only appears to exist. // However that may be, Petersburg not only appears to us, but actually does appear – on maps: in the form of two small circles, one set inside the other, with a black dot in the center; and from precisely this mathematical point, which has no dimension, it proclaims forcefully that it exists: from here, from this very point surges and swarms the printed book; from this invisible point speeds the official circular" (*Petersburg*, 2). The Gogolian Skaz creates a spoken narrative mocking official documents and leaving the reader deprived of authorial guidance.

In *Petersburg* we never know exactly what is to be taken seriously and what is the object of ridicule. The best example is the love entanglement of Nikolai with Sofya. Nikolai tries to attract her attention by disguising himself as a red domino, but he keeps stumbling in his garments. Sofya, ambivalent about the affair, at once wants him and rejects him. She prefers being courted by all sorts of suitors while being safely married to an estranged officer – her mouth is seen from the start as adorned with a suspicious black moustache. When Likutin, her husband, attempts to commit suicide after Sofya has disobeyed his orders not to go to a party in which she will meet Nikolai, he does hang himself but merely cause the ceiling of his room to collapse. Yet, despite its grotesque tonality, this scene suddenly turns into a moment of peace and happiness when the couple reunite in the rosy light of dawn.

Sofya reads both Annie Besant, following whom she organizes spiritualist séances, and Karl Marx (she has memorized the *Communist Manifesto*). It is clear that Biely ironizes his former passion for Alexander Blok's wife, Liubov Dmitrievna, who had flirted with him, hesitated, dallied again, and then rejected him between 1904 and 1906. Irony is dominant and corrosive in a novel whose tone is hard to ascertain even when it touches on themes that are close to Steiner's anthroposophism. Biely wrote the chapter in which Nikolai arms the bomb and then falls asleep, his head on the bomb hidden in a sardine can, just a few hours after having heard a talk by Rudolph Steiner. In this passage, Nikolai enters a sort of trance, sees all his Asian ancestors, Tibetan lamas, Buddha, and Confucius, up to the god Kronos, and decides to equate Nirvana with Nothingness. He will be agent of the destruction of European values by Mongolian hordes . . . This scene of an oniric Last Judgment is thus presented as an aberration, and the epilogue makes it clear that Nikolai had to grapple more deeply with the Egyptian Book of the Dead and with the origins of monotheism. Was the Apocalypse merely a parody then? Biely does not provide a clue, and suggests simply that it will take more than the Russian Revolution to reach a definitive answer.

The only stable certainty is provided by the book's musical structure – and Schopenhauer, who praised music above all other arts, remained Biely's guide, although such certainty bypasses individual psychology. Music offers a resolution of the subjective tensions by creating a state akin to contemplation. Already in 1905, Biely had rejected Dostoevsky for not being musical enough. The musicality of his prose makes this novel a long prose poem, all the while caught in tightly composed plot, with suspense created by the constantly ticking bomb. In that sense, it is more of a novel than *Ulysses*, in which, with the exception of Molly's infidelity, very little happens, whereas *Petersburg* keeps its social and political relevance. It is a modernist novel even if it was written by a "reluctant modernist." The modernism comes to the fore in literary techniques, in the use of a free indirect speech tantamount to inner monologue, in the numerous verbal leitmotifs and ironically repeated phrases and sentences, and in the playfulness of the language that often engages in jokes, puns, and double entendres. Modernist too is the overarching perspectivism that makes the point of view shift all the time, multiplying ambiguities while integrating modern science so as to educate the reader.[21] Mikhail Bakhtin was just beginning his studies at the time, and his concepts of open multi-voicedness and heteroglossia marked the Russian reception of the novel,[22] as they describe well Biely's masterpiece in which symbolism is metamorphosed into a stylistic "heteroglossia." This "explodes" the author's attempts at reinstating his "monologic" vision since a bomb has indeed exploded at the end, shattering the old novel and its stable subject. It was a stylistic bomb as well as the bomb of the Russian Revolution: in the final version, Biely added just one sentence to the novel in the epilogue: "There will be an explosion: everything will be swept away" (*Petersburg*, 292).

Pessoa's Incipient Heteronymity

Another explosion would radically transform Fernando Pessoa in Portugal. It affected his body, his "soul," and his name, and it was dependent upon another revolution. Pessoa had returned to Lisbon from South Africa in October 1906, and in 1913 found himself caught up in a whirl of intense creativity. He had experienced the jolt of the 1910 revolution, which forced Manuel II to abdicate, as a call for freedom and modernization. In 1912,

Pessoa started contributing to new literary magazines like *A Aguia*. He described his mental turmoil in February 1913 to his mentor Sà-Carneiro:

> At present I'm going through one of those crises which they usually call, in agriculture, crises of over-abundance. Ideas come to my mind so fast, so abundantly that I have to carry a notebook, and even then the number of pages I fill is so great that I get lost, because there are too many, and other pages I can't decipher because I wrote them too fast. That I lose ideas is an acute torture for me, and the ideas pursue me, obscurely changed, to torture me more.[23]

The letter lists all the new concepts that jostle, half-realized, in his mind: "Verses in English, in Portuguese, reflections, ideas, projects, fragments about which I understand nothing except that they exist, letters with neither beginning nor endings, critical flashes, metaphysical murmurs . . . A whole literature, my dear Mario, which comes from a mist, passes through a mist, vanishes into a mist . . ."[24] This would become a constant complaint for Pessoa, the feeling of such an exorbitant profusion accounting for the almost inevitable creation of "heteronyms," those literary alter egos, distinctive pseudonyms endowed with a whole identity, a style, a date of birth and even an astrological chart. In the multiplication of potentialities, he was like Roussel, whose had reached a sudden "glory" making him the equal of the greatest. But Pessoa was saved from delirious megalomania (even if he was often afraid of becoming insane) by the very fragmentation of his projects. Indeed, his preferred model was Shakespeare, and what he admired most in the Bard was his utter absence of personality.

In 1913 Fernando Pessoa had not yet invented his main heteronyms; Alberto Caeiro, Ricardo Reis, and Alvaro de Capos came to him in March and June 1914. But it was in 1913 that he fully assumed a creative role in Lisbon. To memorialize this, he started collecting the autobiographical prose fragments of *The Book of Disquietude* in a Lusitanian equivalent of Rilke's *Notebooks of Malte Laurids Brigge*. Pessoa kept adding entries to these notebooks all his life. The first fragment to be written, "In the Forest of Estrangement," was published in a review in 1913. At that time, Pessoa was also busy adapting futurism to his literary aims, filtered as they were through a purely Portuguese context. Curiously, this led him to write, in May 1913, a long poem in English, "Epithalamium" just as he was looking for ways to combine his new-found ventriloquism with movements like neo-classicism, late Romanticism, Whitmanian lyricism, paganism, and modernism. To Pessoa's restless and burning mind, all these styles had to be granted an equal chance of finding a medium of expression. In March 1913 he wrote the influential poem entitled "Impressions of Twilight," better known as "Pauis," a free-verse experiment that gave its name to a short-lived movement, "paulismo," after it was published to great acclaim in *Renascença* in February 1914. It struck his readers as unprecedented in Lusitanian poetry:

> Quagmires grazing qualms of anguish through my soul in gold . . .
> Distant tolling of Other Bells . . . The gold wheat
> Pales in the cinders of sunset . . . A carnal thread runs through my soul . . .
> So identically same, the Hour! . . . Swaying tops of palms . . .
> Silence stared at us by leaves . . . Slim autumn
> Of a vague bird's song . . . Forgotten blue, stagnant . . .
> Oh what mute cry of agony claws at the Hour!
> Wonders in me yearn for something else than these cries!
> I hold out my hands beyond, but holding them I see
> That what I want is not what I desire . . .
> Cymbals of Imperfection . . . So much antiquity
> Of the Hour expelled from self of Time! . . . Receding wave that invades
> A self abandoned by myself until I faint,
> A present I remember so well that I feel myself forgetting! . . .
> Fluid of aureole, transparent Was, hollow from holding to itself . . .
> The mystery knows my otherness . . . Moonlight falls on the
>   uncontainable . . .
> The sentinel is rigid – his lance driven to the ground
> Rises higher than he is . . . What is all this for . . . Day is ground . . .
> Climbing vines of irrelevance licking the Beyonds of every Hour . . .
> Horizons closing eyes to space where errors are linked in a chain . . .
> Opium fanfares of future silences . . . Long trains . . .
> Long gates seen afar . . . through the trees . . . so much iron![25]

The disconnected and hallucinatory images evoke the disjointed ejaculations of Schoenberg's hysterical female narrator in *Erwartung*, with poetic echoes of Rimbaud's synesthetic visions. What stands out in this medley of uncoordinated (although in strictly rhyming lines) impressions is the subtle way in which Pessoa pushes Romantic longing to an extremity of subjective dispossession. He asserts once more that "I *is* another," as Rimbaud famously put it, analyzing with astute precision how one can catch oneself forgetting at the very moment one is remembering, how one can be and not be oneself at once, how it is quite common to realize that one desires one thing and wants another. He hits all at once on what will become his main theme in an excessive, almost parodic poem, which stages the systematic dissociation of the self. The self's baroque explosions find a counterpart, in the literary advantages that can be drawn from the abandon of a classical concept of personality.

Darlene Sadlier has pointed out that the poem, reproduced by itself in Pessoa's poetic collections in Portuguese, should be printed with the first section that accompanied it when it was published in *Renascença*. This section presents a classical evocation of the bell of the village in four rhymed quatrains that seem to be the pretext for the anguished meditation that we have read:

> Oh bell of my village,
> Dolorous in the calm evening,
> Each one of your peals,
> Rings deep within my soul.
>
> And so slow is your ringing,
> So unhappy with life,
> That the first stroke already
> Sounds like a repetition.
>
> For as much as you toll near me
> When errant and sad I pass,
> To me you are like a dream –
> Always sounding distant . . .
>
> For every one of your rings
> Vibrating in the open sky,
> I feel the past farther away,
> I feel a longing [*saudade*] closer by.[26]

The juxtaposition of different stylistic renderings of one canonical theme, the "sad longing" or *saudade* brought about by the melancholy ringing of an evening bell, betrays a dialectical method that is not devoid of histrionic aspects. This came to the fore in 1914 when Pessoa gave voice at once to all his opposite subjectivities, beginning with the neo-classical Ricardo Reis and the "pagan" or Whitmanian Alvaro de Campos. The technique of variation on a theme allows style to reveal its opacity: language cannot be thought of as transparent; it becomes a dynamic and autonomous medium in which the weight of culture is brought to bear on a labile self who morphs completely at the suggestion of poetic iridescences. This is why there was no "first ring": in Pessoa's modernist world-view, repetition comes first and *is* original.

Among the languages in play, none was more important for Pessoa than English, a language in which he had been schooled in South Africa. Among the first poems written in English is the "Epithalamium" of 1913, a paean to sexual desire and profane love extending to 21 sections. As Pessoa wrote to a friend in November 1930, "Antinous" and "Epithalamium" were his only productions that could be called "obscene."[27] Even if he was truly fluent in English, he was aware that his command over the language of Shakespeare was derivative, which accounts for the audacity of these two poems. They form a diptych, "Antinous" (1915) dealing with same-sex love (we hear Hadrian lamenting the death of his youthful lover) while "Epithalamium" starts from an anonymous wedding to sing the joys of heterosexual love. "Epithalamium" describes one single day: it begins with the sun shining in the morning on a young bride still dreaming until she has to dress for the wedding ceremony, which is followed by a dinner and wild party, and then the night comes, bringing more boisterous revelry. The main influences on Pessoa's English poetry were Shakespeare (a little later, he turned out 33 rather competent Shakespearian sonnets), Keats, and Poe. "Epithalamium" reads at times like a retranslation into English of a Portuguese version of the "Eve of St Agnes." What is fascinating is the degree of explicitness that Pessoa allows himself. Here, he evokes the young woman's initial fear of defloration:

> Between her and the ceiling this day's ending
> A man's weight will be bending.
> Lo! With the thought her legs she twines, well knowing
> A hand will part them then;
> Fearing that entering in her, that allowing
> That will make softness begin rude at pain.
>
> (*OP*, 613)

The stilted language is both bucolic and nostalgic, its tonality ranging from Virgil to Dutch paintings suggesting uninhibited license. It is a "Flemish hour" (*OP*, 618) when "the bull climbs on the heifer mightily!" (*OP*, 613). A "red bacchic surge of thoughts" (*OP*, 617) accompanies the delight taken in the pleasures of the flesh. The pagan love song begins with the bride's fears and fantasies in the morning and shifts to the bridegroom's erotic longings during the dinner.

> The bridegroom aches for the end of this and lusts
> To know those paps in sucking gusts,
> To put his hand first on that belly's hair
> And feel for the lipped lair,

The fortress made but to be taken, for which
He feels the battering ram grow large and itch.

(OP, 616)

Sexual delirium is soon shared by all, young and old; older people remember how they "paired and the night sawn / The day come in and [. . .] did still pant close, / And still the half-fallen flesh distending rose" (*OP*, 616). The frenzy turns into a universal plea for unrestrained copulation. The sprinkling of archaic phrases lends to this materialistic paean a surrealist tinge along with its flow of rhythmic clichés: "Put out of mind all things save flesh and giving / The male milk that makes living!" (*OP*, 618). The evocation is not without grandeur:

> Io! Io! There runs a juice of pleasure's rage
> Through these frames' mesh,
> That now do really ache to strip and wage
> Upon each other's flesh
> The war that fills the womb and puts the milk in
> The teats a man did win
> The battle fought with rage to join and fit
> And not to hurt or hit!
>
> *(OP*, 618)

The finale reconciles the participants with the night as the cycle is completed: now, as all the lovers are busily engaged in amorous jousts or, if they sleep, dream of desire. The stars pale, a new day comes in the east, to let "with clamour of joy and life's young din / The warm new day come in" (*OP*, 619–20). It has too often been said that Pessoa's English poems – the only book that he published in his lifetime was a collection of English sonnets – are conventional and do not live up to the excitement generated by his heteronyms. But the English language itself functioned as a heteronym for Pessoa, allowing him to explore issues that he would never have broached in Portuguese. In these poems, he confronts headlong that sense of division out of which he wrote in so many voices. Another English poem from 1913 condenses this mood, this time in the mode of Poe more than of Keats. I'll just quote the beginning:

THE ABYSS

> Between me and my consciousness
> Is an abyss

159

At whose invisible bottom runs
The noise of a stream far from
Whose very sound is dark and cold –
    Ay, on some skin of our soul's deeming,
Cold and dark and terribly old,
    Itself, and not in its told seeming.

My hearing has become my seeing
    Of that placelessly sunken stream.
Its noiseless noise is ever freeing
    My thought from my thought's power to dream.

                          (*OP*, 623)

In 1913 Pessoa gave a unique voice to the alienation brought about by subjective dissociation, especially when it grasps its determination by the unconscious. The cold stream prevents thought from focusing on noble themes like God, the World, or Reality. A decade before Artaud's famous letters to Jacques Rivière, in which the erosion of his very thought is documented at length, Pessoa expresses the modern angst generated by the self's dispossession as a result of the structure of language. "Although I'm constantly in search of myself, nevertheless I'm still afraid to find me, to avoid the chance that I'll find myself to be somebody else," the well-named Pessoa (his name means "nobody") wrote in a typical admission of ambivalence in a letter dated April 8, 1913. Nevertheless, his vaporous or pulverous subjectivity that pulls itself out of the void again and again, often by multiplying its masks, to rise out of a lurking disaster or madness, is the best basis for the launching of a new modernism, both intensely local, therefore full of Lusitanian pathos and *saudade*, and totally cosmopolitan, deliberately open (or "ope" in Pessoa's idiosyncratic English) to the influences of a world culture.

Larbaud's Inner Dialogics

A similar problem was a point of departure for a writer who is rarely associated with Pessoa, Valery Larbaud. Larbaud's beginnings were more auspicious, as he was heir to a fortune in Vichy water, and extremely gifted in languages. This gave him leisure to travel through the whole world at an early age, but he was determined to leave a mark in literature as more than just a gifted amateur or translator. For his first literary endeavors, he chose the mask of an English man, A. O. Barnabooth, supposed to be both a millionaire and a poet. Barnabooth's first poems were written in 1902, after Larbaud had manifested his enthusiasm for Whitman, whose poems he

started translating in 1899, when he was barely 18. In 1908 Larbaud pub-
lished anonymously a collection of poems entitled simply *Poems by a Rich
Amateur*. It was preceded by a biographical note; it added to the poems
supposedly written by Barnabooth an ironical short story making fun of
Barnabooth's infatuation with the daughter of a poor shirt-maker. In 1913,
Larbaud thoroughly revised the book, and decided to sign it with his name.
This became Larbaud's edition of *A. O. Barnabooth, his Collected Works Con-
sisting of his Tale, Poems and his Personal Diary*. Larbaud reduced by half the
original poems, deleted the long biographical note, and added a pseudo-
autobiographical journal, in fact a real novel of about 220 pages written
in the first person. In the end, Barnabooth marries one of the waifs he has
saved from prostitution in London, and returns with her to the place of
his birth, Arequipa, a territory disputed by Chile, Bolivia, and Peru. Now a
citizen of the world, he bids adieu to Europe, whose looming conflagration
he foresees.

The 1913 changes were felicitous: Larbaud modified the image of the
writer, as the original portrait veered uneasily between facile satire (the
"rich amateur" was too outspoken in his contempt for the poor and too
boastful of the infantile gratification of his whims) and a fantasmatic projection in an idealized double (like Larbaud, Barnabooth loved travels less for
the sense of luxury they provided than for the opportunity of multiplying
encounters with low life, stumbling on gritty facts in unexpected contexts,
in short enriching oneself with new experiences). Barnabooth, like Larbaud,
confessed to the pleasure he would take in debased popular culture, snatches
of song, local kitsch. Talking of literature, he said: "I only like second rate
works."[28] Indeed, the poems are replete with direct quotes and oblique allusions to Walt Whitman, many Spanish poets, and lesser French writers.
Afraid that readers would mistake the author for Barnabooth, in 1913 Larbaud
decided to tone down the portrait and make the millionaire less unbearably
pretentious, less satisfied with his money. Like Pessoa, he deals with the
needs of the body, and the poetic part is divided in two parts, *"Borborygmes"*
(stomach rumbles) and "Europe."

The whirl of colored, exotic names that make up most of the poems
would become tedious if it was not underlain by a constant concern for the
demands of the body ("Stomach-rumbles! Stomach-rumbles! . . . / Dull groans
rise from stomach and tripe / Complaints of an always altered flesh / Voices,
the irrepressible whisper of organs, / Voice, the only human voice that doesn't
lie, / That persists even after physiological death . . ."[29]) The travels in luxury
trains, yachts, or steamers throughout the world make us glimpse vignettes
of Venice, the Lipari Islands, Naples, Cahors, London, the Bosporus, Odessa,

Mers-el-Kébir, Schveningen, Barcelona, Kharkov, Copenhagen, Rotterdam, Cordoba, Seville, Montenegro, Colombo, Nagasaki, Croatia, Stockholm, Berlin, San Francisco, and Chicago, and yet in all this tumbling whorl it is Europe that is the main object of the poet's love and critique:

> I sing Europe, its railroads and theaters
> And its constellations of cities, and yet
> I bring in my verses the spoils of a new world . . .[30]

He wishes to bring to Europe the raw colors of other continents, and his muse is a Creole woman. Although Larbaud believed that Whitman could be grafted onto French culture (a program which, as we have seen, was not far from Cendrars' project), he is not entirely sure that he is the man to complete it, which is why this particular poem ends with the wry question: wasn't this just another stomach-rumble?

The adoption of the persona of an idle millionaire was not without risks. Of course, one should not confuse Larbaud and Barnabooth, who, if he was rich enough, was not a millionaire; besides, here and there, Barnabooth accuses a certain V. L. of making fun of him![31] In that sly game with disguises, Barnabooth embodies the dream of absolute freedom; the diary's initial title was "Diary of a Free Man." His unlimited fortune allows him to realize his wildest dreams; yet we see him fail there as well. He indulges his eccentricities, can be as fastidious and blasé as he wants, but remains incorrigibly naive and often duped. At one point, during a stay in Florence, he falls in love with the "plebeian" Florrie Bailey, a beautiful British woman who had sent him a billet-doux signed "Heart's Desire."[32] Seized, as he is regularly, by the desire to marry a plebeian so as to make amends for his useless riches, he proposes to her. He then learns from his accountant that she is nothing but a hired detective who is watching him, that she used to be a prostitute compromisingly immortalized in pornographic photographs. He persists in this project until Florrie herself rejects him: she prefers freedom to living with a millionaire whom she finds serious, dull, and boring. When he finally marries Conception Yarza, the young girl saved from the gutter, his accountant takes this to be another passing whim.[33] We too may wonder whether this move is final, even if it has the redemptive quality that he was looking for. His main wish is to flee the Old World and return to his roots in South America. At the end of the journal, the "rich amateur" notes that he is forgetting French: "I am now losing the habit of thinking in French."[34] Thinking in Spanish is a first step in the decision to "drop everything he has ever owned." He will live on a ranch and promises that he will stop writing a journal – or writing at all. The end of the cosmopolitan dream marks Larbaud's renunciation of masks and heteronyms. His evolution is inversely parallel to that of Pessoa, whose linguistic ventriloquism and stylistic "heteronymity" reconcile modernism, nationalism, and cosmopolitanism.

The poetic epilogue added during the revisions of 1913 states Barnabooth's decision to start a new life outside Europe. This enacted Larbaud's own farewell to poetic writing, for after this last poem he limited himself to the medium of prose. Barnabooth's rejection of Europe does not preclude nostalgia for the England of his youth. This epilogue expresses fears and dark forebodings, as the terrible clash approaches. The poet sees a widening gap between the Roman side and the German side of Europe:

> I will remember European life:
> The smiling past leaning on roofs,
> The bells, the meadows of the commons, the quiet voices,
> The fog and tramways, the beautiful gardens and
> The smooth blue waters of the South. [. . .]
> And I will remember this place where winter
> Inhabits the heart of Summer months:
> This icy place, with black rocks and black skies,
> Where in pure silence,
> High above all Europe.
> Germania and Rome meet.[35]

In this text as in history, only "death's bony hand"[36] could write the real epilogue. It contains just one word: "Finis."

Chapter 7

At War with Oneself: The Last Cosmopolitan Travels of German and Austrian Modernism

Among European countries in 1913, none was more aware of the threat of a looming war than Austria. War seemed all but inevitable; it would be brought about by nationalist aspirations unleashed in parts of the old empire, especially among Slav minorities encouraged by a young, forceful, and arrogant Serbia. Nationalism in its turn had fueled anti-semitism, much as the reawakening of the American South had fueled anti-black racism in the US, and it also generated an aggressive militarism. One of the ironies that were rife in German culture at that time is condensed in one name, Bernhardi. In 1912, Arthur Schnitzler published a controversial play, *Professor Bernhardi*, in which the eponymous hero, a Jewish doctor, refuses to let a priest have access to a dying patient in order to save the latter's peace of mind. The play was immediately censored in Vienna, but soon rehearsed in Berlin and Munich. Early in 1913, Karl Krauss attacked Schnitzler for being too provocative, although he said that he sided with the humanist doctor's point of view.[1] This polemic generated a heated discussion about anti-semitism. Not long after, General Friedrich von Bernhardi from the German army admonished his country openly when he published the blandly titled *Germany and the Next War* in 1913.

It is no accident that the theme of war ran like a red thread through most modernist masterpieces of the period, even if it was a war against oneself, within one poetic or novelistic subject, or within a European totality seen as a subject. Those who believed in the unity of Europe often also believed in a stable subjectivity. As we have seen, the destruction of an Old World cosmopolitanism was accompanied by the release of new energies.

Harnessing the energies of war to new artistic movements was not limited to futurism, as we will see with authors like Rilke, Mann, Kafka, and Hugo von Hofmannsthal.

I will use the issue of international travel as a way of exploring the concept of totality and its limits. In the first decade of the twentieth century one could still travel from England to Prussia, Austro-Hungary, or Italy without a passport; Russia was the only country that demanded passports and visas at the border, and a visa was needed to leave as well.[2] The situation changed after the war, with national passports issued everywhere. In the last autumn of this peaceful progression from country to country, no writer had moved back and forth as often as Rilke. He had visited Russia with Lou Andreas-Salome, and lived in Austria, Germany, France, Italy, Spain, and Switzerland. Like Rilke, Thomas Mann surmised that the Old World cosmopolitanism was dying. In their poems and fictions they staged this slow death. Hofmannsthal and Kafka traveled much less, and pointed out the dangers or the impossibility of mobility. They make us perceive that the danger comes not so much from death itself as from its obscure twin, infinity. They both fear and enact the vertigo of infinite regress. As Hermann Broch wrote about Joyce, with oblique reference to Kafka and Hofmannsthal, when artists take upon themselves the task of "representing totality without believing in it," then the danger of infinity is all the more pressing since "the infinite and death are born of the same mother."[3]

Rilke after Duino: The Spanish Exile

Rilke's life and career are emblematic of the fate of cosmopolitan artists in 1913. Rilke's German family lived in Prague; he was therefore Austrian but spent his life in Germany before settling in Paris, where he had found a master in the famous sculptor Rodin. The year 1913 nevertheless marked a second and final break with Rodin, at a time when we see the poet making a clear decision in favor of autonomy and modernism. He had come to Duino near Trieste, breaking with his usual pattern of restless travels in Europe. In 1912, staying in Duino castle for a second, longer and more productive, visit, Rilke, always the perfect guest, got involved in his benefactor's passion, spiritualism. He was happy enough to play the part of "court poet" to his patroness, the princess of Thurn and Taxis, who organized séances in September and October 1912 in the castle so as to allow her son Pasha to display his power as a medium. Rilke watched, and when the automatic writing produced on an Ouija board connected them with an "Unknown

Lady" beckoning them from a bridge, he immediately recognized Toledo and took this as his cue. Already he was longing to see El Greco's paintings, and almost immediately, in his nomadic fashion, Rilke decided to leave Duino for Spain and made arrangements to spend the winter in Toledo.[4] Behind him he left the straggling first three elegies along with other unfinished drafts. He had to go abroad to learn how to make one single "thing" (a poem, a book) with all his fragments.

The culture of spiritualism belongs fully to modernism, as Helen Sword has demonstrated.[5] Her ample survey testifies to the productive way in which most modernist poets, writers, and artists could invoke famous or anonymous ghosts. Hesitating between urbane skepticism and a "Celtic" suspension of disbelief, poets like Yeats took messages sent from beyond the grave to fan the fires of inspiration. In Rilke's career they would alleviate writer's block. Earlier in 1912, Rilke had had a momentous encounter with an angel, in the form of a voice that came to him from stormy ocean clouds and gave him, mouthed in the pandemonium of a sea-tempest, the famous opening lines of the first Duino elegy:

Wer, wenn ich schriee, hörte mich denn aus der Engel / Ordnungen?

[Who, if I cried out, would hear me then in those angelic / Orders?]

The belief in spirits and otherworldly manifestations allowed modernist poets to adapt ancient ideas of daimonic inspiration to modern times. Whether it be an angel's voice speaking in the clouds or an invisible hand writing words letter by letter in a séance's shadows, mediumistic transmission marked the return of a conception of influence that bypasses Romantic theories of inspiration. As Hölderlin said, even if the gods will not return, they still manifest themselves through subtle signs. Such hope underpins Rilke's sustained meditation on men, angels, and gods that provided the initial impetus for the first Duino elegies. It breaks with the remnants of a distant and estheticized Catholicism by opting for a purely pagan angel, a messenger who brings good tidings by orienting poetic inspiration. The return of inspiration is conveyed in one of the densest statements of Rilkean poetics, the much-admired Spanish trilogy from 1913.

Following the dark woman's injunction, Rilke traveled to Spain at the end of 1912, arriving in Toledo, a city that impressed him more by its architecture and setting than by its artistic treasures. The weather was bad, so he decided to push further south, first to Cordoba and Seville, then on to Ronda. He stayed in Ronda from the end of 1912 till the middle of February 1913. The small city's unique situation, perched atop two high mountains

cut by a deep gorge, was an ideally dramatic setting for solitary walks, during
which he came up with a number of poems. Freed from his old demons and
neurotic ailments, Rilke found peace in extreme solitude as he was the only
guest in the local British hotel. He saw himself turning into a medieval saint
or St. Francis of Assisi. The southern Spanish mixture of Islamic, Christian,
and pagan elements corresponded to the non-confessional religiosity that
he had been groping for in Duino. A time of ecstatic retreat was needed to
make sense of the welter of new images, meditations, and invocations that
had invaded him with the first two elegies, the third one still unfinished.
The "Spanish trilogy" poses the question of *poesis*, asking how it is possible
to make a "thing" out of the diversity of experience and the depth of subjective suffering. It does so in a recognizable Spanish landscape, with
scudding clouds, jagged mountains, deep gorges. All the details of the scenery
bring grist to the poetic mill and create a "something," almost a meteor
whose curve seems to be suddenly meaningful.

> . . . from me alone and all I don't know,
> to make the thing, Lord Lord Lord, the thing
> that, cosmic-terrestrial, like a meteor
> collects in its gravity only the sum of flight:
> weighing nothing finally but arrival.[6]

The second part of the trilogy probes his earlier restlessness, now seen as a
prerequisite for the maturation of poetry. Wondering why he must wander
around always carrying heavy intellectual baggage, the speaker compares
himself to a porter who "hefts from stall to stall the market basket / that keeps
filling up, while he, weighed down, follows / and can never ask: Master,
why this feast?"[7] The physical transmutation of lived experience into "blood"
and "music" depends upon the heroism of the poet who boldly faces the
stars, relinquishing the sensual comfort of a shared bed. The third section
concludes by opposing the chaos of modern life in a metropolis with the
absolute certainty granted by instants of sacred communion with nature.
Having reached a fixed point, the poet will feel secure, protected by a god
who will even abolish death.

> But may I, when again I have the city's crush
> and tangled noise-skein and furor
> of its traffic wrapped around me, alone,
> may I above that thick confusion
> recall sky and the gentle mountain rim
> on which the far-off plodding herd curved homeward.

He sees himself as a shepherd visited by a god:

> Even now a god might
> slip into this form and not be lessened.
> Alternately he moves and lingers, like the day itself,
> and the shadows of the clouds
> pass through him, as though space were slowly
> thinking thoughts for him.

> Make of him whom you will. Like a wind-whipped nightflame
> into the lamp's mantle I place myself inside him.
> A flare grows steady. Might Death
> less darkly find its way.[8]

The mystical heroism discovered in Ronda led to the drafting of the sixth Duino elegy, a meditation on heroes whose death, like the untimely disappearance of children, paradoxically affirms life. All these were symptoms of a great change, a transformation in Rilke's body and soul, as he wrote in January 1913 from Ronda: "I feel these are only interminable peripeteias of a great transformation taking place within me, body and soul completely changing, molecule by molecule . . . if I can succeed in supporting it, eternity will come afterwards, no matter where I find myself."[9] Having overcome his neurotic inhibitions in Spain, Rilke returned to Paris. There, he was able to keep his distance from his erstwhile mentor, Rodin, who stubbornly refused to sit for his ex-wife. The slight tipped the balance, and Rilke never contacted him again. He then finished the third Duino elegy dealing with sexual love, in which "the blood's hidden guilty water-god" is coupled with a mother who lets the child confront his old terrors and dare go out into "violent Beginning."[10] He had successfully outgrown his fin-de-siècle estheticism and opted for high modernism;[11] Rilke would now embark on the last phase of his poetic career, which culminated with the completed elegies and the cycle of the Orpheus sonnets.

Thomas Mann after *Death in Venice*

A similar confrontation with death presided over Thomas Mann's literary activity in 1913. It connected two stays in different places, Venice and Davos. The first concerns the origin of *Death in Venice*, first published as a novella in 1912, then in book form in 1913. It derives from a vacation at the Hotel des Bains in the Lido in Venice with his wife Katja, where Mann was attracted to a beautiful Polish adolescent, Wladislaw Moes. He used this incident as the basis for a story in which he projected himself onto the figure of an aging and successful writer, Gustav Aschenbach. Aschenbach, 17 years older than Mann actually was, fascinated by the beauty of Tadzio, the seductive ephebe, over-extends his stay in Venice despite an epidemic of cholera. Finally, he lets himself die, absurdly rouged and beautified, swooning to death in a last contemplation of the shapely boy. Mann's second stay led to *The Magic Mountain*. From March to September 1912, Katja Mann was treated in Davos for a lung infection that looked tubercular. To be with her, Mann spent three weeks between May and June in a sanatorium there. Having arrived in Davos, where he had planned to complete *Death in Venice*, he felt feverish himself, and the doctor jokingly asserted that he too was tubercular. Although he did not stay, having charge of their four children, the incident yielded the plan of a narrative that would be the antithesis or the "antidote" to *Death in Venice*. What was played out in sensuous detail as the Romantic and Wagnerian fascination for the *Liebestod* motif in the Venice allegory would be transformed into an affirmation of life, when Settembrini's loquacious humanism met Castorp's eagerness to learn and to mature.

As Mann wrote in July 1913, the comedic tone of the sanatorium story should offset the darker Nietzschean tragedy that befalls Aschenbach on the beach of the Lido. Both stories start from a moment that breaks with the humdrum routine of work, and the holiday decided upon either for relaxation or to recover from disease integrates the characters into groups of foreign nationals, while the protagonists' erotic encounters with Tadzio and Clavdia Chauchat affect their willpower and upset their moral balance for good. Castorp had planned to stay for just three weeks when he visited his cousin, but he ends up spending seven years of his life in the Berghof sanatorium. These seven years cover the period leading up to the First World War, and the last glimpse that we have of Castorp, finally cured, is that of a man stumbling in mud, dodging exploding shells in a horrific battle, a collective demise that calls up, among many others, the fate of Freud's patient, the "rat-man," who died in the war just after being cured from his neurosis.[12]

The war forced Mann, like Joyce and Proust, to take longer than expected to complete his novel, which turned into a universal receptacle capable of incorporating a wider range of topics and meditations. It was set aside between August 1915 and April 1919, and finished in 1924. Responding to the political and ethical turmoil created by the world war, Mann engaged in critical debate with his elder brother in his *Reflections of a Non-Political Man* (1918). However, the idea of presenting a cross-section of European cultures and mentalities in the years before 1914 was there from the start, with the French, Dutch, Russian, English, and German inhabitants of the sanatorium. The ideological antagonism between Settembrini and Naphta was there as well. Like Biely, Mann developed the clash between an "Asian" concept of the state coupled with a passive irrationalism, and a "Western" rationalism praising the qualities of individuality and responsibility, developed at length by Settembrini in the speeches articulating his opposition to the proto-fascist Naphta, who only thinks in terms of collective social beings. *The Magic Mountain* may be the most systematic attempt to describe, analyze, and diagnose the components of the pre-war spirit that reigned in 1913.

Such a diagnosis had been prepared by *Death in Venice* (*DV*). The first words of the tale signal the precarious situation of Europe: "On a spring afternoon in 19–, the year in which for months on end so grave a threat seemed to hang over the peace of Europe . . ."[13] The first Balkan war which, as we saw, pitted Serbia, Bulgaria, and Greece against the Ottoman empire, directly impacts the plot, and it is no coincidence that when Aschenbach takes a walk through the cemetery in the overture to the story, he admires both Byzantine decorations and Greek crosses (*DV*, 196). His decision to travel in order to lift his writer's block calls up Rilke's unrest and also taps into a deeper wish to meet the Orient, deploying an orientalist fantasy that should end the confinement of an intellectual who has never ventured beyond Europe and acutely feels the limits of the "European psyche" (*DV*, 198). His itinerary is both typical and allegorical, Aschenbach travels south to Trieste and Pola, stays in Brioni, an island of the Adriatic where he cannot find rest, and finally reaches Venice. When the epidemic catches up with him there, national differences reassert themselves: the Germans and Austrians leave as soon as the word contagion is heard, while the Poles and Russians stay defiantly. An Englishman tells the truth to Aschenbach, for he, true to clichés, is a no-nonsense pragmatist. The plague of cholera takes into its sweep the whole East, as it was born near the Ganges, before moving on to China, Afghanistan, Persian Astrakhan, Moscow, then by boat to Toulon and Malaga, Palermo, Naples, Cabria, and Apulia before attacking Venice. Similar to a spreading war, the pandemic generates a "state of crisis" (*DV*, 354) in the city, and while contradictory rumors proliferate, public morality degenerates, robberies and murders increase, and debauchery is on the rise. It is in this public context that the last dream of Aschenbach acquires its relevance: he indulges in a scene of primitive orgy, phallic worship, and sexual license that seems to come from Stravinsky's *Rite of Spring*. The revelation that Eros does not dwell in language but lurks in the appealing flesh of a young god is shattering for a writer like Aschenbach, who becomes the protagonist of his own short story, "A Study in Abjection." Tadzio turns out to be more than Narcissus or Hyacinthus; he is also a psychopomp who carries him across the Styx to Hades.

Having concluded that his attraction for the boy is unhealthy, Aschenbach prepares to leave Venice for a resort near Trieste. He packs his belongings regretfully. Delaying his departure to catch sight of Tadzio one last time, he takes off in the *vaporetto* bound for the municipal station. Feeling that he is losing something, he is beset by ambivalence and both wants "to catch and to miss" his train (*DV*, 228). In the station he is told that his trunk has been sent by mistake to Como. Instead of getting angry, he is relieved, and a surge of "wild joy" engulfs him. Manically exhilarated, he is brought back to the Hotel des Bains. His fate is sealed, and fate has taken the shape of misdirected luggage: the temporary loss triggers the "relaxation of his will" and delays the recognition of his desire (*DV*, 230–1). A similar theme is sounded in Kafka's "The Stoker" when Karl arrives in New York, and in Hugo von Hofmannsthal's *Andreas* when the hero reaches Venice. All these exotic places bring about a dissolution of the old self; what emerges is mostly frightening, but the shattering of a pre-critical ingenuity is positive in the sense that it allows desire to emerge, and it is imperious, whatever the cost will later be. And desire always comes accompanied, bringing in tow the twin specters of death and the infinite.

The Statue of Liberty's Mighty Sword

"The Stoker" begins as young Karl Rossman is ready to disembark from the transatlantic steamer at a quay in New York. When he realizes that he has left his umbrella below, he asks an acquaintance to look after his heavy trunk. As in a nightmare, he is prevented from reaching the bunk. Instead, he meets a stoker whose bunk is a substitute home but who forces Karl to become embroiled in his own struggles. When Karl worries about his trunk, the stoker says that the trunk has either been stolen or is still there, and will be found where it is.[14] This fatalism acts as a poultice, and Karl forgets again about his luggage. He had to lose his father's box in order to find what he did not expect to see – an American uncle, ready to welcome him, an important man who is a senator. It is not until the third chapter, after Karl has been ignominiously expelled by the now tyrannical uncle, that his luggage miraculously turns up. It is further described in the next chapter: the trunk, none other than his father's old trunk, still contains an old salami, his passport, and family photographs. Not so much a sign of reunion with the family, it in fact contains the "portable altar" one needs in order to achieve true homelessness. Earlier in the "Stoker" chapter, Karl believed that it was right to tell a lie if it was for the sake of "justice," which means simply defending the stoker against various adversaries in the name of a curious paralogism: "If trunks can be stolen in America, one can surely tell a lie now and then as well, he thought in self-justification."[15]

Like Karl, Kafka had no qualms telling a lie about the country in which suitcases can miraculously appear and disappear. The first paragraph describes the Statue of Liberty brandishing a sword rather than a torch, hinting that the bronze woman has become an allegory of Justice rather than of Freedom or the Enlightenment. In his misguided but intense quest for justice, Karl sides with the stoker because he represents the underdog, the humiliated subordinate unable to explain himself in front of figures of authority like the captain and the senator. Karl lies to himself when he identifies with the stoker, whose cause he adopts without having known him for more than a few minutes, especially when the stoker accuses Schubal of evil intentions. Symptomatically, Karl owes the reappearance of his trunk to Schubal, who finds it on the boat and has it dispatched to his uncle.[16] The trunk left behind in the boat contained his coat, whose secret pocket held his passport, now saved by Schubal. Yet Karl sticks to his suspicion of foreigners like Schubal, who is Rumanian, and later has a similarly xenophobic fear of an Irishman with whom he shares a room. The quest for truth is born out of inexperience, and Karl will have to dispose of the rotting German salami left in his father's military trunk. In a similar manner, when the young Andreas arrives in Venice early in the morning on a fine day in 1778, his first contact with the reality of the city is by way of heavy luggage dragged as impedimenta: "'This is a fine thing',' thought young Herr Andreas von Ferschengelder, on September 17, 1778, for his boatman had unloaded his trunk on to the stone steps and pushed off again."[17] He too follows the wrong guides in his travels, as we will soon see.

The Impossible "Reunion" of Hofmannsthal's Andreas

Andreas or the Reunited Ones (*Andreas oder die Vereinigten*) is something of a riddle. It is the only novel in Hugo von Hofmannsthal's prolific career, which began early. In 1890, at the age of 16, he was feted as a child prodigy whose poems became the talk of Vienna. It ended abruptly in July 1929, when he died from a sudden stroke after having heard the news of his son

Franz's suicide. Hofmannsthal spent a lot of time and effort on the book, yet never completed what stands out as his "narrative masterpiece."[18] The novel's very meaning remains difficult to ascertain, even if its importance in German literature is undeniable. It began like the Aschenbach story – in June 1907 Hofmannsthal, who was staying at the Lido in Venice, began drafting a first-person narrative entitled "Venice Travel Diary of the Herr von N. (1779)." In 1912 he added two more fragments, "The Lady with the Little Dog" and "The Venetian Adventures of Herr von N.," each about 25 pages long. And in 1913 he began the main section of the novel, subtitled "The Wonderful Friend," writing some 85 pages, the only continuous part that we have. He kept on adding notes in later years but never managed to complete the novel. The fragments were praised by Stefan Zweig, who said that it was the "torso of possibly the most beautiful novel in the German language," and by Richard Alewyn, who describes "eighty pages of the most vibrant prose that has ever been written in the German language."[19]

The premises are conventional enough, a variation on the pattern of the *Bildungsroman* with Venice as a backdrop. The story follows the 22-year-old Andreas on his journey of discovery. Andreas has been sent to Italy by his rich and noble parents so as to complete his education and see the world. The scene takes place in 1778 at the climax of the rococo period, when Empress Maria Theresa was on the throne, and when Venice, in steady decline, was becoming a closer ally of the Austrian empire as it pushed toward the south. The narrative begins *in medias res*: Andreas reaches Venice early on September 17, where he meets a strange man, half-naked in the street, who takes him to the noble but impoverished palace of the Count Prampero. Andreas is given the elder daughter's room, and is introduced to the members of the family: Nina, the elder daughter, a former actress, now a famous prostitute, and Zustina, the younger one, about to offer her virginity as the prize of a lottery organized to save the family from ruin. While he rests in the room vacated for him by Zorzi the stage designer, Andreas dreams and relives in a long flashback his previous travels through Austria and northern Italy. This is the only self-contained scene of the novel, and it is remarkable.

Having left Vienna and reached Villach on his horse, Andreas meets a young man, barely three years older than he is, who insists on being hired as a servant. Unable to push him away, Andreas allows Gotthilff to accompany him. He is talked into buying a small horse for his companion. Gotthilff is impudent, sexually promiscuous, and treats Andreas to all sorts of obscene gossip. At one point during the next day's ride the flow of salacious remarks makes Andreas fantasize about love-making with a countess so that he pulls on Gotthilff's reins and the other falls from his nag. Gotthilff recommends that they let their exhausted horses stop at a farm. This turns out to be a homestead in which the noble family of the Finazzers lives. Andreas and his servant are welcomed graciously, and he immediately takes an interest in the beautiful daughter, Romana. Gotthilff, more and more truculent, tends to his wounded horse and seduces a maid. Romana shows Andreas the village and the churchyard where her six younger sisters and brothers are buried. The coat of arms of the family is an armed knight with a dog at his feet. They steal a first kiss, and Andreas thinks of entering her bed at night – but she sleeps with a maid nearby. He has a terrible nightmare and is woken up by shrill screams: the wanton maid is strapped half-naked to a bed to which Gotthilff has set fire before fleeing with Andreas' horse and his money sewn in the saddle. This scene of horror and betrayal affects Andreas, who feels responsible for it and wants to pay for the damage. He has a memory of having killed a dog when he was 12, and goes to a wood where he has a mystical vision of his future life with Romana, who asks him where the dog is buried. He has a another, more radiant vision of the future, and feels assured that he can possess Romana no matter where he goes or whether he sees her again or not.

Such a scene is laden with opaque symbols, echoes of past memories and visions of the future that create a simultaneous unity of impression. In the notes accompanying this more and more fragmented narrative, one finds a quote from Jacques Rivière (Alain-Fournier's friend and brother-in-law), who had described the structure of a good poem in a 1913 article:

> In a beautiful poem, there is no progression; the end is always at the level of the beginning; one immediately communicates with it; everything is on an equal footing and one can enter from anywhere. Its lines form a circle, they are turned to one another, look at one another, lock us up in their ring. They mean to disorient us on the spot and make us forget time and its dimension. Poetic emotion is a whirling motion through which is formed in us, even as things race away, a pool of eternity.[20]

This captures the esthetic project of Hofmannsthal, and it engaged him in intractable complexities: what is conceivable in a poem becomes impossible if one wants to write a novel that uses a travel narrative to present a coming-of-age story, both a narrative of sexual initiation and mystical discovery.

Besides, in keeping with an evolution magisterially analyzed by Broch, Hofmannsthal had been the first witness of a crisis in language, a moment dramatically captured in the 1902 "Letter of Lord Chandos."[21] After this linguistic crisis, he decided to move from the purely esthetic sphere to the sphere of ethics. Accordingly, the leitmotif of *Andreas* is guilt: Andreas feels tainted by his servant's sadistic treatment of the farm-girl, a crime which has disgraced him, and he wants to make amends to the family of the woman he plans to marry. Romana had looked at him in horror while they untied the maid from the burning bed, and in his dream too she gazed at him with awe. The terrestrial paradise that he had glimpsed a day before vanishes, and he sets out on his voyage and returns to Villach where he met the valet, who was none other than an escaped convict. Cruelty to animals and to lowly humans was a sin for Hofmannsthal, who had made of the cries of dying rats an emblem of mute and anguished empathy with all creatures, the key to Lord Chandos' story. The irony is that the servant's name means "God's help" at a time when help is cruelly lacking. The "sin" (this is the word used by the maid when freed) in which Andreas has been plunged unawares is compounded by his childhood memories of cruelty to animals. The "fall" that precipitated the story, the moment when Gotthilff's horse stumbles, had already been caused by his sexual excitement at the other's salacious gossip. The ethical moment occurs when someone is "touched by the infinite" – this happens to Andreas when he admits to himself that he killed his dog: "And that was how the infinite came to him" (literally, "touched him").[22]

The meaning of the title, *Andreas or the Reunited Ones*, is another riddle. While it may predict a happy ending in which Romana and Andreas are reunited as his visions seem to promise, it may also mean that the young man is not simply accumulating experiences and wisdom but is trying to find unity in himself. The reconciliation of all urges, from wild sexuality, as in the valet's case, to higher forms of betrothal and courtly love (Andreas will carry Romana's sacred image wherever he goes) takes into account the ethical law. Without this law, the sundering of experience will never be overcome. This is both a Freudian novel, telling the story of how to achieve a healthy balance between all those aspirations, and a Jungian tale of mystical initiation. Andreas goes to Venice in order to choose a good guide, and he finds it in Sacramozo, the Maltese knight who becomes his spiritual mentor until he commits suicide on the very night when Maria and Andreas are sexually united.

Venice brings to the Alpine section the counterpoint of a decadent and theatrical world in which it is difficult to distinguish reality from appearance. Such a confusion is suggested by the story of Maria, the woman in black seen by Andreas, a young widow caught in the middle of a schizophrenic crisis. She is both Maria, who wishes to be dead, and Mariquita, a sensuously

attractive woman. Maria suffers from a deep "psychic malady."[23] Hofmannsthal explains in a note: "The lady [Maria] and the Cocotte [Mariquita] are
both Spanish: they are dissociated aspects of one and the same person, which
play tricks on each other."[24] Hofmannsthal had been inspired by Morton
Prince's 1906 study of *The Dissociation of a Personality*, a book which he
read in 1907.[25] Prince's Miss Beauchamp suffered from multiple personality
disorder, her schizophrenic personality having split up into several distinct
identities – the case later fascinated Joyce and found its way into *Finnegans
Wake* for the portrayal of Issy. Miss Beauchamp transformed herself at
will into a little saint (BI) or a real devil (BIII, also called Sally). Andreas
arrives at the moment when the baroness exchanges her saintly self for
the wicked persona of Mariquita. Mariquita pretends to be called Dolores,
and charms Andreas. A sexual union between Maria/Mariquita and Andreas
was planned, after which she would enter a convent while Andreas went
back to Romana.

Of course, this is only one possible ending among many, since the notes
proliferated, and different incidents were added, with new journeys and
tangential developments. Their modernity lies in their radically open character as they sketch more episodes and meditations. As the years passed,
they incorporated quotes and references to books that Hofmannsthal was
reading on topics as diverse as myth, the unconscious, the history of Venice
and Austria, war, poetry, mysticism, and travel. They allude to authors
as diverse as Goethe, Novalis, Gogol, Lactantius, Diderot, Proust, Hugo,
Lamennais, Rousseau, Des Brosses, Hölderlin, Dante, and Vico. A typical
late sketch for the "novel" (*Andreas* is usually referred to not by title but as a
generic "novel") sketches an opposition between Italy, emblematized by
Goldoni, Gozzi, Alfieri, Ariosto, Tasso, and Vico, and France, where the
names of Voltaire, Rousseau, and Madame de Staël dominate.[26] The last
note for the "novel" is dated November 1927 and limns an ever-broadening
program: "The Novel // should be a compendium. // Philosophy of politics
– going down to the smallest ramifications in biology."[27] It was inevitable
that *Andreas*, battling with the "monster of totality"[28] as Barthes would say,
would suffer the fate of Flaubert's *Bouvard and Pécuchet*, Mallarmé's *Livre*,
Musil's *Man Without Qualities*, and Kafka's main novels. Such radical incom-
pleteness was contained in the incomplete fragments of 1913.

Hermann Broch provided his solution to the riddle of the novel's incom-
pletion: on his view, Hofmannsthal abandoned the narrative because it could
not but turn autobiographical, a drift that Hofmannsthal wanted to curb or
avoid. Indeed, a number of notes refer to Rousseau's *Confessions*, with the
lively account of the Swiss writer's formative years and sexual experiences

in Venice, while another note begins with "Authors of autobiographies."[29] Rilke's *Notebooks of Malte Laurids Brigge* had a strong impact on Hofmannsthal, who heard Rilke read from it and then started a friendship with him. The work of Hofmannsthal is caught up in a tension between a confessional impulse stemming from purely narcissistic urges and a wish to erase narcissism by approaching impersonal myth, religious ritual, apocryphal local folklore, traditional fables, anonymous aphorisms, and ancient canonical forms.

> With *Andreas* Hofmannsthal had set for his narrative production a pinnacle whose height he had underestimated; he abandoned the ascent because, having started with chiefly visual but otherwise insufficient equipment, he would have felt bound to make use of autobiographical elements (which had already accumulated in the preliminary sketches for the novel) – and this was incompatible with his need for "I"-suppression: more important to him than completion and publication was personal self-interpretation, self-contemplation, self-education, which had been his concern in writing poetry from the beginning – with the result that he was always ready to resign himself to the fragmentary.[30]

Accordingly Broch highlights the fact that, in 1913, music was again competing with literature for Hofmannsthal – *Andreas* was left unfinished largely because the writing of *The Woman Without a Shadow* had taken precedence. The theme of *The Woman Without a Shadow* had already been sketched in 1911: a childless and shadowless princess buys her shadow, which entails the ability to procreate from a poor dyer's wife. In March 1913, Hofmannsthal accompanied Strauss in a car trip to Rome during which they discussed the opera. He then wrote the first and second acts, while Strauss immediately composed the music.[31] The opera was completed in 1915, and Hofmannsthal then wrote a prose version of the tale in 1919 – it is as impersonal and allegorical as he had wished. Broch thinks that Hofmannsthal tackled the problem of the integration of childhood and maturity by working on it from another angle, that of the parents. The resolution of his literary dilemma could only be a libretto, just when the strains of the Viennese "joyful apocalypse" were being heard in the background. The masks and plays of the Venetian *commedia dell'arte* (in many notes, Hofmannsthal insists upon an atmosphere of disguise and cheap theatricality) reach back to an older folklore and work with pure allegories. The issue of fertility leads back to common humanity while providing an apt metaphor for renewed creativity. However, they can only blend in the lighter world of the opera. In the medium of the novel, Hofmannsthal had come too close to Kafka's modernism, a modernism fraught with angst and paradoxes. Having glimpsed it he retreated by using the easy Viennese exit: "Music please!" A flare of the orchestra, and the shadows whirl madly on the stage.

Kafka's New Year

Hofmannsthal's unanswered questions were a central issue for Kafka as well. How can one work from oneself but without a self? How can literature overcome subjective division? How can one create a system of beliefs combining esthetics and ethics without falling into endless fragmentation? While Andreas himself tended to look more and more like a Kafka character as time went by, in 1913 Kafka's life turned into the unfinished and unfinishable novel of a young man's sentimental education, an infinite *Bildungsroman* that he decided to perform as an epistolary novel. This generated a masterpiece in epistolary art, his *Letters to Felice*. Ironically, Kafka's only way out of a protracted marital impasse was an epistolary battle with Felice. The battle was almost ended when Kafka's life turned into a plot from *The Magic Mountain*: in August 1917, he started hemorrhaging blood and was sent to a sanatorium. The year of the major literary breakthrough had been 1912, since it saw the writing of *The Judgment* in September, and the beginning of the novel *Amerika*, whose first chapter, "The Stoker," was finished, and for which six other chapters were drafted. Then in November he completed *Metamorphosis*. Kafka gave an ecstatic testimony of how *The Judgment* came to him in one night of sheer creative delight between September 22 and 23, 1912. It was an experience that evinced "a complete opening of the soul and the body." He had thought of Freud when penning the story of a young man's condemnation to death by his despotic father. Kafka would have to move beyond the father–son conflict; for that, he needed a woman with whom he could fall in love.

These last months of 1912 had brought to Kafka ample confirmation that he was meant to be a writer, but he lacked a confirmation in the flesh, which would require a new theater of operations. The opportunity was provided by Felice Bauer, whom he met in August 1912. He started writing to her on September 20 of that year, just two days before his literary "breakthrough." As the correspondence picked up speed and volume (soon Kafka would write to Felice once or twice a day), he found himself devoured by it, and did not write much else in 1913, except for some revisions of the stories, and some work on the unfinishable *Amerika* or the *Man who Disappeared*. The year 1913 brought concrete reassurance of his talent by other means. The evidence that he could find an audience was there: the collection of stories *Meditation* was published late in December 1912 by Rowohlt, and *The Stoker* was issued in book form in May 1913, followed by the publication of *The Judgment* in June 1913. Yet for Kafka 1913 remained a year of transition that ushered in a new way of writing and would allow him to take the measure of his destiny – a task for which he would need the unwitting collaboration of Felice.

Felice came from Berlin to Prague, where she visited Max Brod's family on August 13, 1912. At the end of the dinner at which they met that evening, Kafka promised, half in jest, to accompany her to Palestine the following year. He waited one full month before sending a letter on September 20. Soon, both of them would be entangled in a web of projects, counter-projects, and obstacles, in a frustrating dance of longing and rejection. Things spun quickly out of control, at least on Kafka's side. Already by November 11, 1912, and without having seen her again (they would only meet again in March 1913), he was writing to Felice, shifting abruptly from the formal *Sie* to the intimate *Du*: "I belong to you; there is really no other way of expressing it, and that is not strong enough."[32] That same letter deploys the strategy that Kafka will use for the few years to come: he establishes a perverse contract that is binding but impossible to fulfill. In this case, it has to do with the schedule of the expected letters: they have to reach him on Sundays, since they are too disruptive on weekdays. As Felice had started describing her clothes, confiding her likes and dislikes, Kafka objected that he didn't want to know too much: such details would make her too alluring, too immediately desirable, and then he could not prevent himself from catching the first train to Berlin and rushing to see her; but of course, such a trip was impossible. Reasons would vary: he adduced his health, his work, or his family obligations. In this same letter, he insists that he is "not good enough for marriage, let alone fatherhood" (*Letters*, 37). Then he catches himself, seeing that it is monstrous to inflict pain when he means to be loving and tender. "And how horribly I torment you, and how I compel you, in the stillness of your room, to read this letter, as nasty a letter as has ever lain on your desk! Honestly, it strikes me sometimes that I prey like a specter on your felicitous name!" (*Letters*, 37). Among the degraded images of himself that he conjures, this is a recurrent and powerful one: Kafka is a bloodthirsty Homeric ghost who needs fresh blood from the living and walks in hell. What he feasts on, rather than blood and flesh, are names. He could not have chosen better: Felice means "happy," whereas he knows that he is destined for a life of unhappiness. Unhappily for her, her last name, Bauer, means "peasant" and calls up stability, earthiness, the expectations of a family life, but Kafka cannot comply with the demands of petty-bourgeois normalcy.

Can he even sign "yours," he who began the letter by stating that he was "all hers"? That cannot be taken for granted: "Did I think of signing myself *Dein*? No, nothing could be more false. No, I am forever fettered to myself, that's what I am, and that's what I must try to live with" (*Letters*, 37). He should have added – and he soon will – "that's what *you* must try to live with." All the following letters play a similarly perverse game of seduction and repulsion, an exhausting cat-and-mouse game that Felice will learn to play as well, scoring a few points: usually, when Kafka finally comes to see her in Berlin, she is barely available. The mutual torture will soon be compared to a war – curiously, Franz and Felice, the two eternal lovers who must keep apart to keep on sending passionate missives, invent epistolary trench warfare, just slightly in advance of real fighting. How can there be peace, he already asks in November 1912 – "But is a peaceful solution possible now?" (*Letters*, 37) – when he is at war with himself and fighting against the whole world, beginning with his father and his mother?

Glancing back at the years of correspondence, Kafka later multiplied images from the ongoing war, providing the theme for a fascinating chapter in Frederick Karl's biography of Kafka, "Franz, Felice and the Great War."[33] One example of Kafka's inventive tactics is a fantasy sent to Felice in a letter dated New Year's Eve 1913. There, under cover of sending greetings and regrets that they are not together, Kafka spins out a curious narrative about their reunion. He supposes purely hypothetically that he and Felice have arranged to meet in the flesh. This encounter takes place in Frankfurt, and, on the second evening of their stay together, they would go to the theater. Felice rushes to be on time and is now waiting for Franz, who doesn't appear. Confused, Felice goes back to the hotel.

> And what do you find? I am still lying [. . .] in bed at 8, not tired, not rested; I maintain that I have been incapable of leaving my bed, complain about everything and insinuate even worse complaints; I try to make amends for the terrible wrong by stroking your hand, by seeking your eyes, lost in the dark room, and yet my whole behavior shows that I am quite prepared to repeat the whole thing at any moment. Although I am at a loss to explain myself in words, I am aware of our situation in every detail, and if I were in your place, standing at my bedside, I wouldn't hesitate to raise my umbrella and in my anger and despair break it over my head. (*Letters*, 136)

The scene is both hilarious and infuriating, and provides another way of testing Felice's resolve. Kafka comments that such a scene is "impossible in reality" although it is clear that reality does not count much for him. What he likes is the writing of these letters the distance that they presuppose. In a diary entry from January 24, 1914, Kafka notes that he has never experienced the sweetness of love for Felice except in the letters he writes to her. The same 1913 New Year letter adds a twist of wry humor. Felice has said dramatically that they "belonged together unconditionally." Kafka snaps back that he has no dearer wish than being bound to her by their tied-up wrists. He even fantasizes, seeing himself and Felice as a couple led to the guillotine during the French Revolution. Marriage was indeed capital punishment for Kafka, who blamed this strange humor on the odd "13" of the New Year (*Letters*, 137).

Such fantasies do not mean that Kafka had metamorphosed into a huge beetle! He can also laugh, as he describes in another letter more than four pages long. This was triggered by an incident in his workplace. Being the youngest clerk, he had to make a speech of thanks to the president of the insurance company. The president took a funny pose to listen, with legs crossed, hand on the table, beard lowered to his chest, protruding stomach heaving gently. Kafka was attacked by fits of giggles that could pass for a tickle in the throat. Then the president stared at him and he felt terror but was still unable to contain the devilish laughter surging from him. The president gave his own speech of thanks, and then Kafka abandoned whatever control he had so far managed to exert:

> At first I laughed only at the president's delicate little jokes; but while it is a rule only to contort one's features respectfully at these little jokes, I was already laughing out loud; observing my colleagues' alarm at being infected by it, I felt more sorry for them than for myself, but I couldn't help it; I didn't even try to avert or cover my face, but in my helplessness continued to stare straight at the president, incapable of turning my head, probably on the instinctive assumption that everything could only get worse rather than better, and that therefore it would be best to avoid any change. And now that I was in full spate, I was of course laughing not only at the current jokes, but at those of the past and the future and the whole lot together, and by then no one knew what I was really laughing about. (*Letters*, 147)

To hide the general embarrassment, a colleague began another speech revolving around his pet ideas. Under the strain, he became ridiculously animated; his exertions were too much for Kafka, who roared with laughter: "the world, the semblance of the world, which hitherto I had seen before me, dissolved completely, and I burst into loud and uninhibited laughter of such heartiness as perhaps only schoolchildren at their desks are capable of" (*Letters*, 147–8). Utter silence greeted this outburst; the president nobly exonerated the culprit by blaming it on his own jokes before dismissing everyone hurriedly. It was impossible to stop Kafka: "Undefeated, roaring with laughter yet desperately unhappy, I was the first to stagger out of the hall" (*Letters*, 148). Coughing and wheezing, he rushed to his desk to write a letter of apology, believing that he would never be pardoned.

Kafka's pervasive laughter was emphasized regularly by close friends like Gustav Janouch (much more than Max Brod, who was too serious himself) and it is no coincidence that Kafka mostly laughed at figures of authority. He was at one point tempted to join Rudolf Steiner's anthroposophical movement, as Biely had done. When he met Steiner in March 1911, he explained what in the school attracted him, asking Steiner whether one could be a writer and a theosophist at the same time. The diary does not quote Steiner's answer; it merely notes the fact that while listening, Steiner kept "working his handkerchief deep in his nose, one finger at each nostril."[34] The diary stops there, without further comment: it reduces Steiner to being a nose-picker, not a mystic, while Kafka thumbs his (literary) nose at him. This scene can be superimposed on the preceding one. Abject impotence and nervous *fou-rire* make one laugh and generate consternation at the same time, which is akin to the mood created in Felice. In both cases, social farce is transformed into letter-writing: Kafka had to write to the president to apologize for his laughter and beg his favor. This worked well enough as he was the most efficient agent of the Workers' Accident Insurance Institute, an important governmental service overseeing the increasing number of work accidents generated by the industrialization of Austria. Kafka's forte was the technical language of accident prevention, a task for which he was often distinguished by his superiors; in March 1913 Kafka was promoted to vice-secretary, and became a "Prokurist" like Joseph K. in *The Trial*.

The letters to Felice explored what it meant to be mystically married to writing. Kafka measured his new power when he perceived the limitations of his first stories collected in *Meditation*, which he considered as a mere stylistic exercise in 1913. He could not have worded the abrupt and magnificent definitions of his role as a writer if he hadn't felt threatened at the core of his very being by a loving woman. At one point, Felice, meaning well, confided that she would like to be next to Franz when he writes – a suggestion that he rejected with customary horror. His type of writing demanded absolute solitude and infinite quiet. "Writing that springs from the surface of existence – when there is no other way and the deeper wells have dried up – is nothing, and collapses at the moment a truer emotion makes that surface shake. This is why one can never be alone enough when one writes, why there can never be enough silence around one when one writes, why even night is not night enough" (*Letters*, 156). In another fantasy, he imagines that he is in a deep cellar, that food is brought regularly, his only exercise being to get the food. Yet, should the wish be granted, he would have to fear impotence, despair, and madness.

Since his relation to writing was akin to a mystical marriage, a marriage with God, he asks Felice whether she feels the presence of God in her life:

> Are you aware [. . .] of a continuous relationship between yourself and reassuringly distant, if possible infinite height or depth? He who feels that continuously has no need to roam about like a lost dog, mutely gazing round with imploring eyes; he never yearns to slip into a grave as if it were a warm sleeping bag and life a cold winter night, and when climbing the stairs to his office he never need imagine that he is careering down the well of the staircase, flickering in the uncertain light, twisting from the speed of his fall, shaking his head with impatience. (*Letters*, 186)

The humorous language describing human concerns and relationships in terms of a dog's life is symptomatic. Felice must choose between being the servant of a madman chained in a cell or an addressee, a meaningful absence. If marriage abolishes the needed distance, then he cannot sustain his nothingness, the "nothingness that I am" (*Letters*, 289) and the consequence is his destruction and that of Felice. This dialectical negativity can only convert itself into the plenitude of literature: "I have no literary interests, but am made of literature, I am nothing else, and cannot be anything else" (*Letters*, 304). In the same letter of August 1913 he quotes a review of *Meditation* that defines his art as a "bachelor's art" and asks slyly: "What do you think of that, Felice?" (*Letters*, 304).

Such endless self-torture is as exhausting for the reader as it was for Felice – until her friend Grete was added to spice up the mix. Kafka found an even more tortuous way of preventing marriage, by setting two girlfriends in competition for a monster who can only live when he is writing. Interestingly, these letters reveal an author who is never entirely sure of what he meant when writing a story. This is true of *The Judgment*: "The 'Judgment' cannot be explained. [. . .] The story may be a journey around father and son, and the friend's changing shape may be a change in perspective in the relationship between father and son. But I am not quite sure of this, either" (*Letters*, 267). The breakthrough of 1912 revealed the depth of creativity in him, but the epistolary war of 1913 was necessary to understand what he wanted to do with his newly found literary virtuosity.

Once he could defend his position as a writer more than the meaning of what he had to say, he could continue his intransitive exercise without having to justify what was meant or not meant. The double-binds of life were not stronger than the double-binds of fiction if, by writing letters, one could inflict real pain, make people fall in love, or reach life-altering decisions. Thus Kafka found that literature touches the heart of life by way of sublimation, the sublimation of narcissism (as we saw it in Hugo von Hofmannsthal), or the sublimation of sadistic impulses lurking in the world of the obsessional. Having penetrated there, not unduly bothered by the need for traditional plots and characters, he would take as his theme the fragility and the lability of a divided self, fractured in the struggle against a terrifying social order in which victimization, humiliation, and alienation are the norm. The myth of totality has been exploded as another Romantic illusion. And there is no need to travel to America, even in one's imagination, to verify this. A land surveyor named by a simple initial will do. Literature has thus become infinite, it is an endless *felix culpa*, the inexpiable happy sin contained in an interminable letter that Kafka was sending to himself while addressing all men and women.

Chapter 8

Modernism and the End of Nostalgia

The "Gilded Age," a phrase coined by Mark Twain and Charles Dudley Warner in 1873, was launched at exactly the same time as the United States adopted the Gold Standard, following Britain, which had adopted it as early as 1820, soon to be imitated by most industrial nations. What was denounced by the populists as "the crime of 1873" facilitated the growth of American capitalism while encouraging early globalization. The "Gilded Age" ended in the first decade of the twentieth century, some historians say with the panic of 1907. Its real death sentence was issued on February 3, 1913, when the 16th Amendment, introduced in 1909, was finally voted, making income tax official. This was a time when everything had a fixed price, but could be taxed as well. This also applied to family contracts like marriage; values as weightless as freedom could be bought, had to be bought even, and the most solidly entrenched fortunes could yield something for the benefit of the community. This was one of the sobering lessons drawn from American capitalism and applied to social customs and personal ethics in Edith Wharton's *The Custom of the Country*. The novel was serialized in January 1913 while she was still completing it, then published as a book in October 1913. This is also one of the lessons learned by Proust's narrator at the end of his long quest for artistic autonomy. For Wharton, it meant above all solving the issue of divorce – her own divorce from Teddy Wharton, a difficult, ill suited, and disappointing husband, and the divorces of her heroine Undine Spragg.

Proust's utter devotion to his work was to entail the end of his nocturnal social life and its dangerous pleasures. Freedom was gained when he could replace his adolescent fascination for elite society with a stubborn dedication to his novel – when life served art, and not the reverse. Proust and Wharton have often been linked, and not only by the fact that they were in possession of a huge fortune; at some point, Wharton hoped that Proust would finish the French translation of *The Custom of the Country*, a translation begun by Robert d'Humières, who was killed in action in 1915. Proust discussed the translation with Gide but went no further.[1] R. W. B. Lewis, Wharton's biographer, notes that Proust's and Wharton's social lives never overlapped even though they frequented the same salons:

> In the high reaches of Parisian social life, they missed each other as though by divine planning. Proust entered the Faubourg world in 1894, at the age of 23. After becoming the familiar of the ducs and duchesses, the comtes and the comtesses he would draw upon, splice and reshape for his epic novel, he withdrew abruptly following the second trial of Alfred Dreyfus in 1899. [. . .] By the time, in 1906, that Edith Wharton was introduced to the aristocratic milieu, Proust had been absent from it for some years. The war and a need for broader human contact lured Proust back into the world, in particular to the center of social gravity at the Ritz Hotel. At this stage it was Edith Wharton who had largely retired from the scene – racking personal problems had already caused her to curtail her social involvements, and her refugee work reduced them even more drastically.[2]

Besides their involvement in the Dreyfus case (like Proust, a staunch pro-Dreyfusard, Wharton believed in the innocence of Captain Dreyfus in spite of the anti-Dreyfusard prejudice of old friends like the novelist Paul Bourget), there was someone who acted as a messenger, a former lover of Edith Wharton, Walter Berry. Berry dined with Proust twice a week by the end of the war. Proust admired Berry's solid culture, his sophisticated cosmopolitanism, and his dry wit, and thought that the American involvement in the war was due to Berry's efforts. He dedicated his 1919 *Pastiches et mélanges* to him: "To Mister Walter Berry, lawyer and man of letters, who, since the first day of the war, facing an America that was still undecided, pleaded with incomparable energy and talent the cause of France, and won his battle."[3] On her side, Edith Wharton sent a copy of *Du côté de chez Swann* (*Swann's Way*) to Henry James two months after its publication in 1913. At her injunction, James devoured it and saluted a "new master."[4] An important bridge between American and French modernism had been established.

Their common interests go beyond spatial or social proximity. The commonality of themes becomes obvious if one thinks of the unsparing analysis of jealousy in *The Custom of the Country* and in *Swann in Love*, the novel within the novel in *Swann's Way*, the first published book of the enormous project of *La Recherche*. Critics often oppose Proust's modernism to Wharton's alleged classicism. Wharton would be a realist writer who never strayed far from the tradition of late nineteenth-century social Darwinism, allied with a Nietzschean satire of modern manners. Thus Robin Peel's *Apart from Modernism* argues that Wharton cannot be considered as a modernist, even though she flirted with literary experimentation, because her political world-view was ultimately conservative. She remained a "Tory," hence ultimately dependent upon a notion of classical representation in art.[5] Whatever her politics, she had more in common with Proust. With this contiguity in mind, I will focus on the books published in 1913, *Swann's Way* and *The Custom of the Country*.

Wharton's Comedy of Remarriage

The plot of *The Custom of the Country (CC)* is simple: it describes the social ascension of a beautiful and unscrupulous upstart from the Midwest who, by seducing and marrying rich and respectable husbands in New York and Paris, reaches a coveted position of social eminence. This same summary could also trace the ascension of a Proustian heroine like Odette de Crécy, if we translate American local and social topography into their French equivalents. Wharton's predatory heroine bears the ridiculous name of Undine Spragg, a name that blends jarring elements: Spragg evokes the uncouth origins of Undine, born in Apex with a father who is a self-made man; her first name, we soon learn, was not chosen for the Romantic associations stemming from La Motte Fouqué's subtle romance; it owes its existence to an electric appliance. Undine's second husband, the well-born and sensitive Ralph Marvell, begins associating the name with Montaigne's self-characterization as "ondoyant et divers," when his reverie is cut short by Mrs. Spragg's matter-of-fact etymology – "Why, we called her after a hair-waver father put on the market the week she was born" – and he adds: "It's from *undoolay*, you know, the French for crimping; father always thought the name made it take."[6] The satire is clear, showing an example of the obscene appropriation of cultural icons by American capitalism. The commercial recycling of myth and classical echoes leads to the launching of a hair waver a week after her birth. Thus one of her main physical assets is Undine's wavy and abundant red hair. At the same time, we know that she has been caught up from her birth in a network of modern commodification with its attendant marketing strategies. Undine is her father's true daughter: she is "launched" on a social scene that is a market; society, like a stock exchange, affixes price-tags to her and her suitors. Like Lily Bart in *House of Mirth*, she must calculate the right investment and not make a mistake – in a sense, her ruthlessness avenges Lily's failure and suicide. Undine's name gives shape to her fate, its classical echoes keep ringing as she is also often compared to Atalanta, a mythical identification combining respect for antiquity (and this is the key to the respectability that she is searching for) and her flair for the new, underpinning her total lack of scruples and her go-getter mentality. This culminates when she sells priceless antique tapestries hanging in de Chelles' manor. Undine is indeed "*undoolay*," a protean figure capable of undergoing many metamorphoses: the mimetic or "doxic"[7] character of this social chameleon is both her strength and her weakness.

The first husband we see Undine catch is Ralph Marvell, a privileged scion of the old New York aristocracy based in Washington Square. Ralph has less money at his disposal than his rich brother-in-law Peter Van Degen, who married Ralph's cousin although she was secretly in love with Ralph. Ralph is the most delicately drawn figure in the novel. The failure of their marriage is inevitable, as we see when Undine and Ralph spend their honeymoon in Italy. While his upsurge of amorous intensity rekindles his creative flame, she is hot, bored, and maneuvers to join well-to-do friends in a fashionable resort in Switzerland. Once pregnant, Undine shows little aptitude for her maternal role, bitterly regretting that this prevents her from wearing the new dresses bought in Paris. Things go downhill for the couple: Ralph has to work in an office to pay for Undine's expensive lifestyle, which she later uses as a pretext to divorce him: he was too absorbed by business. Meanwhile she allows herself to be courted by Peter Van Degen, which proves to be a mistake, since after he has seduced and possessed her he gets tired of her. Nevertheless, the sale of precious pearls, his parting gift, pays for her to return to Paris, where she captures the French nobleman Raymond de Chelles. Using her son Paul as a bartering tool, she forces Ralph to consent to a divorce, after which he commits suicide. Free to marry de Chelles, she discovers that living with this ancient family is as boring and empty as her walks in Italy with Ralph. She decides to return to Elmer Moffatt, the husband from Apex who has become a millionaire and an art collector. The divorce and wedding are rushed through, and at the end we witness Undine's unsatisfied desire: she now longs to be an ambassador's wife. Undine's ethical failure is measured by her son, Paul, in whom she shows no interest. Already in New York, she forgets his second birthday, and after her estrangement with Ralph she agrees to let him live with his father until he becomes an exchange chip. Paul is closer to both Elmer Moffatt and Raymond de Chelles, whom he calls daddy, than to his mother. The diagnosis is severe and has crucial implications for Wharton's judgment on the defects and qualities of the "modern."

It is Ralph who feels acutely that he is "not modern" enough. Modernity entails the disappearance of the old New York, trodden underfoot by the invasion of new barbarians who flaunt their money and are devoid of manners. Ralph pictures this evolution in terms of the conquest:

> Ralph sometimes called his mother and grandfather the Aborigines, and likened them to those vanishing denizens of the American continent doomed to rapid extinction with the advance of the invading race. He was fond of describing Washington Square as the "Reservation," and of prophesying that before long its inhabitants would be exhibited at ethnological shows, pathetically engaged in the exercise of their primitive industries. (CC, 47)

Nevertheless, he relinquishes his ironic distance to identify with the spirit of respectable thrift since it provides a bulwark against the "chaos of indiscriminate appetites which made up its modern tendencies" (CC, 48). He straddles the fence, at least by his unfortunate choice of a bride: "He too had wanted to be 'modern,' had revolted, half-humorously, against the restrictions and exclusions of the old code" (CC, 48). This explains his failure to be realistic about Undine's true nature and wishes as well as his inability to marshal his energies and creative impulses. Ralph the sentimentalist is caught in a contradiction between his belonging to a new generation and his half-hearted adherence to old-fashioned ideals. The scientific language of ethnology or heredity cannot mask a widening ethical gap.

In a telling verbal echo, those who are described by Ralph as the "Aboriginals" become for Undine the "originals": "Even in Apex, Undine's tender imagination had been nurtured on the feats and gestures of Fifth Avenue. [. . .] In Mabel's world she sought in vain for the originals, and only now and then caught a tantalizing glimpse of one of their familiars . . ." (CC, 19). Dreaming of gaining access to this closed society she needs Mrs. Heeny, their manicurist, to understand that Ralph is more of an "original" than the "familiars" like the popular painter Popple. She learns further distinctions, like the social divide between Fifth Avenue and Washington Square, and in Paris, the gap between the Faubourg Saint-Germain and the newer Champs-Elysées area. Her quest for the ancient, the true, and the authentic (a regressive quest for the "aura" in Walter Benjamin's terms) makes her something of an anti-modern. Nevertheless, Undine is "modern" precisely because she is so mimetic and thus destroys the very aura she craves.

Her capacity for imitation is boundless, and Wharton shows this with a bantering humor that gives a unique tone to her social critique. Undine is a living paradox: she embodies relentless energy in the pursuit of her goals, while being subservient to other people's definitions of what is desirable: "Undine was fiercely independent and yet passionately imitative. She wanted to surprise every one by her dash and originality, but she could not help modeling herself on the last person she met, and the confusion of ideals thus produced caused her much perturbation when she had to choose between two courses" (CC, 13). In fact, her wish to conform by imitating those she deems superior is driven by desire. We see this clearly in the scene in which, upset by what she mistakes as a slight from the Marvell family and by Ralph's indifference, she impulsively visits an art show. Her radiant beauty attracts men's gaze more than the paintings, and she adopts a pose: "She flung herself into rapt attitudes before the canvases, scribbling notes in the catalogue in imitation of a tall girl in sables, while ripples of self-consciousness played up and down her watchful back" (CC, 31). She pretends to admire the pictures when keenly noting the appearance of the smartly dressed members of the audience. She has a "watchful back" as her gaze is really directed at the people around her. Among them is a lady who looks at the paintings through an eye-glass deftly hanging from a pearl chain. This immediately triggers an irrepressible desire for that object in Undine: "It seemed suddenly plebeian and promiscuous to look at the world with a naked eye, and all her floating desires were merged in the wish for a jeweled eye-glass and chain" (CC, 32). The sheer violence of this urge makes her bump up against a man who is none other than Peter Van Degen; later she realizes that the owner of the precious eye-glass was Peter's wife, Ralph's cousin.

An equivalent scene in Swann in Love shows Swann, whose eyesight is failing, wearing glasses at home and a monocle at dinners. Odette believes that he does this to look "smart" (as she often says in English) and exclaims: "I really do think for a man it's very smart! How it suits you! You look like a real gentleman. All you're missing is the title!"[8] The irony is that Swann is a true gentleman, the friend of the duke of Wales and Grévy, the French prime minister, and he does not need a title to look important, as the lesser and uneducated nobles she takes as lovers do. Here, as with Undine, her admiration cuts two ways, since she implies that there is always a higher rung to reach on the ladder of social success. Her steady ascension is inter-rupted here and there but goes steadily thanks to a process of happy guess-work. When Undine is in Paris attempting to seduce Raymond de Chelles after the separation from Ralph, making useful connections with dubious noble women, she is still trying to "guess what they would expect her to say, and what tone it would be well to take" (CC, 242). She adopts a behavior that combines Apex dash and New York dignity, and finds out to her relief that the cocktail is appreciated.

During their honeymoon trip to Italy, Ralph thought that happiness was at hand: for him "the cup of life seemed to brim over" (*CC*, 90). He has reached his own "Apex," soon after to discover that Undine's beauty hides nothing. Her habit of pretending more or less competently in society is of no help in a couple's protracted tête-à-tête. Even her "pliancy and variety were imitative rather than spontaneous" (*CC*, 92). Is Undine really as devoid of interiority as she seems? Is it just a lack of inner fire, or that she has not followed own desire? A little later, once she is married to Raymond de Chelles, the archetype of old French nobility, Madame de Trézac warns her: at a French society dinner, beauty does not suffice; women have to work more, they have to appear intelligent as well as seductive. Undine has nothing to say except vague formulaic responses, and the reproach is biting: "well you don't work hard enough" (*CC*, 339). Nevertheless, Undine is "adaptable" and willing to learn; one guesses that in her next incarnation, if she does marry an ambassador after Moffatt, she will pretend to follow intellectual discussions. Indeed, after her aborted fling with Van Degen, like Madame Bovary, Undine starts reading sentimental novels: "her novel-reading had filled her mind with the vocabulary of outraged virtue" (*CC*, 236).

Her father has advised her to send the jewels back, which deepens the uncertainty caused by her mixture of personal shallowness and independence. She fantasizes that she will express her scorn of the rich Van Degen by throwing back his jewels at him. Of course, she keeps them, sells them, and invites her parents to accompany her to Paris just to look respectable. In such scenes, Wharton seems to provide a clinical diagnosis of the American go-getter and social gold-digger. It is a form of controlled hysteria. Undine often suffers from her tender "nerves" and cannot be contradicted. She terrifies her parents, who are powerless in the face of her infantile rages. In her aggressive striving after power, money, and prestige, all the elements that define "cultural capital" according to Bourdieu, Undine takes after her father, whose desire she repeats and imitates but in another domain, and in a feminine key. She unites ruse (she tells her father when he asks whether she has sent back the pearls that Mrs. Heaney took them, which is technically true) with common sense. Undine manages to convince her father to agree to her whims while reproducing his acquisitive passion, even in his less honest dealings. His rise to riches came from his selling valueless tracts of land to the city's water company, which evinced a cunning mixture of altruism (Apex is cured of recurrent epidemics of typhoid fever) and interest (previously valueless land suddenly becomes marketable). In this novel, Wharton has put to productive use her own undiagnosed hysteria, a hysteria for which she had been treated in Philadelphia by Dr. Weir Mitchell, the leading specialist in the treatment of hysteria for women.[9] A few years later, it was her husband's turn to suffer from complex hysterical symptoms, from which he never fully recovered after they had moved to Paris.

To call Undine a clinical hysteric would be a gross exaggeration, although she shares notable features with Charcot's hysterics of the turn of the century. As Lacan has shown in Dora's case, the main case of hysteria analyzed by Freud, she desires by proxy and is deeply identified with her father. Dora falls in love with Mrs. K., who is her father's illicit object of affection.[10] Undine's imperious desires follow the general lines of her father's business strategies. This is confirmed when she maneuvers to escape from a stifling marriage, planning to go on her own to Paris. Undine is described as "too sternly animated by her father's business instinct" (CC, 148) to actually pay heed to his financial difficulties. The hysterical couple linking father and daughter is reconstituted when she confides that she wants to go there to get free from her marriage; at this instant, Moffatt appears and asks whether they have been quarrelling. She answers: "we never quarrel any more: he always agrees with me" (CC, 125). In conformity with the Lacanian notion of hysterical desire as a desire without a clear object but structured like an imitation of the father's desire, Undine's idea of what she wants is vague and radical; she tells Ralph that she expects marriage to bring her *"everything"* (CC, 61), while admitting to the derivative nature of her wants: "I want what the others want" (CC, 64). Like most hysterics, she produces desire all the time and hence the means to acquire its objects, without being interested in the enjoyment that possession is supposed to bring. She is in quest of a master-signifier that remains elusive, and is not to be confused with wealth or power for instance. What she is after is, in purely Freudian terms, the drive.

A passage in which Undine rages against her father highlights the intensity of her drive. She compares herself to a "tornado," a word also applied to Wharton by her close friend Henry James. It is crucial to note that this simile comes from her own mouth; Undine unleashes her anger because her father has realized that Ralph is not rich enough to sustain the lifestyle to which his daughter has been accustomed, and he recommends canceling the wedding. This irritates Undine, who will agree much later with her father's prescience. Her diatribe is reproduced in one page of free indirect style: "Everything had gone down before her, as towns and villages went down before one of the tornadoes of her native state. [. . .] Did he suppose she was marrying for *money*? Didn't he see it was all a question, now and here, of the kind of people she wanted to 'go with'?" (CC, 78). Ironically, she is indeed not marrying for money; what she wants is power and respectability.

Most of Undine's words are in quotes to show that she reproduces other people's expressions in a sliding social scale that makes her language self-conscious. Swann has the same habit, as the narrator observes: he cannot say "hierarchy" without putting the word between inverted commas for instance (*SW*, 100). These quotes point to the codes that one has to master if one wants to live in polite society. In conformity with the pattern laid down by hysteria, Undine does not seem interested in sex. When she lets Peter Van Degen hold her hand, she behaves like her father: "So Mr Spragg might have felt at the tensest hour of the Pure Water Move" (*CC*, 184). When she lets him kiss her, she is not excited in the least: "But her physical reactions were never very acute: she always vaguely wondered why people made 'such a fuss', were so violently for or against such demonstrations" (*CC*, 184). Is Undine the mere product of social forces over which she has no control, or a very gifted social climber who has finally learned to master the forces and games that destroy Lily Bart in *House of Mirth*?

With this novel, it seems, Wharton has invented the genre of the "comedy of remarriage," to quote Stanley Cavell's brilliant phrase,[11] a filmic genre that dominated post-Depression Hollywood in the thirties and forties. Cavell coins it for romantic comedies in which a man and a woman end up marrying the same partner after a break-up or a divorce, as in the *Philadelphia Story*. This generic inscription should make us pay attention to an important deviation from the norm established by Cavell: in *Custom of the Country*, in what is Wharton's deliberate manipulation of the narrative, the reader is not told until late in the story that Undine has been married before. Undine, whom we tend to see as naive, inexperienced, and juvenile, is in fact a small town divorcee whose secret is exposed slowly. The first pages of the novel give vague warnings ("so completely had silence closed in on the subject that to Mrs. Spragg it had become non-existent," p. 9). Moffatt is introduced ominously: is he a blackmailer? Why must Undine avoid him? The parents' point of view prevents us from guessing their responsibility, while it looks as if Elmer has kept a soft spot for Undine since the broken marriage; his efforts at amassing a fortune could just be a way of getting her back.

If this interpretation is accurate, then the novel is a "comedy" since all ends "well," even when the last marriage, which is a remarriage, turns into farce – it is expedited at full speed in Reno, with a judge who jumps into their car to play the role of best man (*CC*, 366–7). One of the ironies of the book, as Stephen Orgel points out, is that when Undine shocks Ralph's parents by her candid admission that divorce is convenient for a wife who is unhappy with her husband, she is not naive but "subversive,"[12] although we are not aware of it. Undine seems to blurt out ingenuous remarks; it is only later that we understand why she was so interested. When Ralph's mother tries to convey to her why divorce is anathema in good society, the point is lost on her. However, the comedy of remarriage turns to tragedy after Ralph discovers the truth from Moffatt. What leads Ralph Marvell to commit suicide is not the fight over Paul's custody but the sudden revelation that he was not her first but her second husband. He has shared Undine's body with a man whom he despises. Suddenly, all becomes a lie, and the very source of his inspiration collapses. Undine embodied joy and radiance, all of which is irremediably corrupted all at once.

Could it be that the social comedy of serial divorce turns into the tragedy of failed marriages? This hesitation determines the meaning of the novel. Its very "modernism" depends upon the resilience of the ambiguity: the more one dwells upon the alternative, the less "classical" its social satire becomes. For there are many modernist elements in *The Custom of the Country*, some in the alert narrative technique, others in the themes treated. An abundance of cuts and jumps in the narrative startles the reader; no recapitulation of what is happening is ever provided, the pace of the narrative is increased by the fact that Wharton rarely pries into her characters' thoughts. When Undine is wounded by the failed affair with Van Degen, she has only popular novels to give shape to an unspeakable frustration. Wharton refuses to meddle with the psychology of her characters – a feature that contributes to the satire while corresponding with a modernist eschewal of explicitness and sentimentality. Thus we may wonder at the end whether Undine had been in love with Moffat all the time and had used the other two husbands pragmatically, so as to reach a superior life, before acknowledging her "true love" (this is the romance version), or whether she uses Moffatt as another stepping-stone which will bring her higher, as she had done with him in Apex (the cynical version). We are spared this simplistic alternative when she dreams of marrying an ambassador – the only truth, Wharton suggests, is desire.

The main modernist feature is the novel's ethical ambivalence: whereas some critics speak of satire, others conclude that we are not to judge Undine. Indeed, satire there is if we take at face value the violent diatribe launched by de Chelles when he vehemently rejects the idea that Undine might sell the priceless tapestries that have hung for centuries in his castle. De Chelles underlines the principle of imitation as opposed to authenticity when he rails against American women:

> You come among us speaking our language and not knowing what we mean; wanting the things we want, and not knowing what we want them; aping our weaknesses, exaggerating our follies, ignoring or ridiculing all we care about –

you come from hotels as big as towns, and from towns as flimsy as paper, where the streets haven't had time to be named, and the buildings are demolished before they're dry [. . .] and we're fools enough to imagine that because you copy our ways and pick up our slang you understand anything about the things that make life decent and honourable for us! (*CC*, 341–2)

Yet we cannot take the criteria of French aristocracy as absolute, as an ultimate shelter from the encroachments of American capitalism. The values associated with honor, decency, and tradition have been hollowed at the core by the narrative itself, at least in so far as Wharton has consistently and convincingly evoked the tedium of everyday life in the castle of the aptly named "Saint Désert" (*CC*, 317–27). It is expected that Undine be content with a dull routine; her life being an endless repetition of empty rituals; her only reprieve will be found in bickering with the servants or her mother in law. It is Raymond's unquestioned prerogative to go to Paris when he pleases to entertain mistresses. Undine's victory when she enters the most closed circles of French aristocracy is shown as empty indeed. De Chelles' angry diatribe is justified, yet it is not the novel's last word.

It is no coincidence that it was the alleged cynicism of this novel that cost Wharton the Nobel Prize in 1927.[13] While "cynicism" may not be the right term, there is a deep ambivalence in Wharton regarding her heroine. Should we absolve Undine because she is only reproducing the "custom of the country"? One guesses at times that Wharton will say, like Flaubert with Emma Bovary, "Undine, *c'est moi!*" However, Undine is not happier or flattered when she has a lover, as is Emma, who is sensually delighted at first. What Undine wants is not sex, but marriage and respectability. Wharton's double-edged critique is close enough to *Madame Bovary*, in which Flaubert attacks the petty-bourgeois world of respectability with a heroine who has no other way of ending marital boredom than adultery. Like Flaubert's, Wharton's critique is mixed with empathy, even if her style has very little to do with Flaubert's. This empathy explains why we are ready to condone the remorselessness of Undine and Emma.

The root is not just the critical analysis of social mobility announcing the triumph of the modern spirit, when money replaces birth, order, and tradition. Undine is beautiful and relentless in her dissatisfaction. Earlier Wharton had discovered Nietzsche's works, which she read in German, and read them passionately at the time of her adultery with Morton Fullerton. Undine's attitude harbors a Nietzschean radicalism, the rationale of her behavior is an unconscious urge to destroy the ancient values. In May 1908, having fully enjoyed her extramarital affair and at last discovered the pleasures of the flesh, Wharton noted: "How strange to feel one's self all at once 'Jehnseits von Gut und Böse' [Beyond Good and Evil]."[14] That very spring she devoured in succession *Beyond Good and Evil*, *The Will to Power*, and *The Genealogy of Morals*.[15] Undine is a Nietzschean heroine who is not afraid of destroying a semblance of order as she struggles for her independence and freedom. Her weapons are the only ones that society provides for a woman – appearances. The novel repeatedly echoes the Nietzschean *Umwertung aller Werte*. Again and again, Undine discovers that "Once more all the accepted values were reversed" (*CC*, 180): each time some measure of stability is gained, Undine needs to break with it so as to move to another level. Trying to master the codes of the French aristocracy, she learns not to associate status with appearances as she naively did in New York, but finds that social elevation does not correspond with morality: "but that [Princess Estradina] should boast of her intimacy with Madame Adelschein, and use it as a pretext for naming herself, overthrew all Undine's hierarchies" (*CC*, 242). The satire of vulgar American capitalism goes beyond a denunciation of the commodification of all values when combined with modernist experimentation in ethical uncertainty and varying narrative distance. This is why one cannot follow Peel's conclusion about Wharton's avoidance of modernism when he says that "Her fiction is, paradoxically more modern now than it was in 1915,"[16] an admission that weakens the whole of his argument. It is not because between 1900 and 1915 Wharton became entrenched in reactionary discourse that she cannot be called a modernist, especially if we read her as a modernist today. Such a dichotomy misses the link between historical contextualization and the critical ascertaining of the meaning of a text. Wharton's fiction *is* more modern today just because we have less reluctance to call it modernist.

The idea that marriage provides the only way for women to progress in society constitutes the backbone of the bourgeois novel, a genre that, since Jane Austen at least, stages the conflict between the prose of social values (the laws of the market) and the poetry of the heart (the lyrical illusions of the thwarted protagonists), as Hegel famously stated. In *The Custom of the Country* and *Swann's Way*, the parallel progression of Odette de Crécy and Undine Spragg shows something that goes beyond the opposition between endogamy and exogamy by turning the tables against a system in which, as Lévi-Strauss said, social life is defined by the ways in which men exchange words, goods, and women. Here, women do not exchange or produce goods, as they tend to be imitative in their use of words and not really work, but they do exchange men. This is also true in Proust's world. In Wharton's novel we are told what the "custom of the country" means: it is a system in which women are not allowed to take any interest in the endeavor by which men are supposed to pay for their wives' pleasures (*CC*, 129). Even Ralph, who is presented as a notable exception because of his old-fashioned Romanticism, must "conform to an environment where all the romantic values are reversed" (*CC*, 130).

Wharton does not spare Ralph Marvell either; endowed with all the qualities, like Ulrich in *The Man Without Qualities*, in fact he has none. He is cultivated, gentle, affectionate, unpretentious, but lacks precisely what Undine has, namely her drive. In that sense, he appears similar to Swann, although Swann is far richer: both are at bottom dilettantes, with interests too broad, too diffuse. They fail as writers and never find a medium to express their creative impulses. Much as Swann toils desultorily on his Vermeer monograph, Ralph's poetic musings are never convincing. He does write two chapters of a novel, just before being hit by the news of Undine's first marriage, and then commits suicide. Is there a link between both characters' failure to write and their fascination with radiant beauty? The lack of vitality displayed by Ralph Marvell, especially when he feels a gap opening between him and his wife, makes the reader long for Undine's untutored spontaneity and wild energy. However, her solution is not to become a libertine (she is not an "immoral woman," p. 222); she just wants a stronger protector. She will not play the role of idealized muse inspiring a poet, who once indeed felt "the releasing power of language" (*CC*, 88), but soon after he lets his "magic wand" lie so as to contemplate his wife's sublime emptiness. His gentle passivity is deepened by this fascination with Undine; he is, in fact, the "coy master" much more than she is the "coy mistress" sung by his namesake, the English poet Marvell. When he tries his hand at a novel he could succeed, had he had the strength to defy convention and perhaps marry Clare, his beloved cousin. Marriage has not worked for Ralph: it has not made him more mature or ready to act upon his desires. Even after Undine has left for Paris alone to enjoy herself in dinners and select salons, he believes that she "was still in the toy age" (*CC*, 193), a statement that applies in fact to himself. Deluded by appearances, he misses the opportunity to become an adult though marriage or adultery, while failing to find freedom through divorce.

Proust's Literary War

Quite the reverse would be true of Swann, although this is never stated explicitly. Swann marries Odette only after he stops being madly in love with her. As Deleuze would say,[17] we move from the sign-system of love, which is described as a disease whose main symptom is morbid jealousy, to the reassuring semiotic system of worldliness, family concerns, and social aspirations. This is why hurried readers are baffled, when they reach the ironical ending of *Swann in Love*, by Swann's coarse dismissal of the whole affair: "To think that I wasted years of my life, that I wanted to die, that I felt my deepest love, for a woman who did not appeal to me, who was not my type!" (*SW*, 396). It takes some readjustment to understand that they did marry later, then had a daughter, Gilberte, who is the narrator's first object of infatuation. The volume published in 1913 is united by Swann: in the first part, his visit disturbs the Oedipal rituals of going to bed and prevents the mother from giving a kiss to the young boy, and later, in the third part, he appears next to his daughter, when the narrator's parents have cut him out because of his marriage to a disreputable woman. Nevertheless, as this volume ends, the narrator seems attracted to Odette, the mother, as she parades in the Bois de Boulogne, saluted by all her former lovers, much more than to the daughter, who fades away, later to marry his best friend, Saint-Loup. Undine and Odette are linked by an eternal beauty that attracts all men despite their vulgarity of expression.

The social comedy of manners is more developed in Proust's *Swann in Love* than in *The Custom of the Country* as the narrative begins *in medias res* with the picturesque and ridiculous Verdurin set, whose salon is the site of the meetings between Swann and Odette, and later a place of torture when Swann is excluded. Proust reproduces at some length the silly mannerisms of the little group, which apes the higher circles while pretending to find them utterly "boring." Odette's lack of culture passes for gentility in this low-brow group, whereas Swann has to downplay his connections with the higher spheres. Wharton indulges in similar comedy at the beginning of *The Custom of the Country*, as when Undine blurts out that she has seen "Sarah Burnhard" perform in a theater, acting in "Leg-long" and "Fade" (*L'Aiglon* and *Phèdre*) (*CC*, 25). Her disappointment with the famous actress, whom she has found to be much older than she expected, echoes the narrator's disappointment in *Swann in Love* when he first sees La Berma (in whom we recognize the same Sarah Bernhardt) as Phèdre in *In the Shadow of Young Girls in Flower*. He too, finds her old and mannered, despite the high praise she had elicited from Bergotte, the famous novelist, and Swann. Just moments later, he naively confesses his disappointment, but the enthusiasm of his father and Mr. Norpois makes him change his mind. The fundamental law of the Verdurin salon is that it has to exclude all other coteries and that it embodies the elite despite Cottard's stupid puns and the nonsensical conversations.

Swann's disgrace comes when he refuses to publicly disown the noble company he keeps. In the sharper light provided by *The Custom of the Country*, we can guess Odette's motivations: she needs to get married as she is tired of her life as a kept woman with many lovers, among whom are a few women. Only a rich and superior man like Swann can fall for this since he has never frequented the lower social circles in which she has been notorious.

Wharton and Proust are modernist writers for different reasons. There is a radical difference between Wharton's rapid completion of her novel and Proust's launching of an almost interminable project. Wharton was a well-known novelist who had no trouble serializing *The Custom of the Country* in *Scribner's Magazine* in January 1913. When the book came out in October, the press was laudatory and the sales brisk. She was immediately acclaimed as the best living American novelist. Not so with Proust. The year 1913 began with new rejections of the first part of *Lost Time*. In 1912, Proust had tried Fasquelle, Gallimard, and Ollendorf; the latter famously replied in February 1913 that he didn't see why a man "should take thirty pages to describe how he turns over in bed before he goes to sleep." Finally Proust signed with Grasset and paid for all expenses. The book was not finished at this point, the final title being found only in May 1913. When the first volume was published in November 1913, despite a campaign of press interviews, the responses of critics were lukewarm, most readers being baffled by the book's complexity. For a novelist like Gide, one of the Gallimard editors who rejected it, this was due less to his famously long sentences than to Proust's reputation as a rich amateur interested in consorting with the nobility of the Faubourg Saint-Germain.

It was typical that the overture should have attracted most criticism. The opening of Proust's novel plunges us into a character's expanded subjectivity. We are told in intricate and fantastic detail how the narrator, who goes to bed early ("For a long time, I went to bed early," *SW*, 3), regularly wakes up without knowing where he is, and changes his self as his surroundings whirl in his mind, or becomes the characters of a book just finished before he fell asleep. This wonderfully crafted initiation is a hymn to the lability of the self, its endless "metempsychosis" unfolds the myriads of selves granted by dreams and fiction to whoever sleeps, reads, or writes. These ruminations constitute a musical overture that slowly involves the reader in the book.

And, half an hour later, the thought that it was time to try to sleep would wake me; I wanted to put down the book I thought I still had in my hands and blow out my light; I had not ceased while sleeping to form reflections on what I had just read, but these reflections had taken a rather peculiar turn; it

seemed to me that I myself was what the book was talking about: a church,
a quartet, the rivalry between François I and Charles V. (*SW*, 3)

The full significance of the conceit that the narrator is the subject of the very
book that he is reading becomes obvious at the end, when we follow the
narrator in his pledge to narrate it all. Proust had thought of *A la recherche du
temps perdu* as a diptych in which the second half would give all the keys to
the riddles left by the first, but the delays imposed by the war forced him to
revise, distend, and increase the scope of his magnum opus.

Wharton's and Proust's novels of 1913 belong to an early modernist
moment of discovery, as both probe the links between form and technique.
Both were aware of the difficulty of expressing the "new" when the old world
was still alive and dominated the social game. The "new" can only be brought
about by unexpected breaks with routine, which was the case with *A la
recherche* when Proust decided to include the Great War in *Time Regained*.
This forced him to multiply last-minute readjustments, to place Combray
on the front line and thus move the village from Normandy to the north
of France, further away from Balbec. During these revisions, the term "modernism" symptomatically cropped up, often used in a derogatory way. At
one point, Charlus links literary critics and war strategists in a denunciation
of modern follies: "To make things worse, the public, after resisting the
modernists of literature or art, is falling into line with the modernists of
war."[18] His pro-German views go deeper, surely, than Cottard's nationalistic
propaganda. Similarly, Bloch praises Rachel's "modernistic diction"[19] as the
younger actress triumphs over the Berma, which marks the triumph of fake
values after the war. The war upsets social relations, bringing low noble
individuals and allowing Bloch, Brichot, Odette, and the Verdurins to prosper
while the noble Saint-Loup has died at the front. The passing of time has
generated a complete reversal of values: we learn that, after Swann's death,
Odette became Madame de Forcheville, having married Swann's old rival.
She appears in the last party as the official mistress of the very old but
still hearty Duc de Guermantes. The most striking transformation concerns
Madame Verdurin. She has lost her husband, married a destitute cousin of
the Prince de Guermantes, and finally, after he died as well, married the
prince himself. Madame Verdurin has become the Princesse de Guermantes
at the end. Proust's main characters repeat the social game of draughts to
which Wharton had reduced serial remarriage: it takes only three or four
well-calculated moves to become the queen.

This process creates a spiral in both cases: Undine is eager to continue the
game by marrying the next available ambassador just as the Proustian reader

re-enters the book just completed. This "bathmology" or "science of degrees," to quote Roland Barthes' term,[20] is allegorized in the noble name of de Chelles, which calls up the French *échelles* (ladders). The game of snakes and ladders is not just cynical: the true meaning of previous epiphanic revelations is given to the narrator at the close of the Guermantes' afternoon reception. All this is grist to the book's endless mill as time will be abolished by art in the end. If the last dinner-party turns into a spectral dance, the vision of the ravages of time leads to esthetic equanimity by steering away from a radical modernity that would have no patience with the "lost" or "wasted" past. Lost time is never lost, because it will be used by fiction. This is how artist and readers become one with the book. The narrator leaves the upper reaches of the social world whose main symbol is the final convergence of the two "ways," that of Swann and that of the Guermantes. As with Wharton, both sides are caught up in the social melting-pot in which remarriage is the strongest ferment of dissolution and recombination. This also makes us hear a submerged pun on the family that stands out for ancient social values before it, too, is caught up in inversions and transformations. The sacred name of Guermantes suggests in echolalia that wars give the lie to apparently steadfast social hierarchies (*les guerres mentent* – "wars are a lie"). No doubt, Walter Berry was inspired when he gave Proust an eighteenth-century volume bearing the arms of the Guermantes family.[21] This was a true memento that he, Wharton, and Proust could share and exchange.

Le Grand Meaulnes and the End of Nostalgia

For Proust, the magical power of ancient nobility was condensed in a name like "Guermantes" while, for Alain-Fournier, the source of fascination was contained in "Yvonne de Galais," the heroine of *Le Grand Meaulnes* who embodies the fading splendor and the sexual charm (*galant*) of ancient France, when it was almost Roman Gaul. This titled past was fast vanishing in 1913, as Proust and Alain-Fournier knew. Yvonne was borrowed from Yvonne de Quièvrecourt, the sprightly young woman wearing a wide-brimmed hat who caught Alain-Fournier's eye on June 1, 1905, as she sauntered down the steps of the Grand-Palais. Entranced, he followed her to a *bateau-mouche*, and thence to the streets until she entered an impressive residence on Boulevard Saint-Germain. The vision morphed into fiction when Meaulnes stumbles into a masked ball and, like a sleepwalker, accompanies his lady on a boat trip. After that initial epiphany, Alain-Fournier saw Yvonne praying in church on Pentecost Sunday. The gift of the tongues was extended to him, and he confessed his love, although he was unable to overcome her resistance. His work revolves around this failure and the initial epiphany whose potentialities he teases out endlessly. He hoped to sway Yvonne when he sent her his first published piece, a slim essay from 1907, "The Body of Woman," which extols purity and advocates that women's bodies remain clothed. The flaunting of weak Catholic estheticism allied with the idealization of motherhood turned out to be counterproductive: Yvonne, a devout Catholic, already engaged, got married in 1906, and became a mother in 1909. If "The Body of Woman" failed to woo her, Le Grand Meaulnes seduced generations of French readers. "The Body of Woman" makes the dubious claim that the vision of a woman praying in a cathedral is most propitious to shape male desire because femininity appears there "mingled with a mysterious, infantile and Christian past."[22] This note of whimpering religiosity has heaped more scorn on Alain-Fournier than any writer active in 1913, and Le Grand Meaulnes has remained associated with adolescence, in the same way as Catcher in the Rye condensed American nostalgia for an authenticity lost by post-World War II baby boomers. Nevertheless, Le Grand Meaulnes merits serious evaluation because it condenses most of the uncertainties and potentialities of the emerging modernism of 1913.

The social spectrum invoked by Alain-Fournier resembles the vision of Irish politics that Yeats developed in 1913 when he imagined that the alliance of the old aristocracy and the educated children of the peasantry would regenerate a country ruined by colonialists, capitalists, and corrupted politicians. In that sense, Le Grand Meaulnes remains close to the center of gravity of France, a country that was predominantly rural before the war. Alain-Fournier depicts the intertwined worlds of instruction in the primary school of a small village and the aristocratic domain of the local squire tucked away close by. Most of the action takes place in rural Sologne, a region of hunting and fishing far from Parisian sophistication. It was the France that Alain-Fournier knew well. He had grown up there, the son of the local schoolteacher, before moving to Paris as a student. The plot is deliciously corny: a young boy arrives at the school and cuts a different figure. He is the "big" or "great" Meaulnes, a natural leader doubled with an incorrigible dreamer and quester. His arrival signals a break in the humdrum lives of the schoolboys. Soon, he feeds their newly triggered excitement when he has an "adventure." Having run away from school, he chances upon a strange property in which a mysterious ritual is in progress. Bluffing, he mixes freely with hired actors and dressed-up children. Then he sees the beautiful Yvonne, with whom he falls in love at first sight. He has to leave when the party is cancelled, not without having glimpsed a distraught and suicidal Frantz. This is Yvonne's brother, who had planned to bring his fiancée to the party; but the wayward woman, Valentine, slipped away, afraid of looking vulgar in such a nobly festive context.

Later on, Meaulnes, obsessed with his vision of the ideal woman during this party, launches a wild-goose chase that leads him to Paris. There he meets Valentine, with whom he has a rather sordid affair. Meanwhile, the narrator has discovered that Yvonne is not very far away, and prepares her for a reunion with Meaulnes. When they meet again, Meaulnes and Yvonne decide to marry, but a secret weighs on Meaulnes' mind and he behaves horribly to his young wife after the marriage. A call from Frantz reminds him of an oath concerning Valentine and sends him on the road again. When he comes back, having succeeded in finally reuniting Franz and Valentine, he learns that Yvonne has died after a difficult birth. Left with a baby daughter, he is ready to engage in "new adventures."

The plot appears to be predicated on the pattern of courtly love, adapting the Romantic fascination with chivalrous ordeals. The chosen woman is idealized, out of reach, and literally "impossible," even after one has married her – once Meaulnes has attained the object of his desire, he leaves: dreams must remain dreams. This finds a parallel when Valentine explains to Meaulnes that she had no choice but to leave Frantz although he loved her, because he admired her too much: "He only saw me in imagination and not as I was."[23] It is inevitable that sexual desire should connect Meaulnes and Valentine, as she offers a degraded image of femininity. In the novel she asks Meaulnes: "Do you want to ask for my hand in marriage, you too?" (p. 367); in the first draft, she says: "At last, what do you want? To sleep with me?" (p. 545). Each time, Meaulnes answers affirmatively. The world in which women are either idealized figures or perverse whores is familiar, and the number of such clichés is increased when the second half of the novel shows a weakening in style and narrative technique. The overall story fails to live up to the evanescent charms of the blurred epiphanies of the first part. Meaulnes, like Tannhäuser, has to atone for a sexual sin, and he will pay the full price when he comes back to a dead wife.

Meaulnes' double is Frantz de Galais, lost in dreams and disguises; he has indulged in regressive escapism since childhood. The "mysterious party" which ravished a schoolboy like Meaulnes is later exposed as a failed attempt at dazzling a young proletarian woman whom Frantz intends to marry, a strategy that radically misfires. It seems that the noble de Galais family needed fresh blood from a lower-middle-class youth like Meaulnes. In fact, Frantz's alter ego is François, the narrator whose French name gets translated into the German of early Romanticism as "Franz". François embodies the scribe, the intellectual as mediator who dreams by proxy and who often speaks of Meaulnes' "adventure" as "our adventure" (p. 338). After Yvonne has given birth and is struggling between life and death, François expresses his despair eloquently: "We had found the beautiful young woman again. We had conquered her. She was the wife of my companion and I, I loved her with the deep and secret friendship that never speaks its name" (p. 357) This allows the reader to glimpse from very close up her charming and doomed silhouette.

Like *The Custom of the Country*, *Le Grand Meaulnes* embodies the travails and difficult birth of modernism in 1913. It gestures to the modern without being able to free itself from the nets of the past. Not strictly speaking a "modernist" novel, as David Ellison has argued in a convincing analysis,[24] it plays with the clichés of modernity as opposed to the faded charms of the past. Ellison resorts to the category of the Romantic "beautiful soul" to do justice to Alain-Fournier's infectious charm in the first part of the novel while acknowledging his limitations as a narrator afterwards. On this view, the main limitation of the novel is its recourse to belated Romantic clichés at a time when modernism had rendered them unavailable. Alain-Fournier's novel, according to Ellison, should be considered as placed in the "crucial transition that occurs, in the period around 1913, between the decline of Romanticism and the explosion of new forms which constitutes what is generally called European Modernism."[25] Ellison thus compares it with two contemporary works, Proust's *Swann's Way* and Rilke's *Duino Elegies*, by situating it differentially as heir to the Romantic tradition of the "beautiful soul." Yet, even if the novel indeed recycles the theme of the "beautiful soul" developed by Schiller, Goethe, and Hegel, it seems too simple to categorize it as a belated version of Romanticism.

The earlier felicities of the text lead to an esthetic error compounded by an ethical failure: "the beauty of the book masks its existential immobility," Ellison writes, taking the unresolved issue of moral choice as a stumbling block. He adds: "The problem of choices and responsibility, as well as the passage to adulthood, are all eluded, bypassed. Poetic imagery (*das Bild*) covers up and stifles moral progress (*die Bildung*)."[26] Nevertheless, Ellison admits that the reason given for Meaulnes' abandonment of his dream, once it has almost been realized, is an ethical sense of having betrayed another dreamer, his brother-in-law Frantz. The real trick played by the novel's narrative is to delay this disclosure, making Meaulnes look like a Romantic who cannot live in peace with his ideal once he has attained it, whereas he has just had as a mistress his future sister-in-law. Understandably, he cannot enjoy domestic bliss without some inner turmoil. This concerted delusion or obfuscation is increased by the narrator's misleading perspective. Witnessing Meaulnes' unease regarding his wife, François segues into Romantic projections that sound like the purple prose of *Great Gatsby* (a novel which displays important affinities with *Le Grand Meaulnes*): "What took place then in that obscure and wild heart? I have often wondered and knew only when it was too late. A remorse that he had ignored? Some unexplainable regrets? The fear of seeing the happiness he was holding in his hand fade away too soon?" (p. 339). The Germanic *Blutbruderschaft* with Frantz triumphs over staid enjoyment of marital happiness, with all the homosexual echoes one can imagine in this case. One of the keys of the novel is provided by the game of projection and identification in which the three male figures are engaged. Repeatedly, Frantz is denounced as immature, and the promise made to him by Meaulnes is "infantile" (p. 340). This puerility is highlighted and denounced several times by François, who cannot stand the "childishness" and "fantasmagorias" of Frantz, a prematurely aged child who oscillates between flights of fancy and sudden despair (p. 335). François is himself infected by the Romantic virus, as I will suggest. One can wonder whether Meaulnes has matured at the end, when he returns, his mission accomplished. To be sure, he has grown a beard and sounds even more elliptic in his utterances. And the *deus ex machina* effectively steals the "joy" upon which the narrator had counted – being the surrogate father of Yvonne's daughter. We will all be frustrated in the end.

François the narrator remains an incorrigible Romantic who embodies the "beautiful soul" more surely than Meaulnes. When the text mentions the distant "beautiful souls," it is not so much Meaulnes who dreams as François, who imagines his friend's fantasies: "He departed. [. . .] No doubt, over there, on the lawns, attentive young girls spoke of love. One could imagine, over there, their souls, beautiful souls."[27] Insofar as François stands for the reader and does not permit us to see things clearly, the book can be called Romantic and ethically deficient. Yet such a reading tends to be too gullible and take the book's narratological sleight of hand for granted. I would argue that its modernity is to be discerned not in its initial beauties but in the radical way in which the second part resorts to hackneyed plots and clichés handed down from popular literature. The debased world of juvenile adventures enacts a thorough debunking of Romanticism just when the novel becomes more like Stevenson than like d'Annunzio.

Indeed, the book's initial style recalls the poetic prose of a d'Annunzio, or the style invented by Joyce to render Stephen's progression through sexuality and estheticism in *A Portrait of the Artist as a Young Man*. Alain-Fournier's strategy is no doubt less subtle, but when he lets his novel progress through different styles it cannot be called an accident: it does not suggest either the weakening of earlier stylistic felicities or moral deficiency. Like Joyce's *Bildungsroman*, *Le Grand Meaulnes* stages its own temporality as it struggles with a Romantic nostalgia whose parody is literalized by language. What could be better adapted to the debasement of "infantile" ideals than the hackneyed world of popular fiction? The second half of the novel is wooden and clumsy with a purpose. The clumsiness is increased as we stick to the privileged point of view of François, the narrator, so as to be privy to Meaulnes' most intimate thoughts. This interesting technical dilemma has not been solved well by Alain-Fournier; however, in this treatment by proxy, the narrator reframes nostalgia, shows us that even nostalgia has aged badly, thus forcing us to question the earlier staging of mystery, purity, and perfection. The starting point of the quest, the bizarre ceremonial seen by Meaulnes who has wandered into the magic of a "mysterious domain" in which children are disguised and adults wear old-fashioned costumes, embodies his deepest dreams and desires, but it is consciously and systematically debunked. When we learn that the masked ball was a misguided ploy through which Frantz wanted to dazzle a reluctant fiancée, who is put off by the old-fashioned display, we understand that the novel depicts less the miracle of enchantment than its very destruction. The costumes and disguises used by the actors in a family charade are just that: old-fashioned devices that can be discarded.

Le Grand Meaulnes exemplifies emergent modernism in 1913, a modernism which is still uncertain, hesitant because caught up in nostalgia while struggling to get rid of it by shaping a modern idiom. It harks back to a Romantic yearning for Novalis' blue flower or Nerval's *chimères*, all the while trying to adapt to the dire realities of modern life. Most of the novel takes place in a countryside setting, with the grainy evocation of quaint villages and devoted schoolteachers; we are still in the nineteenth-century *Bildungsroman*, and follow a hero who emerges from confined surroundings before reaching the frustrations and disappointments of the metropolis. *Le Grand Meaulnes* thus attempts to denounce its own "puerilities," even when it has to admit that such "puerilities" are the best of what it has to offer in terms of language and style. The difficult balance struck between nostalgia and disillusionment derives from the legacy of Flaubert, as shown by the deeply ambivalent portrayal of Frédéric Moreau in *Sentimental Education*: Valentine is a younger Rosanette while Yvonne is a doomed Madame Arnoult. Joyce struggled with similar issues of artistic and ethical distance regarding Stephen in *A Portrait of the Artist as a Young Man*, as all post-Flaubertians who had passed through symbolism knew: novels would play on Romantic clichés that were critiqued at several levels simultaneously. If "adventure" triumphs in the end – it is the novel's last word, it is because it cannot but remain in the future mode. As for us, we are left with the dire limitations of François, the half-reliable narrator. Alain-Fournier was killed in action in September 1914, leaving us another type of sadness since we are forced to see his novel less as a "novel of adolescence" than as the juvenilia of a gifted writer who died just before he turned 28, an age at which Joyce had only completed *Dubliners* and a collection of poetry, the pale and antiquated *Chamber Music*.

Conclusion

Antagonisms

The violent energies of an unspent and therefore ghostly Romanticism were soon to find an outlet in the Great War. Meaulnes' last adventure, had he been a real person, would have brought him inevitably to the muddy trenches of Verdun, and it is likely that his little daughter would have been an orphan in 1918. What has struck, and continues to strike, historians is the bellicist enthusiasm that took advanced countries like France, England, Italy, Austria, and Germany by storm in the summer of 1914. Sophisticated, cosmopolitan, and internationalist artists and writers like Cendrars, Gaudier-Brzeska, and Apollinaire expressed one wish – to go fight the enemy. All three could have easily avoided the draft, for reasons of nationality (Cendrars and Apollinaire only received French nationality after they had enlisted) or distance (Gaudier was living in London and could have avoided being drafted because of his family situation). Is it simply that Romanticism was not dead yet, or, more disturbingly, that modernism also contributed to the general unleashing of this passionate aggressivity?

We need to distinguish between a Europe-centered modernism and a more expansive geography that encompasses the whole world caught in the throes of the early globalization that I have hoped to sketch. If the American public remained at some distance from the European conflagration and was split between Republican interventionism and Wilson's reluctance to join the war, it was still informed of the crisis in Europe. The newspapers reported the race in shipbuilding and the production of new armaments between Britain, Germany, and France. In May, Winston Churchill offered a one-year truce, only to be rebuked when the Kaiser announced plans to build an even stronger armada. Yet some sought reassurance in the belief that socialist leaders like Jaures in France and Liebknecht in Germany would oppose any drift to war with a general strike. As early as January 1913, the *Atlantic*

Monthly asked its regular contributor, the Italian journalist and prolific cultural critic Guglielmo Ferrero, to present "The Dangers of War in Europe" to its public. In this wide-ranging and premonitory article, written while the Tripoli campaign had not yet been concluded, Ferrero sketches a whole history of Europe. He contrasts the optimism of the previous century, marked by a successful fight against absolutism and the rise of liberalism, to the deepening gloom of the first decade of the twentieth century. In the middle of the nineteenth century, the utopia of the bourgeois liberals had almost come true when power had shifted from the princes, kings, and courts to democratically elected parliaments. They believed that the old wars of conquest triggered by ambition, family feuds, ancient glory, and royal caprice would end: the populations, newly freed and enlightened, represented in parliaments, would grasp that imperialist wars were against their best interests. True, they would want to defend themselves against aggression while trying to live in peace with neighbors animated by similar ideals. However, according to Ferrero, this promise proved to be false, for instead of peace being given to nations freed from the royal yoke, general warfare now threatened from all sides.

Ferrero's thesis comes close to Fullerton's views as expressed in *Problems of Power*, although the Italian writer downplays the economic factor. For Ferrero, the triumph of post-1848 liberalism led directly to the bellicose situation in 1913; in most countries, democracy had come too quickly, preventing public opinion from maturing. This, coupled with the increased power of the press, unleashed a dangerous nationalism that infected populations much more than their rulers: "It is the people who are fired with a desire for war, while their governments, together with their sovereigns, devoted to the preservation of peace, resist as long as they can the pressure of public opinion, even at the risk of losing their popularity for which they so eagerly strive."[1] Thus Italy's war against the Turkish empire in Libya had been launched by popular assent, defended by a massive press campaign, whereas the king remained cautious: "The war in Tripoli was made by the people and those newspapers which were the people's organs . . ."[2] Ferrero points out similarly that in Germany, it was Kaiser Wilhelm II who saved international peace during the 1905 Moroccan crisis with France, against public opinion. This paradoxical situation was all the more fraught with danger as the older mental categories did not apply. In the new situation, the masses appeared more conservative, more entranced by tradition, more easily swayed by nationalistic frenzy, whereas the political rulers tended to be realistic. The ideals inherited from the Enlightenment were shared by elite groups only, and these tended to lose touch with the excitable majority.

When public opinion is prejudiced in favor of war and imperialist aggression, any educated appeal to reason is all but impotent. Thus, foreseeing the rise of a populist fascism after the war, Ferrero blames war on an ineradicable Romanticism that blinds people to the collective sufferings brought about by war: "we now see in Europe that the Christian and humanitarian education of centuries has not succeeded in eradicating from the masses their warlike propensities, while a prolonged season of peace, with the omnipresence of newspapers, and the superficial instruction of the elementary schools, easily deceives the popular imagination by representing war under a romantic aspect, as a kind of national sport, creating at once entertainment and glory."[3] Tellingly, Ferrero analyzes the image of the Abyssinian war created by the Italian popular press: magnified as an epic legend, the lurid romance turns into a paean to patriotic fervor, remaining blind to the dire realities of the mass slaughter of civilians and general devastation.

From this perspective, war would be the consequence of the paradoxical conflation of a modern evolution towards democracy in a period of industrial revolution and scientific progress, and the spectral resurgence of an ancient heroic Romanticism, a compromise between the fruits of the French Revolution and the return of the nationalist myths. Democracy had not succeeded in educating the masses or raising their political consciousness. The belligerent situation of Europe in which seven or more nations, armed to the teeth, were ready to slaughter each other, demonstrated a weakening of democratic ideals. Yet each nation was both afraid of its neighbors and confident that war would bring an immediate victory. The huge reshuffling of Europe begun by Napoleon had reached completion in 1913, and its outcome looked terrifying. Ferrero concluded by arguing that the solution lay in more democracy and more socialism. He stressed that there was an urgent need for competent political elites capable of understanding the new situation, of leading enlightened governments instead of looking for personal wealth in commerce and industry.

If this diagnosis is accurate, it helps us to understand the plight of the modernists: they could not revert to the old rationalism that had been debunked by Nietzsche, Bergson, and the left-wing post-Hegelians and Marxists, and they could not partake of the Romantic myths of blood, the earth, and the nation; they therefore had few weapons at their disposal. One of these was irony, and it often missed its aim, or was liable to be misunderstood. A good example of this can be found in the critique of eugenics attempted by Jean Cocteau in 1913. We have seen with Yeats and Alain-Fournier how the idea of a rejuvenated nation created by the blood alliance between the "races" of the peasants and the nobility was still tempting. This ideology often led to the concept of wars as regenerating bloodbaths. The young and gifted Cocteau was completely opposed to such an idea. In 1912 he created a ballet for Diaghilev's Ballets Russes entitled *The Blue God*. Having outgrown his conflicted and jealous friendship with Proust and his infatuation with Nijinsky, in 1913 he was still looking for his voice as a writer. He accompanied Stravinsky to Switzerland while working on his *Potomak*, a series of 60 or so drawings accompanied by textual vignettes. He had begun it in 1912 when staying in Jacques-Emile Blanche's country house in Offranville, under Gide's interested and paternal gaze (he guessed that Cocteau was imitating his earlier witty parable of *Paludes*). Blanche would say on this occasion that "everything shows that we are running headlong to a cataclysm, even the young Cocteau, with all his youth, can feel it."[4] The *Potomak* was published as a book after the war, with a dedication to Igor Stravinsky insisting on the fact that the main trigger for such an experimental book was the *Rite of Spring*:

My dear Igor,

It is not by accident that I am offering this book to you.

After THE FIREBIRD, that, coming from the snows, crossed Siegfried's forest to land among us, and the poor puppet Petrushka who died one Andersen evening at the sound of harmonicas, THE RITE OF SPRING celebrates its rituals. [. . .] Your masterpiece resembles an egg because it is full of life and mystery. I remember calling it after the first performance "The Georgics of Prehistory." I now add: His pastoral. A ferocious eclogue. [. . .] The Album of the Eugènes imposed itself to me in a country estate where, every day, your music was played to me. One heard the heavy stumping of heels hitting the earth . . .[5]

The genesis of this patchwork book is complex.[6] In 1912, Cocteau started drawing funny sea-monsters to amuse Blanche's young nephew. Gathered in an album, they soon took on a life of their own and were given human clothes, huge paunches, and voracious habits. These disquieting little Ubus would eat up humans, especially relishing their entrails, gobbling them up whole at night or during concerts. They preyed on the stereotypical couple of the Mortimers who first seemed unaware of these proliferating parasites, then started evincing anguish facing the "Thing." "Eugène" was one of Cocteau's first names, and he used the grotesque creatures to deride petty-bourgeois rituals and the conventions of married life. The Mortimers are devoured again and again, in a sexual ingestion that betrays a libidinal ambivalence. Cocteau himself pointed out the pun on *gêne*, meaning embarrassment, while a more relevant echo can be heard: the Eugènes embody "eugenics" with a vengeance. "Eugène," meaning literally "well born," is a sarcastic joke played on the idea of birth and propriety. The perverse couple made up of the Mortimers and the Eugènes points to the traumatic nature of physiological functions, including sexuality and reproduction (in all its senses, thus art as well), as well as nutrition. Thus Cocteau tells contemporaries like Alain-Fournier: "Eat up your nostalgia!" The *Potomak* puts an end to the regressive dreams of an original race, and forces French readers to swallow their national pride and eat an Anglicized "dead mother" (one can hear *morte mère* and *mortifère* in Mortimer).

The *Potomak* also parodies the psychoanalytic scenario in which Cocteau himself was caught, between the dim memory of a father who had committed suicide and an all-too-present mother, so devoted that she smothered him. However, as early as 1915, when Cocteau had enlisted in the ambulance corps, he would adapt these grotesque drawings to a propagandist aim: the "War Eugènes" became traditional German "ogres" or "Huns" with a recognizable spiked helmet.[7] Although he adapted the Eugènes saga to the war effort, Cocteau later felt the need to tone down such patriotic readings. In the second edition of 1924, he mocked reductive allegorization and insisted that in 1915 he was still reading Nietzsche and listening to Bach.[8] Once more, modernist derision had been hesitant and finally misunderstood. Nevertheless, *Potomak* stands out as Cocteau's first real book, a book whose zany arabesques and disconcerting verbal pyrotechnics announce the spirit of Dada. There, both the ideology of the modern and its opposite, romantic nostalgia, are mercilessly ridiculed: the bourgeois who go sightseeing and try to understand the opera belong to a "couple" also made up of those ghoulish devourers. Significantly, Cocteau names one literary predecessor, Gertrude Stein, when he quotes an incident that took place in 1913. He heard a group of friends giggling, shocked by what they took to be the most preposterous sentence ever: "Dining is West."[9] Far from sharing their scorn at Gertrude Stein's nonsense, he saw the liberating potential of those apparently absurd words: "A single epithet should suffice to trigger dreams, a light shoulder neck, a single signpost. What annoyed this group, the American farce, on the contrary seemed to me a proof of confidence. // Already, better than a ruin, the new touched my heart and sailed off, rounded, towards risk. The new harnessed with mystery, that was what I was turning around, before the cell of a choice restricted its potential."[10] In an ironic homage, the choice of the American river, deliberately misspelled with its final *k*, obeys a similar logic of openings and disruptive non sequiturs while acknowledging Stein's avant-gardist assurance.

212

After making a decision in favor of risk, the *Potomak* mounts a satire of biology and eugenics via the monstrous Eugènes. They announce the rather sinister Mr. Eugenides, the Smyrna merchant met in London and who invites the narrator of *The Waste Land* to a special weekend in Brighton. Cocteau shared Stein's disgust with the dominant ideology of normalcy, especially when it led to racial theories. In a letter, Cocteau made the connection before dismissing it for being only partly relevant: "Think just for a second of the 'well born,' of the Eumenides even, and then let's forget about it, please."[11] Like the Eugènes, the Greek Eumenides were named by antiphrasis "the kindly ones," whereas they were the three Furies, the agents of the vengeance of the gods when they wanted to punish humans. Thus, in Sophocles' version, Orestes is struck by them after the murder of his mother, pushed by Antigone. These neo-classical tragic echoes would attract Cocteau to Orpheus and Antigone after the war, while suggesting an ancient crisis, a mythical substratum to an inevitable war. In the *Potomak*, he simply titles an autobiographical paragraph "Antigone's lamentations," just before sketching his new "minimalist esthetic."[12]

Antigone's name condenses opposition to generation (*anti-gone*) and suggests radical feminine antagonism to the values of the *polis*, according to Hegel's famous analysis in the *Phenomenology of Spirit*. The notion of a war of women had been denounced virulently but also given wider credence by the British biologist whom we have already encountered, Walter Heape. In his hugely popular *Sex Antagonism* (1913), he began by analyzing the current "discontent" in matters of sex that seemed to permeate society. Anticipating Freud's later *Civilization and its Discontents*, Heape listed three main sources of unrest in civilization: class, sex, and race. "The origin of this universal unrest may be traced broadly to three sources, Racial antagonism, Class antagonism, and Sex antagonism."[13] Heape developed this trinity of struggles, passing rapidly on racial conflicts, while seeming more tolerant of class antagonism. He stated that "class readjustment" is not a "national evil" but "a sign of the vigour of a people."[14] He added: "this is a class war that we are experiencing," and he saw no immediate end to this phenomenon. By contrast with the first two, "sex antagonism" seemed a more recent phenomenon, although Heape demonstrated throughout his book that it had always existed. To do so, he deployed a genealogy of exogamy and totemism that provided a framework in which social constraints about sexual objects were to evolve over time. In the end, Heape asserted the pre-eminence of biology over history when he deemed women inferior because of their different sexual constitution. Heape was evidently not a progressive, although his highlighting race, class, and gender as the three realms of a continuous social struggle is a good reminder that the outbreak of the Great War in 1914 put an end, at least temporarily, to these unresolved quarrels. The military war silenced or suppressed them, until they came back in the twenties – this time, women won the right to vote in most advanced countries, even if there was still a lot to be desired on the race and class fronts. In 1913, however, class war seemed incompatible with nationalistic war. This proved to be a decisive factor in the policy of the German intelligence services regarding Stalin, Trotsky, and Lenin; they helped these revolutionaries, allowing them to go back to Russia in order to preach class warfare, bring about a revolution, and prevent the tsarist regime from waging war on the eastern front.

It would be an unfair exaggeration to say that all the modernists were rabid warmongers: Pound, Broch, Joyce, D. H. Lawrence, and a few others voiced their rejection of militarism, and their suspicion of the "red herring" of nationalism, as Pound would say. Pound, an American living in London, was immediately struck by the enormity of the loss when friends such as T. E. Hulme and Gaudier-Brzeska were killed. Those who resisted the drift to war usually did so because their internationalist ethos led to a double critique of Romanticism and modernity. This was demonstrated most clearly in an early poem written by Hermann Broch. In 1913, Broch, then under the influence of Karl Kraus' pacifism, penned a poem entitled "Cantos 1913" in which he denounced the bellicose nationalism of Austria and Germany. This wholesale attack on militarism was later used as a prologue for a collection of stories in which he denounced the ethical lack of responsibility that led to the rise of Hitler, *The Guiltless*. Broch changed the title to *Voices 1913* in 1950 because of the publicity being given at that time to Pound's *Cantos*, a poem which he found to be deeply tainted by fascism. His poem begins with a dialogue between a father and a son: the father expresses a naive trust in progress, and represents the values of the nineteenth century; the son is more skeptical and afraid, as he sees the return of the repressed as ghosts. The father insists that "progress is real and limitless" and that there is no need to talk about ghosts. The son reasserts that progress has been "a gift and a curse to the human race," since it has shattered even our "ground" and the very "space" in which we live.[15] The father denounces his son as a "reactionary" whereas the son laments the unmooring of the infinite in a new world-view that has shattered being. Confusion, anguish, and panic lead populations to the mistaken belief that salvation will come from war alone. Meanwhile, the scions of the bourgeoisie enjoy the last parties and look down on the uneducated masses without feeling any kind of responsibility for the situation:

214

And so the year thirteen has passed away
With empty sound and operatic stance.
The light-slung arch, however, still holds sway
recalling festivals and rites of high romance,
lace, corsets, crinolines, and stand-up collars that choke,
last gentle farewell year of the Baroque.[16]

More than this deluded "farewell to Europe," the object of Broch's scorn is utter stupidity. Stupidity would later be denounced as kitsch by the Austrian writer, and it consists in idealizing everything:

For stupidity is lack of imagination;
it mouths abstractions, babbles holy concepts,
native soil and country's honor, women and children
to be defended. But faced with the concrete, it
loses its tongue, no more able to imagine
men's shattered bodies, faces, limbs,
than the hunger it imposes on
their faithful wives and dear little
children.[17]

Stupidity does not spare poets and philosophers who praise war, even when it is class war: there, too, the "bravely flying flags on barricades" (Broch was opposed to the Spartacists but close to the trade unionist with whom he held a dialogue after the war) betray, according to him, the same kind of dangerous lyrical illusion. Fundamentally, Broch agrees with Ferrero, and both illustrate Cocteau's diagnosis: the Eugènes are the greedy ghosts who invade our dreams; it is after all not necessary to see them turn into German soldiers rather than any other type of enemy. The coupling of romantic yearning and modernistic forays into the absurd should not blind us to the ethical function of the writer. In Broch's historical and metaphysical scheme, 1913 is the first stage in the progression of three "dishonest decades" that culminated in 1933 with the generalization of terror , especially in Germany.

While not leaving aside these ethical and political concerns, I would like simply to note that the emerging modernism of 1913 attempted precisely to make us imagine things differently – which is why it has kept its value as a testimony, even if it has been unable to make people and governments change much (if at all). For 1913 gives us a glimpse of modernism before it was canonized, systematized, or institutionalized, a process that would take place rapidly in the late twenties, and which continued until the mid-fifties. This early modernism arose before any distinction was made between progressive form and regressive content (even though Adorno tried to introduce this gap in a later assessment of *The Rite of Spring*, as we have seen). True, it often remained a witness to the ongoing modernization process that led to globalization, a globalization that, in its turn, rendered war all but inevitable. The same inevitability also made modernism the dominant form in the arts and literature. After 1913, a whole world of references, echoes, and allusions suddenly became as obsolete as corsets and stand-up collars. This year should thus still be taken as a point of reference for what we consider as "new" today, and this is why a recent poetry magazine has taken it as a title: what the journal *1913*[18] exemplifies perfectly is the need to return to that moment and understand it more fully, to replay its stakes and appreciate all of its nuances in order to assess better the originality and relevance of present-day endeavors. In brief, 1913 gives access less to an ur-modernism than it discloses a privileged moment in the history of modernity, a time full of foreboding and instruction for future generations, a time when literature and culture uniquely wrestled with a world that seemed on the brink of chaos and uncertainty.

Notes

Introduction

1   Morton Fullerton, *Problems of Power* (New York: Scribner's Sons, 1913), 282–3. I will return to this book soon.

2   Leonardo Sciascia, *1912 + 1* (Milan: Edizioni Adelphi, 1986).

3   Modris Eksteins, *Rites of Spring: The Great War and the Birth of the Modern Age* (New York: Houghton Mifflin, 1989).

4   A very good discussion of *Erwartung* will be found in Christopher Butler's *Early Modernism: Literature, Music and Painting in Europe in 1900–1916* (Oxford: Oxford University Press, 1994), 111–15.

5   See Allen Shawn, *Arnold Schoenberg's Journey* (New York: Farrar, Straus & Giroux, 2002), 148.

6   Michael North, *Reading 1922: A Return to the Scene of the Modern* (Oxford: Oxford University Press, 1999).

7   Marc Manganaro, *Culture, 1922* (Princeton: Princeton University Press, 2002).

8   Hans Ulrich Gumbrecht, *In 1926: Living at the Edge of Time* (Cambridge, MA: Harvard University Press, 1997).

9   Ibid. 426, in italics in the text.

10   Marjorie Perloff, *The Futurist Moment: Avant-Garde, Avant Guerre and the Language of Rupture* (Chicago: University of Chicago Press, 1986).

11   Liliane Brion-Guerry, ed., *L'Année 1913: Les Formes esthétiques de l'œuvre d'art à la veille de la première guerre mondiale*, 3 vols (Paris: Klincksieck, 1971).

12   Frederic Morton, *Thunder at Twilight: Vienna 1913/1914* (Cambridge, MA: Da Capo Press, 2001).

13   Alan Valentine, *1913: America between Two Worlds* (New York: Macmillan, 1962).

14   Virginia Cowles, *1913: An End and a Beginning* (New York: Harper & Row, 1968).

15   Brion-Guerry, "Pourquoi 1913?", in *L'Année 1913*, vol. 1, 8–13.

16   Sir Charles Petrie, *The Drift to World War 1900–1914* (London: Ernest Benn, 1968), 7.

17 Paul Virilio, *Speed and Politics: An Essay on Dromology* (1977; New York: Semiotext(e), 1986); *War and Cinema: The Logistics of Perception* (London: Verso, 1989); *The Virilio Reader*, ed. James Der Derian (Oxford: Blackwell, 1998); and Steve Redhead, *Paul Virilio: Theorist for an Accelerated Culture* (Toronto, University of Toronto Press, 2004).

18 *New York Times*, Apr. 21, 1912, quoted in Stephen Kern, *The Culture of Time and Space 1880–1918* (Cambridge, MA: Harvard University Press, 1983), 67.

19 I have used several websites dedicated to the "origins of the First World War" to condense this synthesis. Among the historical summaries, next to Petrie's *The Drift to World War*, one can consult Richard C. Hall, *The Balkan Wars 1912–1913: Prelude to the First World War* (London: Routledge, 2000).

20 Hall, *The Balkan Wars 1912–1913*, 118.

21 See Michael Hardt and Antonio Negri, *Empire* (Cambridge, MA: Harvard University Press, 2000), and, by the same authors, *Multitude: War and Democracy in the Age of Empire* (New York: Penguin, 2004).

22 Doug Henwood, "What is Globalization Anyway?", in Amitava Kumar, ed., *World Bank Literature* (Minneapolis: University of Minnesota Press, 2003). For a wholesale rejection of Hardt and Negri's arguments, see Ellen Meiksins Wood, *Empire of Capital* (London: Verso, 2003).

23 Niall Ferguson, *Empire: The Rise and Demise of the British World Order and the Lessons for Global Power* (New York: Basic Books, 2002).

24 Fullerton, *Problems of Power*, vii. Edith Wharton had read the first drafts of *Problems of Power* when it was originally called *Internationalities*. See Marion Mainwaring, *Mysteries of Paris: The Quest for Morton Fullerton* (Hanover, NH: University of New England Press, 2001), and Dale Bauer, *Edith Wharton's Brave New Politics* (Madison, WI: University of Wisconsin Press, 1994).

25 Karl Marx and Friedrich Engels, *The Communist Manifesto*, in Karl Marx, *Selected Writings*, ed. David McLellan (Oxford: Oxford University Press, 1977), 224–5.

26 See Michel Decaudin's preface to Jules Romains, *La Vie unanime, Poème, 1905–07* (Paris: Gallimard, 1983), 18.

27 See on this point Walter Benjamin's *Charles Baudelaire: A Lyric Poet in the Era of High Capitalism*, trans. Harry Zohn (London: Verso, 1997).

28 See Hardt and Negri, *Empire*.

29 For this account, I have used the excellent biography by David Levering Lewis, *W. E. B. Du Bois: Biography of a Race*, vol. 1: *1868–1919* (New York: Henry Holt, 1993), 408–500.

1 The New in the Arts

1 Richard Ellmann, *James Joyce* (1959; rev. edn, Oxford: Oxford University Press, 1982), 301.

2   See Robin Waltz's "The Lament of Fantômas," in *Pulp Surrealism: Insolent Popular Culture in Early Twentieth Century Paris* (Berkeley: University of California Press, 2000), 42–75.

3   Quoted in Stephen Kern, *The Culture of Time and Space, 1880–1918* (Cambridge, MA: Harvard University Press, 1983), 260.

4   Guillaume Apollinaire, "The New Spirit and the Poets" (1917–18), in *Selected Writings*, ed. Roger Shattuck (New York: New Directions, 1971), 230.

5   Ibid. 228.

6   *Sacre* means literally "coronation" while *Massacre* means "slaughter." The easy pun acquired more relevance in August 1914 . . .

7   Richard Buckle, *Diaghilev* (New York: Atheneum, 1979), 182.

8   Gertrude Stein, *Writings*, vol. 1: *1903–1932*, ed. Catharine. R. Simpson and Harriet Chessman (New York: Library of America, 1998), 797–8.

9   Quoted in Buckle, *Diaghilev*, 253.

10 See André Boucourechliev, *Igor Stravinsky* (Paris: Fayard, 1982).

11 T. W. Adorno, *Philosophy of Modern Music*, trans. Anne G. Mitchell and Wesley V. Blomster (London and New York: Continuum, 2003), 145 and 140.

12 Ibid. 146.

13 Ibid. 150–1.

14 Ibid. 160.

15 For an account of this evolution, see Max Paddington, "Stravinsky as Devil: Adorno's Three Critiques," in Jonathan Cross, ed., *The Cambridge Companion to Stravinsky* (Cambridge: Cambridge University Press, 2003), 192–202.

16 See Roger Shattuck's *The Banquet Years: The Arts in France 1885–1918* (New York: Harcourt, Brace & Co., 1958), 113–45, for a good analysis of the last two decades of Satie's life. Satie died in 1924. See also Anne Rey, *Satie* (Paris: Seuil, 1995).

17 See Lawrence Rainey, *The Annotated Waste Land* (New Haven: Yale University Press, 2005), 96–9, for the whole score.

18 Jean Cocteau, *A Call to Order*, trans. Rollo Myers (London: 1926), 43.

19 Adorno, *Philosophy of Modern Music*, 138 and 191.

20 See Christine Poggi, *In Defiance of Painting: Cubism, Futurism, and the Invention of Collage* (New Haven: Yale University Press, 1992).

21 In Guillaume Apollinaire, *Chroniques d'Art 1902–1918* (Paris: Gallimard, 1960), 350–7.

22 Apollinaire reviewed the show's catalog in November 1913: ibid. 425.

23 "Mr Bennet and Mrs Brown" (1924), in *A Woman's Essays*, ed. Rachel Bowlby (London: Penguin, 1992), 70. See also Peter Stansky, *On or About December 1910* (Cambridge, MA: Harvard University Press, 1996).

24 Virginia Woolf, *Roger Fry: A Biography* (1940; London: Harvester, 1976).

25 Ibid. 300.

26 Ibid. 669.

27 Virginia Woolf, "Walter Sickert," in *Collected Essays*, vol. 2 (London: Hogarth Press, 1966), 236.

28 Ibid. 240.

29 Ibid.

30 Ibid. 237.

31 Ibid.

32 "Modern Art," *The New Age* (Jan. 22, 1914), in Walter Sickert, *The Complete Writings on Art*, ed. Anna Gruetzner Robins (Oxford: Oxford University Press, 2000), 338.

33 "The Cubist Room," in *Wyndham Lewis on Art: Collected Writings 1913–1956*, ed. Walter Michel and C. J. Fox (New York: Funk & Wagnalls, 1969), 57.

34 Ibid. 56.

35 Ibid.

36 Ibid. 57.

37 About *Lacerba* and Papini's evolution, see Walter A. Adamson, *Avant-Garde Florence: From Modernism to Fascism* (Cambridge, MA: Harvard University Press, 1993).

38 See appendix II, "Exhibitions Arranged by Stieglitz 1902–46," in Sue Davidson Lowe, *Stieglitz: A Memoir/Biography* (New York: Farrar, Straus & Giroux, 1983), 429–37.

39 Milton W. Brown, *The Story of the Armory Show* (New York: Abbeville Press, 1988), 43–4. See also Abraham A. Davidson, *Early American Modernist Painting 1910–1935* (New York: Harper & Row, 1981).

40 Brown, *The Story of the Armory Show*, 137.

41 Clement Greenberg, "Convention and Innovation," in *Homemade Esthetic: Observations on Art and Taste* (Oxford: Oxford University Press, 1999), 55.

42 Ibid.

43 Ibid. 56.

44 See Stephanie Barron and Maurice Tuchman, eds, *The Avant-Garde in Russia 1910–1930: New Perspectives* (Cambridge, MA: MIT Press, 1980).

45 I quote and translate from K. S. Malevitch, *Le Miroir suprématiste*, trans. and ed. J.-C. and V. Marcadé (Lausanne: L'Age d'Homme, 1977), 41. See also Serge Fauchereau, *Malevitch*, trans. Alan Swan (New York: Rizzoli, 1993).

46 *Le Miroir*, 42.

47 Quoted in Fauchereau, *Malevitch*, 18.

2 Collective Agencies

1 Louis Latzarus, "La Journée Brisset," *Le Figaro* (Apr. 13, 1913), article reproduced on the Jean-Pierre Brisset website.

2 Ibid. Latzarus concludes by dissociating himself from such a cruel practical joke that put on an innocent old man's head a "crown of derision."

3 See Jean-Pierre Brisset, *La Science de Dieu*, in *La Grammaire logique, suivi de La Science de Dieu*, ed. Michel Foucault (Paris: Tchou, 1970), 155. See also Jean-Pierre Brisset, *Œuvres complètes*, ed. Marc Décimo (Dijon: Les Presses du Réel, 2001).

4 *La Science de Dieu*, 110–11.

5 See Roger Shattuck, *The Banquet Years*, rev. edn (New York: Random House, 1968), 63–6.

6 From Marcel Duchamp's 1946 interview with J. J. Sweeney, in *Marchand du Sel: Ecrits de Marcel Duchamp*, ed. Michel Sanouillet (Paris: Le Terrain Vague, 1958), 113. See also Marc Décimo, *Jean-Pierre Brisset: Prince des penseurs, inventeur, grammairien, et prophète* (Paris: Les Presses du Réel, 2001).

7 Quoted in François Caradec, *Raymond Roussel*, trans. Ian Monk (London: Atlas Press, 2001), 135.

8 Jean-Jacques Lecercle, *Philosophy through the Looking-Glass: Language, Nonsense, Desire* (London: Hutchinson, 1985).

9 See Ferdinand de Saussure, *Words upon Words*, ed. Jean Starobinski (New Haven: Yale University Press, 1979).

10 Brisset states that the ancient Romans already spoke Italian; then for some reason, such as the need to hide meanings, they decided to "invert" it. See the section "Latin Is Artificial" in *La Grammaire logique*, 87.

11 Jules Romains, *Les Copains* (Paris: Gallimard, Folio, 1984), 116.

12 See Jacques Derrida, *Politics of Friendship*, trans. George Collins (London: Verso, 1997).

13 Guillaume Apollinaire, *Œuvres en prose complètes*, vol. 2, ed. Pierre Caizergues and Michel Decaudin (Paris: Gallimard, Pléiade, 1991), 960–3.

14 Guillaume Apollinaire, *La Vie anecdotique*, in *Œuvres en prose complètes*, vol. 3, ed. Pierre Caizergues and Michel Decaudin (Paris: Gallimard, Pléiade, 1993), 54.

15 See Marcel Proust, *Remembrance of Things Past*, trans. C. K. Scott Moncrieff, Terence Kilmartin, and Andreas Mayor (New York: Random House, 1982), 916–17.

16 V. I. Lenin, "Conversation" (Mar./Apr. 1913), in *Collected Works*, vol. 19 (Moscow: Progress Publishers, 1977), 45.

17 See Frederic Morton, *Thunder at Twilight; Vienna 1913/1914* (Cambridge, MA: Da Capo Press, 2001), 19–23.

18 It was published in *Prosveshcheniye*, nos 3–5 (Mar./May 1913).

19 Apollinaire, *Œuvres en prose complètes*, vol. 3, 138–40.

20 Ibid. 1191 n.

21 See Calvin Tomkins, *Duchamp: A Biography* (New York: Henry Holt, 1996), 221–2.

22 Apollinaire, *Œuvres en prose complètes*, vol. 2, 937–9 and 1675–82 for the handwritten manuscript.

23 Ibid. 6.

24 Ibid.

25 This was in the eleventh issue, June 1, 1913; see Noëmi Blumenkranz-Onimus, "*Lacerba* ou le nouvel ordre du désordre," in Liliane Brion-Guerry, ed., *L'Année 1913: Les Formes esthétiques de l'œuvre d'art à la veille de la première guerre mondiale*, 3 vols (Paris: Klincksieck, 1971), vol. 2, 1124.

26 "Zone," trans. Samuel Beckett, in Beckett, *Collected Poems in English and French* (New York: Grove Press, 1977), 107.

27 See Guillaume Apollinaire, *Alcools*, ed. Garnet Rees (London: Athlone Press, 1993), 39.

28 Beckett, *Collected Poems in English and French*, 107.

29 Quoted in Cecily Mackworth, *Apollinaire and the Cubist Life* (New York: Horizon Press, 1963), 150–1.

30 For a very attentive analysis, see Marjorie Perloff, *The Futurist Moment: Avant-Garde, Avant Guerre and the Language of Rupture* (Chicago: University of Chicago Press, 1986), 3–43.

31 Blaise Cendrars was a witness of the revolutionary agitation of 1905: see his daughter's biography, Miriam Cendrars, *Blaise Cendrars* (Paris: Balland, 1993), 97–129.

32 This is the title of chapter 9 of Shattuck's *The Banquet Years*, 253–97.

33 See Ezra Pound, "A Retrospect," in *Literary Essays*, ed. T. S. Eliot (London: Faber & Faber, 1963), 3–14.

34 *The New Freewoman* (Aug. 15, 1913), repr. by Kraus Reprint Corporation (New York: 1967), 88.

35 See Ezra Pound, *Selected Letters 1907–1941*, ed. D. D. Paige (New York: New Directions, 1971), 17–18.

36 Ibid. 10, and David E. Moody's forthcoming biography of Ezra Pound (Oxford: Oxford University Press) for the second quote.

37 Pound, *Selected Letters 1907–1941*, 22.

38 Quoted in Jane Marcus's Editor's Introduction to *The Young Rebecca: Writings of Rebecca West 1911–17* (Bloomington: Indiana University Press, 1982), 4.

39 Bruce Clarke, *Dora Marsden and Early Modernism* (Ann Arbor: University of Michigan Press), 1995.

40 *The New Freewoman*, 1/2 (July 1, 1913), 27.

41 *The New Freewoman*, 1/5 (Aug. 15, 1913), 86.

42 *The New Freewoman*, 1/9 (Oct. 15, 1913), 162.

43 Rachel Blau Du Plessis, *The Pink Guitar: Writing as Feminist Practice* (New York: Routledge, 1990), 45.

44 *The New Freewoman*, 1/1 (June 15, 1913), 1.

45 Max Stirner, *The Ego and His Own*, trans. S. T. Byington, ed. J. J. Martin (New York: Dover, 1973), 3

46 Dora Marsden, "Views and Comments," *The New Freewoman*, 1/1 (June 15, 1913), 3.

47 Ibid. 5.

48 *The New Freewoman*, 1/2 (July 1, 1913), 25.

49 *The New Freewoman*, 1/10 (Nov. 1, 1913), 204.

50 *The New Freewoman*, 1/13 (Dec. 15, 1913), 260.

51 Ibid. 244.

52 Ibid.

53 Ibid.

54 Fritz Mauthner, *Beiträge zu einer Kritik der Sprache* (1901–2), 3 vols (Frankfurt: Ullstein, 1982). Mauthner had also published a catalog of abstract notions in philosophy, which he then submitted to a radical philosophical and skeptical debunking: see his *Wörterbuch der Philosophie* (Berlin, 1910–11).

55 T. S. Eliot, *Letters*, vol. 1: *1898–1922*, ed. Valerie Eliot (London: Faber & Faber, 1988), 315.

56 The answer to this (rhetorical) question is given in Shaw's afterword to *Pygmalion* (1913): "Galatea never does quite like Pygmalion: his relation to her is too god-like to be altogether agreeable." This might throw some light on the difficult but obdurate relationship of H.D. and Pound. See Bernard Shaw, *Pygmalion* (Baltimore: Penguin, 1964), 125.

3 Everyday Life and the New Episteme

1 Robert Musil, *The Man Without Qualities*, vol. 1, trans. Sophie Wilkins and Burton Pike (New York: Random House, 1996), 3.

2 From an Austrian point of view, Romanticism defined the whole of the 19th century – see Broch's trilogy *The Sleepwalkers*.

3 *The Man Without Qualities*, 5.

4 See Virginia Cowles, *1913: An End and a Beginning* (New York: Harper & Row, 1968), 188–9.

5 Rainer Maria Rilke, *Die Aufzeichnungen des Malte Laurid Brigge* (1910), in *Werke in drei Bänden*, vol. 3 (Frankfurt: Insel Verlag, 1966), 110.

6 Georg Simmel, "The Metropolis and Mental Life" (1903), in *On Individuality and Social Forms*, trans. Edward A. Shils, ed. D. N. Levine (Chicago: University of Chicago Press, 1971), 53.

7 See Stephen Kern, *The Culture of Time and Space 1880–1918* (Cambridge, MA: Harvard University Press, 1983), 12–15.

8 *The Man Without Qualities*, 4.

9 Robert Musil, "Das Fliegenpapier," in *Three Short Stories*, ed. Hugh Sacker (Oxford: Oxford University Press, 1970), 107–9, and, for an English version, *Posthumous Papers of a Living Author*, trans. Peter Wortsman (Hygiene, CO: Eridanos Press, 1987), 5–7.

10 Robert Musil, "Der mathematische Mensch" (Apr./June 1913), in *Gesammelte Werke*, vol. 8: *Essays und Reden* (Hamburg: Rowohlt, 1981), 1004–8.

11 Ibid. 1004.

12   A phrase used by the Bourbaki group in the thirties; quoted in Eric Hobsbawm, *The Age of Empire: 1875–1914* (London: Weidenfeld & Nicolson, 1987), 245.

13   Quoted in Ronald W. Clark, *The Life of Bertrand Russell* (New York: Knopf, 1976), 213.

14   Robert Musil, *On Mach's Theories*, trans. Kevin Mulligan, ed. G. H. von Wright (Munich: Philosophia Verlag, 1982), 39.

15   Ronald Clark, *Einstein: The Life and Times* (New York: Avon Books, 1984), 204–5.

16   See Michio Imai, "Musil between Mach and Stumpf," in *Ernst Mach's Vienna 1895–1930*, ed. J. Blackmore, R. Itagaki, and S. Tanaka (Dordrecht: Kluwer, 2001), 187–209.

17   See Alice Calaprice, *The Einstein Almanac* (Baltimore: Johns Hopkins University Press, 2005), 36–46, and, for the "temporary impasse" of 1913, Ronald Clark, *Einstein: The Life and Times*, 199.

18   Michel Foucault, *The Order of Things: An Archeology of the Human Sciences* (New York: Vintage, 1973), xxiii.

19   Quoted in Cowles, *1913*, 35.

20   Ibid. 175.

21   As Jane Farrell-Beck writes about America: "By the mid-1910s, brassieres rather than corsets had become the source of increased business in foundation departments . . . Expansion of women's work, recreation, public roles, and health care further disposed them to trade in old-style corsets for these new foundations." Between 1906 and 1917, brassiere manufacturers distributed their wares regionally and nationally through retail chains, specialty shops, merchants' catalogs, and department stores. *Uplift: The Bra in America* (Philadelphia: University of Pennsylvania Press, 2002), 11.

22   Cowles, *1913*, 175.

23   See Guillermo Gasio, *Jean Richepin y el Tango Argentino en Paris en 1913* (Buenos Aires: Corregidor, 1999).

24   Cowles, *1913*, 235.

25   Quoted in Alan Valentine, *1913: America Between Two Worlds* (New York: Macmillan, 1962), 82.

26   Floyd Dell, *Women as World Builders: Studies in Modern Feminism* (1913; repr. Westport, CT: Hyperion Press, 1976), 13–14.

27   See Hobsbawm, *The Age of Empire*, 207.

28   See Valentine, *1913*, 85–94, for a vivid evocation of the march.

29   Allen G. Roper, *Ancient Eugenics* (Oxford: Blackwell, 1913).

30   As Vernon L. Kellogg would ask in "Eugenics and Militarism," *The Atlantic* (June/July 1913), and in *Beyond War: A Chapter in the Natural History of Man* (New York: Holt & Co., 1912).

31   David Bradshaw, "Eugenics," in id., ed., *A Concise Companion to Modernism* (Oxford: Blackwell, 2003), 39.

32   Henry H. Goddard, *The Kallikak Family: A Study in the Heredity of Feeblemindedness* (New York: Macmillan, 1912), and *Feeblemindedness: Its Causes and Consequences* (New York: Macmillan, 1914).

33   See Tim Armstrong, *Modernism, Technology and the Body: A Cultural Study* (Cambridge: Cambridge University Press, 1998), 133–83.

34   Havelock Ellis, "Sexo-Aesthetic Inversion," *Alienist and Neurologist*, 34 (1913), 156–67 and 249–79.

35   Walter Heape, *Sex Antagonism* (New York: Putnam's Sons, 1913).

36   Ernest Jones, *The Life and Work of Sigmund Freud*, vol. 2: *Years of Maturity 1901–1919* (New York: Basic Books, 1955), 350.

37   *The Freud/Jung Letters*, abridged, ed. William McGuire (Princeton: Princeton University Press, 1994), 252.

38   Ibid. 253.

39   Ibid. 255.

40   Ibid. 244.

41   Jones, *The Life and Work of Sigmund Freud*, vol. 2, 353. See also Frederic Morton, *Thunder at Twilight: Vienna 1913/1914* (Cambridge, MA: Da Capo Press, 2001), 10–11, 49–55, 96–108, 203–6, 213–15, and *passim* for an interesting comparison between Freud's strategy facing the "secession" of Jung and his followers and the attitude of the Emperor Franz Joseph in 1913–14.

42   Jones, *The Life and Work of Sigmund Freud*, 354.

43   Ibid.

44   See Peter Gay, *Freud: A Life for our Time* (New York: Doubleday, 1988), 314–15.

45   Sigmund Freud, "The Moses of Michelangelo," in *Writings on Art and Literature* from the *Standard Edition*, ed. Neil Hertz (Stanford: Stanford University Press, 1997), 124.

46   Ibid. 146.

47   Quoted in Clark, *The Life of Bertrand Russell*, 161.

48   Ibid. 186.

49   Ibid. 172.

50   Ibid. 194.

51   Miguel de Unamuno, *The Tragic Sense of Life in Men and Nations*, trans. Anthony Kerrigan, ed. William Barrett (Princeton: Princeton University Press, 1972), 356.

4 Learning to be Modern in 1913

1   It was called "The Love Song of J. Alfred Prufrock (Prufrock among the Women)" and "Prufrock's Pervigilium." See T. S. Eliot, *Inventions of the March Hare: Poems 1909–1917*, ed. Christopher Ricks (New York: Harcourt Brace, 1996), 39–46.

2   Ezra Pound, *Selected Letters 1907–1941*, ed. D. D. Paige (New York: New Directions, 1971), 40.

3   T. S. Eliot, *Letters*, vol. 1: *1898–1922*, ed. Valerie Eliot (London: Faber & Faber, 1988), 36.

4   From a letter to Verdenal, Apr. 22, 1912, ibid. 34.

5   I am indebted to Piers Gray's "The Life of Theory," in *T. S. Eliot's Intellectual and Poetic Development, 1909–1922* (Brighton: Harvester Press, 1982), 90–107.

6   T. S. Eliot, "Draft of a Paper on Bergson," quoted in M. A. R. Habib, *The Early T. S. Eliot and Western Philosophy* (Cambridge: Cambridge University Press, 1999), 53. Habib dates the "Draft" to 1912–13.

7   T. S. Eliot, *Collected Poems 1909–1962* (London: Faber & Faber, 1963), 17.

8   Ibid. 41.

9   D. H. Lawrence, *Sons and Lovers*, ed. David Trotter (Oxford: Oxford University Press, 1995), 316.

10   Ibid. 337.

11   See Brian Finney, "The Psychoanalytic Perspective," in *Sons and Lovers* (London: Penguin, 1990), 22–32.

12   James Joyce, "Notes for Exiles," in *Poems and Exiles*, ed. J. C. C. Mays (London: Penguin, 1992), 346–7.

13   Ibid. 45.

14   I have tried to analyze the functional relevance of doubt in *Joyce Upon the Void: The Genesis of Doubt* (Houndmills: Macmillan, 1991), 21–42.

15   D. H. Lawrence, *Complete Poems*, ed. V. de Sola Pinto and W. Roberts (London: Penguin, 1993), 45.

16   Ibid. 915.

17   See R. F. Foster's masterful biography, *W. B. Yeats: A Life*, vol. 1: *The Apprentice Mage 1865–1914* (Oxford: Oxford University Press, 1997), 438–9 and 473–6.

18   Quoted in James Longenbach, *Stone Cottage: Pound, Yeats and Modernism* (Oxford: Oxford University Press, 1988), 19.

19   Quoted in Foster, *W. B. Yeats: A Life*, vol. 1, 476.

20   "September 1913," in W. B. Yeats, *Collected Poems* (London: Macmillan, 1965), 121.

21   These comments were made in the late fifties by Williams to John Thirlwall, who copied them into the margins of the poems. William Carlos Williams, *Collected Poems*, vol. 1: *1909–1939*, ed. A. Walton Litz and C. MacGowan (New York: New Directions, 1986), 473–5.

22   William Carlos Williams, *The Tempers* (1913), ibid. 15–16.

23   Ezra Pound, "Robert Frost (Two Reviews)," in *Literary Essays*, ed. T. S. Eliot (London: Faber & Faber, 1963), 382.

24   Robert Frost, *Early Poems*, ed. Robert Faggen (London: Penguin, 1998), 33.

25   Pound, *Literary Essays*, 388.

26   "1913: Philadelphia," in *Willa Cather in Person: Interviews, Speeches and Letters*, ed. L. Brent Bohlke (Lincoln: University of Nebraska Press, 1986), 6–11.

27   Ibid. 10.

28   This is the last sentence of *O Pioneers!*. Willa Cather, *O Pioneers!* (New York: Random House, 1992), 159.

29 Gertrude Stein, *Writings*, vol. 1: *1903–1932*, ed. Catharine R. Stimpson and Harriet Chessman (New York: Library of America, 1998), 378–96. Subsequent citations in the text are to volume 1 of *Writings*.

30 Gertrude Stein, *The World Is Round*, in *Writings*, vol. 2: *1932–1946*, ed. Catharine R. Stimpson and Harriet Chessman (New York: Library of America, 1998), 537.

31 Gertrude Stein, *How To Write* (New York: Dover, 1975), 131.

32 Gertrude Stein, *The Autobiography of Alice B. Toklas*, in *Writings*, vol. 1: *1903–1932*, 798–9.

33 See "Le Ballet des architectes" by Claude Loupiac, in *1913: Le Théâtre des Champs-Elysées*, ed. Thérèse Barruel and Claude Loupiac (Paris: Editions de la Réunion des Musées Nationaux, 1987), 22–52. Most of my documentation comes from this exhibition catalog.

34 See *1913: Le Théâtre des Champs-Elysées*, 55, and Nikolaus Pevsner, *Pioneers of Modern Design* (Harmondsworth: Penguin, 1977), 252.

35 Hanno-Walter Kruft, *A History of Architectural Theory from Vitruvius to the Present*, trans. Ronald Taylor, Elsie Callander, and Anthony Wood (Princeton: Princeton Architectural Press, 1994), 395.

36 Guillaume Apollinaire, review of the Salon des Indépendants, Mar. 1913, in *Chroniques d'Art 1902–1918* (Paris: Gallimard, 1960), 379.

37 Quoted in Hans L. C. Jaffé, *Piet Mondrian* (New York: Harry Abrams, 1970), 64.

38 See Carel Blotkamp, *Mondrian: The Art of Destruction*, trans. Barbara Potter Fasting (New York: Harry Abrams, 1995).

39 Apollinaire, *Chroniques d'Art 1902–1918*, 419.

40 See *Paolo De Chirico: The Metaphysical Period, 1888–1919*, trans. Jeffrey Jennings (New York: Bullfinch Press, 1997), 197.

41 Clement Greenberg, *Collected Essays*, vol. 2: *1950–1956*, ed. John O'Brian (Chicago: University Press of Chicago, 1993), 135.

42 James Joyce, *Giacomo Joyce*, ed. Richard Ellmann (New York: Viking, 1968).

5 Global Culture and the Invention of the Other

1 See Marina Scriabine's survey of magazines like *La Vie heureuse* and *Luxe de Paris* in "Réflexions sur l'esthétique de la vie quotidienne en 1913," in Liliane Brion-Guerry, ed., *L'Année 1913: Les Formes esthétiques de l'œuvre d'art à la veille de la première guerre mondiale*, 3 vols (Paris: Klincksieck, 1971), vol. 1, 923–49.

2 Marcel Proust, *Remembrance of Things Past*, vol. 3, trans. C. K. Scott Moncrieff, Terence Kilmartin, and Andreas Mayor (New York: Vintage, 1982), 376.

3 See *The Invention of Tradition*, ed. Eric Hobsbawm and Terence Ranger (Cambridge: Cambridge University Press, 1993), especially Terence Ranger's "The Invention of Tradition in Colonial Africa," 211–62.

4 Translated in Samuel Beckett, *Collected Poems in English and French* (New York: Grove Press, 1977), 121.

5   Guillaume Apollinaire, *Selected Writings*, ed. Roger Shattuck (New York: New Directions, 1971). Subsequent references are given in the text.

6   Beckett, *Collected Poems in English and French*, 111.

7   See Mary Fenollosa's preface to Ernest F. Fenollosa, *Epochs of Chinese and Japanese Art* (1st edn, 1912; 2nd edn, 1913; New York: Dover, 1963), vii–xxii.

8   Pound, *Selected Letters 1907–1941*, ed. D. D. Paige (New York: New Directions, 1971), 27.

9   Allen Upward, "Sayings of K'ung the Master," *The New Freewoman*, 1/11 (Nov. 15, 1913), 205.

10 The subtitle of *Cathay* duly acknowledges the intermediaries: "For the most part from the Chinese of Rihaku, from the notes of the late Ernest Fenollosa, and the decipherings of the professors Mori and Ariga." See Steven G. Yao, *Translation and the Languages of Modernism* (New York: Palgrave, 2002).

11 Ezra Pound, "Vorticism," *The Fortnightly Review*, 102 (Sept. 1914), 462.

12 *"Noh" or Accomplishment*, in Ezra Pound, *Poems and Translations*, ed. Richard Sieburth (New York: Library of America, 2003), 402.

13 Quoted in Probhat Kumar Mukherji, *Life of Tagore* (New Delhi: Indian Book Company, 1975), 111.

14 *A Tagore Reader*, ed. Amiya Chakravarty (Boston: Beacon Press, 1961), 305.

15 Humphrey Carpenter, *A Serious Character: The Life of Ezra Pound* (London: Faber & Faber, 1988), 186.

16 Pound, *Selected Letters 1907–1941*, 14.

17 R. F. Foster, *W. B. Yeats: A Life*, vol. 1: *The Apprentice Mage 1865–1914* (Oxford: Oxford University Press, 1997), 470.

18 Pound, *Selected Letters 1907–1941*, 19.

19 Ibid.

20 Ibid. 106.

21 See Wilson J. Moses, "The Poetics of Ethiopianism," in *Modern Critical Views: W. E. B. Du Bois*, ed. Harold Bloom (Philadelphia: Chelsea House, 2001), 57–69.

22 Quoted in David Levering Lewis, *W. E. B. Du Bois: Biography of a Race*, vol. 1: *1868–1919* (New York: Henry Holt, 1993), 101.

23 Ibid.

24 W. E. B. Du Bois, *The Quest of the Silver Fleece* (Philadelphia: University of Pennsylvania Press, 2004), 251.

25 I am quoting the full text reproduced in Moses, "The Poetics of Ethiopianism," 64–5. Du Bois' abridged version of the pageant is given in *The Oxford W. E. B. Du Bois Reader*, ed. Eric J. Sundquist (Oxford: Oxford University Press, 1996), 305–10.

26 See David Krasner, "The Pageant Is the Thing: Black Nationalism and *The Start of Ethiopia*," in *A Beautiful Pageant* (London: Palgrave Macmillan, 2002), 31–94.

27 W. E. B. Du Bois, *The Negro* (New York: Holt, 1915), 48.

28 Ibid. 159.

29 Ibid. 272.

30 "The African Roots of the War," in *Writings by W. E. B. Du Bois in Periodicals*, vol. 2: *1910–34*, ed. Herbert Aptheker (New York: Kraus-Thomson, 1982), 97.

31 Ibid. 98.

32 Ibid.

33 Ibid. 104.

34 Ezra Pound, "A Visiting Card" (1942), in *Selected Prose 1909–1965*, ed. William Cookson (London: Faber & Faber, 1973), 300.

35 Leo Frobenius, *Unter den unsträflichen Aethiopen* (Berlin: Deutsches Verlaghaus, 1913).

36 Ibid. xxiv.

37 Leo Frobenius, *The Voice of Africa; being the account of the travels of the German Inner African Exploration in the years 1910–1912* (1913; repr. New York: Arno Press, 1980). Subsequent references, to *VA*, are given in the text.

38 *Unter den unsträflichen Aethiopen*, 6.

39 Ibid. 508.

40 "A Philosophy for 1913," from *The Crisis*, 5 (Jan. 1913), quoted from *Selections from the Crisis*, ed. Herbert Aptheker (Millwood, NY: Kraus-Thomson, 1983), 47.

6 The Splintered Subject of Modernism

1 W. E. B. Du Bois, *The Souls of Black Folk* (New York: New American Library, Signet 1982), 45.

2 Trans. Babette Deutsch, in *Primal Vision: Selected Writings of Gottfried Benn*, ed. E. B. Ashton (New York: New Directions, 1960), 213.

3 Ibid. 219, trans. Michael Hamburger. I have modified the punctuation.

4 See the first of the Rönne pieces dating from 1916, "The Birthday": ibid. 3–12.

5 See Gottfried Benn, *Gedichte (In der Fassung der Erstdrucke)*, ed. Bruno Hillebrand (Frankfurt: Fischer, 1988), 42–74.

6 "Songs," trans. Babette Deutsch, in *Primal Vision*, 229.

7 Ibid. 223–5, trans. Richard Exner; punctuation modified.

8 Trans. Robert Grenier, in *Georg Trakl: A Profile*, ed. Frank Graziano (Lockbridge-Rhodes, Durango, 1983), 27.

9 Quoted ibid. 105.

10 Trans. Christopher Middleton, ibid. 33.

11 See Frank Graziano's introduction to *The Dark Flutes of Fall: Critical Essays on Georg Trakl* (Columbia: Camden House, 1991), 20.

12 *Georg Trakl: A Profile*, 26.

13 Alexander Blok, foreword to *Retribution* (1919), in *Selected Poems*, trans. Alex Miller (Moscow: Progress Publishers, 1981), 262. Subsequent references are given in the text.

14 Rainer Maria Rilke, *Duino Elegies*, trans. David Young (New York: Norton, 1978), 19.

15 Osip Mandelstam, *Stone*, trans. and annotated by Robert Tracy (Princeton: Princeton University Press, 1981), 127.

16 Robert Tracy notes that there was a special law school on the Fontanka canal that was open only to scions of noble families; see *Stone*, 228. Subsequent references in the text are to page number.

17 Michael Groden, *Ulysses in Progress* (Princeton: Princeton University Press, 1977).

18 For more details see the excellent study by Roger Keys, *The Reluctant Modernist: Andrei Belyi and the Development of Russian Fiction 1902–1914* (Oxford: Clarendon Press, 1996), 162.

19 Quoted ibid. 229.

20 Andrei Biely, *St. Petersburg*, trans. John Cournos (New York: Grove Press, 1959), 37. Andrei Biely, *Petersburg*, trans. and annotated Robert A. Maguire and John E. Malmstad (Bloomington: Indiana University Press, 1978). References in the text are to the 1978 edition.

21 See Timothy Langen, *The Stony Dance: Unity and Gesture in Andrey Bely's Petersburg* (Evanston: Northwestern University Press, 2005), 91–3. The creation of a reader is for Langen an indisputable feature of high modernism.

22 See Caryl Emerson's *The First Hundred years of Mikail Bakhtin* (Princeton: Princeton University Press, 1997), 149. Bakhtin was close to the Free Philosophical Association of Petersburg co-founded by Biely in the twenties, but never shared Biely's post-symbolist trust in the demiurgic powers of language.

23 Quoted in L. C. Taylor, "The Life and Times of Pessoa," in Eugenia Lisboa and L. C. Taylor, eds, *A Centenary of Pessoa* (New York: Routledge, 2003), 131.

24 Ibid. 132.

25 I have slightly modified the fine translation given by Darlene J. Sadlier in *An Introduction to Fernando Pessoa: Modernism and the Paradoxes of Authorship* (Gainesville: University Press of Florida, 1998), 34–5. The original text is in Fernando Pessoa, *Obra poética* (Rio de Janeiro: Nova Aguilar, 1986), 108.

26 I have slightly modified Darlene J. Sadlier's translation in *An Introduction to Fernando Pessoa*, 34.

27 "Nota preliminar" to "Poemas ingleses," in *Obra poética*, 587.

28 "Propos de table et anecdotes de M. Barnabooth," from the 1908 edition of *Poèmes par un riche amateur*, in Valery Larbaud, *Œuvres*, ed. G. Jean-Aubry and Robert Mallet (Paris: Gallimard, Pléiade, 1989), 1151.

29 "Les Borborygmes," in *Œuvres*, 43.

30 "Ma Muse," ibid. 60.

31 Ibid. 117.

32 Ibid. 109 and 119.

33 Ibid. 301.

34 Ibid. 303.

35 Ibid. 305.

36 Ibid. 306.

7 At War with Oneself

1 See Wendelin Schmidt-Dengler, "Literarische Streiflichter 1913," in Karen Witt and Christoph Becker, eds, *1913: Aufbruch in unsere Welt* (Vienna: Löcker Verlag, 1993), 25–38.

2 Virginia Cowles, *1913: An End and a Beginning* (New York: Harper & Row, 1968), 107.

3 Hermann Broch, "James Joyce und die Gegenwart," *Schriften zur Literatur*, vol. 1: *Kritik*, ed. Paul Michael Lützeler (Frankfurt: Suhrkamp Verlag, 1975), 90.

4 Ralph Freeman, *Life of a Poet: Rainer Maria Rilke* (New York: Farrar, Straus & Giroux, 1996), 350.

5 See Helen Sword, *Ghostwriting Modernism* (Ithaca: Cornell University Press, 2002).

6 Rainer Maria Rilke, *Uncollected Poems*, trans. Edward Snow (New York: North Point Press/Farrar, Straus & Giroux, 1996), 31.

7 Ibid. "Master" could be translated as "Lord" (*Herr*), as it was for the first part.

8 Ibid. 35. The poem is dated "Ronda, early January 1913."

9 Letter of Jan. 16, 1913, trans. in Donald Prater, *A Ringing Glass: The Life of Rainer Maria Rilke* (Oxford: Clarendon Press, 1986), 220.

10 I am quoting from A. Poulin's translation of the third Duino elegy, in Rainer Maria Rilke, *Duino Elegies and the Sonnets to Orpheus* (Boston: Houghton Mifflin, 1977), 19 and 23.

11 For a systematic analysis of this complex process, see Judith Ryan's invaluable *Rilke, Modernism and Poetic Tradition* (Cambridge: Cambridge University Press, 1999).

12 Freud added a note to "The Rat-Man" in 1923: "The patient, who had recovered his psychic health as a result of the analysis described here, was – like so many other promising and estimable young men – killed in the Great War." Sigmund Freud, *The "Wolfman" and Other Cases*, ed. Adam Philip, trans. L. A. Huish (London: Penguin, 2003), 202.

13 Thomas Mann, *Death in Venice and Other Stories*, trans. David Luke (New York: Bantam Books, 1988), 195. References in the text are to this edition.

14 Franz Kafka, "The Stoker," trans. W. and E. Muir, revised by A. S. Wensinger, in *The Sons*, ed. Mark Anderson (New York: Schocken, 1989), 22.

15 Ibid. 34.

16 Franz Kafka, *Amerika*, trans. Willa and Edwin Muir (New York: Schocken, 1996), 95. This is the continuation of the story in the novel.

17 Hugo von Hofmannsthal, *Andreas*, in *Selected Prose*, trans. Mary Hottinger and Tania and James Stern (New York: Pantheon Books, 1952), 3.

18 Hermann Broch, introduction to Hofmannsthal, *Selected Prose*, xxiii.

19 David H. Miles, *Hofmannsthal's Novel Andreas: Memory and Self* (Princeton: Princeton University Press, 1972), 103.

20 This fragment is entitled "The mystical element of poetry: the abolition of time." Jacques Rivière's essay was published in *La Nouvelle Revue française*,

vol. 1, VII (1913), quoted in Hugo von Hofmannsthal, *Sämtliche Werke, 30: Andreas*, selections from the Archives, edited by Manfred Pape (Frankfurt: Fischer, 1982), 111.

21 Hofmannsthal, *Selected Prose*, 129–41.

22 Ibid. 40, and *Sämtliche Werke*, vol. 30, 71: "So rührt ihn das Unendliche an."

23 *Selected Prose*, 112.

24 Ibid. 87.

25 Richard Alewyn, *Ueber Hugo von Hofmannsthal* (Göttingen: Vandenhoeck & Ruprecht, 1967), 142–60.

26 *Sämtliche Werke*, vol. 30, 179.

27 Ibid. 218.

28 A note from 1919 (*Sämtliche Werke*, vol. 30, 189) states Hofmannsthal's ambition to create a "totality" through art, an endeavor that is impossible since in real life everything is confusedly mixed up. Totality implies an abolition of time transforming the text into pure space, literature's true ambition, according to Hermann Broch.

29 *Sämtliche Werke*, vol. 30, 127.

30 Introduction to Hofmannsthal, *Selected Prose*, xxxi.

31 A detailed account of the genesis of *The Woman Without a Shadow* is provided in Hofmannsthal, *Sämtliche Werke*, vol. 25, 1, *Operndichtung* 3.1, ed. Hans-Albrecht Koch (Frankfurt: Fischer, 1998), 117–46.

32 Franz Kafka, *Letters to Felice*, trans. James Stern and Elisabeth Duckworth (New York: Schocken, 1973), 37. Subsequent references, to *Letters*, are given in the text.

33 Frederick Karl, *Franz Kafka, Representative Man: Prague, Germans, Jews, and the Crisis of Modernism* (New York: Fromm Editions, 1993), 308–419. The 800 pages of this book take as much space as Kafka's collected works, but Karl's attention to textual details, his awareness that one should not put Kafka on a pedestal but situate him in the larger picture of international modernism, and his novelistic re-creation of situations make this biography one of the best guides to Kafka's oeuvre.

34 Quoted in Karl, *Franz Kafka*, 266.

8 Modernism and the End of Nostalgia

1 R. W. B. Lewis, *Edith Wharton: A Biography* (New York: Fromm International, 1985), 400–1.

2 Ibid. 401.

3 Marcel Proust, *Contre Sainte-Beuve* (Paris: Pléiade), 3.

4 Lewis, *Edith Wharton: A Biography*, 402.

5 Robin Peel, *Apart from Modernism: Edith Wharton, Politics and Fiction before World War I* (Cranbury: Associated University Presses, 2005).

6 Edith Wharton, *The Custom of the Country*, ed. Stephen Orgel (Oxford: Oxford University Press, 2000), 51. Subsequent references, to *CC*, are given in the text.

7   Roland Barthes' term for someone who does not have any opinions of his or her own and merely echoes the dominant opinion (or doxa) in a given milieu. For an excellent analysis of Undine's mimetic character, see Nancy Bentley's chapter, "Wharton and the Alienation of Divorce," in *The Ethnography of Manners: Hawthorne, James, Wharton* (Cambridge: Cambridge University Press, 1995), 160–211.

8   Marcel Proust, *Swann's Way*, trans. Lydia Davis (New York: Viking, 2003), 255. Subsequent references, to *SW*, are given in the text.

9   See Lewis, *Edith Wharton: A Biography*, 82–4.

10 I have discussed this in "Dora's Gift, or Lacan's Homage to Dora," in *Psychoanalytic Inquiry, Freud and Dora: 100 Years Later*, 25/1, ed. Susan Levine (2005), 84–93.

11 Stanley Cavell, *Pursuits of Happiness: The Hollywood Comedy of Remarriage* (Boston: Harvard University Press, 1981).

12 See Stephen Orgel's superb introduction to *The Custom of the Country*, vii.

13 Robin Peel quotes Kenneth Clark's autobiography to make this point in *Apart from Modernism*, 203.

14 Lewis, *Edith Wharton: A Biography*, 221.

15 Ibid. 230.

16 Peel, *Apart from Modernism*, 279.

17 See Gilles Deleuze's groundbreaking study *Proust and Signs* (1964), trans. Richard Howard (Minneapolis, MN: University Press of Minneapolis, 2001).

18 Marcel Proust, *Remembrance of Things Past*, vol. 3: *Time Regained*, trans. Andreas Mayor (New York: Random House, 1982), 804.

19 Ibid. 236.

20 In *Roland Barthes by Roland Barthes*, "bathmology" (from *bathmos*, degree) is glossed as "a new science, the science the degrees of language." Roland Barthes, *Roland Barthes*, trans. Richard Howard (New York: Hill & Wang, 1977), 67. To exemplify this principle, one might say that Raymond de Chelles is right when he attacks American vulgarity since he defends his class interests, but that he is wrong when he enslaves Undine to a male patriarchal system that she is right to reject, whereas he is right at a superior level when upholding moral dignity above commercialization.

21 Lewis, *Edith Wharton: A Biography*, 401. Edith Wharton and Walter Berry, both avid readers of *Swann's Way*, had adopted the habit of referring to the Guermantes as real characters (ibid.).

22 "Le Corps de la femme" attacked the materialist libertinism of Remy de Gourmont, Hippolyte Taine, and Pierre Louÿs. See *Œuvres d'Alain-Fournier: Le Grand Meaulnes, Miracles, Le Dossier du grand Meaulnes*, ed. Alain Rivière, Françoise Touzan, and Daniel Leuwers (Paris: Garnier, 1986), 88. Subsequent citations are to this edition.

23 Ibid. 367.

24 David Ellison, "The 'beautiful soul': Alain-Fournier's *Le Grand Meaulnes*," in *Ethics and Aesthetics in European Modernist Literature: From the Sublime to the Uncanny* (Cambridge: Cambridge University Press, 2001), 121.

25 Ibid. 121.

26 Ibid. 131.

27 "On imaginait, là-bas, des âmes, de belles âmes" (*Œuvres d'Alain-Fournier*, 376).

Conclusion

1 Guglielmo Ferrero, "The Dangers of War in Europe," *The Atlantic Monthly* (Boston) (Jan. 1913), 2.

2 Ibid.

3 Ibid. 4.

4 Quoted in Claude Arnaud, *Jean Cocteau* (Paris: Gallimard, 2003), 121.

5 Jean Cocteau, *Le Potomak* (Paris: Passage du Marais, 2000), 53–4; my translation.

6 For more details, see Arnaud, *Jean Cocteau*, 122–4.

7 See "The War Eugènes," appendix in *Le Potomak*, 215–49.

8 *Le Potomak*, 42.

9 This comes from *Tender Buttons*, written in 1912 and published only in 1914. Cocteau's friends saw one sentence on a single page. It is the only sentence in the sub-section entitled *"Dining."* Gertrude Stein, *Writings*, vol. 1: *1903–1932*, ed. Catharine R. Simpson and Harriet Chessman (New York: Library of America, 1998), 342.

10 *Le Potomak*, 34.

11 Quoted from the first 1919 version of *Le Potomak*, 25.

12 *Le Potomak*, 33–4.

13 Walter Heape, *Sex Antagonism* (New York: Putnam's Sons, 1913), 1.

14 Ibid. 2.

15 Hermann Broch, "Voices: 1913," in *The Guiltless*, trans. Ralph Mannheim (London: Quartet Books, 1990), 8. See Hermann Broch, *Die Schuldlosen. Roman in elf Erzählungen*, ed. Paul Michael Lützeler (Frankfurt: Suhrkamp, 1974), 331–2, for the genesis of this section.

16 *The Guiltless*, 10.

17 Ibid. 8–9.

18 *1913, a Journal of Forms*, nos 1 and 2 (2005) (New York: 1913 Press).

Index

Page numbers in italic refer to illustrations.